Volume 30, Number 1

differences

Sexual Politics, Sexual Panics

Guest Editor
Robyn Wiegman

Introduction: Now, Not Now

*H*ere is what we know: feminist political optimism in the United States is difficult to come by in the current environment. The revolution (let's call it what it is) of our lifetimes veers hard right as the u.s. state engages open warfare on air, water, land, and wildlife along with every category of minoritized persons: Muslims, immigrants, the poor, women, people of color, queers. It is easy to sound hyperbolic, and there are numerous pundits and paid professionals, especially from the liberal Left, who will quickly declare such language over the top, if not out of bounds, because it is not predicated on fidelity to the ever receding high notes of political rationality. You have heard their instructions: avoid "abolish" when talking about Immigration and Customs Enforcement (ICE); it is too extreme. Veer right when you see "socialist"; it is best to cultivate the mainstream. Hush all talk of impeachment; it arms the GOP. No to "inequality," yes to "opportunity." Annul identity: "all lives matter."

To be sure, the rhetorical message that sells in the commodified sphere of politics is an easy target for academic feminists adept at reading the logics that shape and inform popular discourse. But we, too,

Volume 30, Number 1   DOI 10.1215/10407391-7481162

have shown concern about the timing and tenor of feminist interventions into the hypermediated domains that now serve as public political culture. Much ink was spilled—or more accurately, many keys were furiously hit on social media forums—in the fall of 2017 in debating the academic's ethical relation to the unfolding scene in which #MeToo rose to prominence in an industry that had long banked its value on brand and spectacle. Could we address the corporate logics that prompted the surprisingly swift dismissals of accused abusers by boards of directors and CEOs, especially as the news of the abuser's behavior had been well known and highly protected to industry insiders all along? Or would this undermine the political urgency of exposing such behavior by casting suspicion on the motives of the corporation when no other institution—certainly not the state apparatus led by a serial predator—was willing to act as arbiter of justice and public morality? And how could we begin to measure the political consequences of recruiting discourses of morality to feminism's side when we had spent decades studying the way these very discourses had worked overtime to undermine feminism's political potency?[1]

The matter of putting faith in the corporation was not the only or even the most pressing concern for scholars who sought to engage the unfolding present through queries about the way that sexuality, violence, and the demand for justice were being claimed, narrated, and circulated. In numerous conversations both public and private, and in blogs and comment sections no less than in Facebook posts and on Twitter feeds, many academic feminists found themselves worrying not so much about *what* needed to be discussed as *when* we could safely do so without imperiling the project of public protest and mass education underway.[2] How soon could we address the collapse of distinctions between harassment and assault or raise issues that drew on the legacy of pro-sex feminism in a media environment more heightened than ever to the profit-generating anthems of scandal and outrage?[3] How soon could the conversation deepen beyond liberal critiques of representation and inclusion when it came to the racial politics in which the white actress emerged as star victim of a movement that originated in the organizing labor of black feminist Tarana Burke a decade before? How soon would it seem constructive and not deflating—or worse antifeminist—to discuss the gender essentialism of the female victim and male perpetrator dyad and the heterosexual scenarios in which this dyad lived? And when could we consider the legacy of the feminist sex wars and the powerful but difficult contestations that ensued in their wake about feminism's own carceral impulses and their ricocheting effect on minority communities (both racial and sexual), along with the risk of sacrificing the conversation about women's sexual freedom to the political terrain of "danger" once again?[4]

The first meaning of the title of this introduction, "Now, Not Now," is meant to evoke the temporal question animating academic feminist conversations in the early months of 2018 when the editors of *differences* offered to dedicate this volume to explorations crafted at the intersection of insistence and caution. Insistence: that the time was now for an unwavering engagement with everything that we have come to know about the complexity and complicity of feminism, especially when it tries to make space for itself in the discursive venues of the political mainstream. Caution: that there was good reason to deliberate carefully about the relationship between alliance and critique, especially given the ease with which academic feminism had forged its political authority by anatomizing public feminism's faults.[5] For second-wave warriors, #MeToo promised to revive the meat-and-potatoes feminist issue of sexual discrimination, harassment, and violence while offering student generations a larger venue for the protests they staged on college campuses that had institutionalized an approach to sexual assault largely as problems of public relations and underage drinking. For many women, some of whom held no special attachment to feminism as a necessary politics, #MeToo made visible forms of everyday coercion that had been sedimented in workplace cultures, dating protocols, and domestic intimacy. Most readers here will remember the quick succession in which a number of highly visible and powerful men—most of whom were politically liberal and ethnically white—lost their jobs in the face of various charges, from unsolicited touching and verbal harassment to quid pro quo, assault, and rape: Harvey Weinstein, Kevin Spacey, Louis C. K., Jeffrey Tambor, Charlie Rose, Matt Lauer, Garrison Keillor, Al Franken, and John Conyers.[6] All this took place while evangelical politician Roy Moore, accused predator of teenage girls, was endorsed by the man occupying the White House, himself a serial denier who more than once floated the idea that it was not really his own bragging voice on the Access Hollywood tape that went viral before the 2016 election.

To mention Donald Trump is to enter the labyrinth of all kinds of sexual offenses, from the routine sexism that dribbles from his lips to his reliance on nondisclosure agreements that give cover to the open secret of his extramarital affairs to the more criminalizing accounts of his proclivity for groping and assault. It is no exaggeration to say that anger over the impunity granted to Trump has fueled the feminist response to each new accusation against a leading figure, simultaneously magnifying the longstanding cultural and legal refusal to take sexual predation seriously in all its manifestations while offering a mechanism to express ongoing public indignation that the Predator-in-Chief has been held to no ethical or legal standard whatsoever. Wendy Brown has called the ascendancy of Trump and Trumpism "the libidinal pleasure of freedom as dis-inhibition," a characterization that rather brilliantly captures the thrill Trump delivers to the wounded world of white heteromasculinity with his poke-'em-in-the-eye and grab-'em-by-the-pussy bravado ("Populism").[7] For the rest of us, the sadism that Trumpism unleashes into the shrunken core of liberalism's civil society is chilling, as it sharpens nationalism's racist and militarist teeth while enshrining the state's strategic intention to govern through both threatened and materialized violence. Compounding the visceral effect of all this is the accompanying drum beat of Trump's daily Twitter habit—over 8,500 tweets since inauguration (as of this writing)—which functions as a living archive of desublimation, one whose menace is heightened and stoked by the profit-generating overload of the twenty-four-hour news cycle. This situation is more than a far cry from the soothing notes of liberalism, which performed its magic as a social depressant by masking violence through the language of democracy, shared national culture, and American exceptionalism. The shock to the system of the Trumpian alternative instead works through amplification, ridicule, and grievance—creating an affective mode of governance we might call mania as state craft.[8]

What kind of feminist sexual politics is adequate in this hideously electrifying and endlessly exhausting environment? For contributors to this volume, this is the most urgent question, one that requires attention not just to continuities between past and present but to how certain aspects of the current terrain of sexual politics have no precise historical precedent. Take the matter of sex panic. Feminist scholarship has long focused on the way sex panics—like moral panics in general—operate by amplifying fear, spreading paranoia and suspicion, and inciting demands for ever greater forms of state regulation and "protection." Their potency is in direct proportion to their ability to travel in mediascapes on the profit-generating currencies of scandal, melodrama, and sensationalism. They are routinely understood to be episodic inflammations caused by social transformations that disrupt the established order, which means that they are resolutely conservative and seek to quell their insecurities by reinforcing bourgeois sexual norms and excising the social body of its purported impurities. The most important feminist text on the history and anatomy of sex panic is Gayle Rubin's 1984 "Thinking Sex," which tracked the continuities between three different episodes in u.s. history: the 1880s, the 1950s, and her contemporary moment. In discussing the 1970s and 1980s, Rubin importantly traced the way the energies that stoked both the Moral Majority—"God's Own Party"—and the secular project of antipornography feminism converged in a politically antagonistic but paradoxically mutual desire to wield the institutions of the state for increased sexual regulation (Williams iv).[9] Today, of course, the tentacles of what was once the Moral Majority have reached deep into social institutions, political parties, educational practices, and the economic foundations undergirding all of these—no less than into the corridors of the White House, the Supreme Court, and Congress. Extensive in social scope and without discernible borders, the sex panic of the religious Right releases its anxieties about reproduction, homosexuality, sex trafficking, gay marriage, and diverse genders into the cultural bloodstream in a modality completely acclimated to daily routine. Normalized, no longer episodic; elemental to media culture and not a momentary flare-up: what we are living in today is an institutionalized sex panic that threatens never to end. Pay no mind to the profane bombast of Trump and Trumpism when the promise is the moral purity of a white Christian holy land.

And what of #MeToo and the viral intensity that has powered it?[10] For some feminists, its political rise has eerily reflected the major themes of sex panic: yoking sexuality to criminality, inflaming public emotion, promoting scandal, and spreading its message through media spectacle. But it has been the movement's commitment to a set drama of guilt and innocence that has raised the most alarm as it forges an allegiance to the narrative ecology of panic: on one side, the emotionally moving and politically powerful enunciation of (female) sexual victimization; on the other, an equally singular narrative of (male) predation, one that flattens differences between categories of sexual harm in a domino-like logic that renders sexual misconduct as sexual harassment as sexual assault as rape. And yet, even as the lack of sexual definition and the hypermediated spread of emotion are consistent with the known traits of sex panic, one prominent characteristic—and a crucial one at that—is wholly absent in the current conjuncture: #MeToo is not a conservative political production addressed to the moral disciplining apparatus of the state and designed to enhance the institutions of repressive sexual management that had long served as the wet dream of the right wing. On the contrary, many of its first successes have bypassed the state apparatus altogether as corporations suspend or fire those who have been accused (sometimes with but often without internal investigations). This is the panicked power of the brand, which wields publicity to secure the corporation's agency in adjudication. Is this the anatomy of a sex panic in neoliberal times, orchestrated from the Left and weighing justice through employment contracts, not jail time? And if so, how can we attend to the contradictions that unfold here, as both the political charge of sexual panic and the historical frame for understanding feminist sexual politics shift?

It will surely surprise no one that the contributions in this special issue do not settle these questions. What we do agree on is that the affective atmosphere of the present not only favors but induces outrage and that there is as much truth as cause for concern in the frequent declarations that ours is the *age of outrage*. For as much as we might want to recruit outrage to our side, it is an equal opportunity emotion, available to every political position. Even those propelled by nostalgia for liberalism's managerial rhetoric of rational debate can express *outrage over outrage* as a necessary, if paradoxical, entreaty for democratic repair. In their book, *The Outrage Industry: Political Opinion Media and the New Incivility*, Jeffrey Berry and Sarah Sobieraj do just this. For them, the age of outrage has been manufactured by the entity their title names, "the outrage industry," which creates both a political media environment of enormous profit as well as a media genre that draws on the popularity of reality TV and celebrity culture. This media environment is driven by personality (think Rush Limbaugh, Sean Hannity, Rachel Maddow, and Chris Hayes) and is not only reactive and ideologically selective but conspiratorial and politically bombastic—no matter the specific political leanings of programming hosts. By producing information as melodrama, provoking anger, and forecasting doom, the outrage industry shapes and promotes a public culture that "takes the form of verbal competition, political theater with a scorecard" (7). While people may find it entertaining—or more accurately *because* people find it entertaining—the outrage industry cashes in on "incivility" and partisanship at the expense, Berry and Sobieraj write, of "political dialogue that is rational, inclusive, impartial, consensus-oriented, and fact-based" (7, 19). The book aims to expose the industry's antidemocratic greed in order to dull its power, reclaiming deliberation and reason for the restoration of democracy to come.

It is difficult to imagine readers of *differences* siding with the analysis that *The Outrage Industry* promotes when it marshals the affective norms of liberal democracy to wage battle with the histrionics of the outrage industry. But a central feature of nearly every conversation about outrage, whether academic or not, does seem to be configured by questions concerning the evisceration of norms, the diminution if not the displacement of a shared public sphere, and the supremacy of affects (as opposed to critical thought) as the blood (and pus) of contemporary politics. It seems inadequate to lay the blame, as some do, at the feet of mass mediated culture, but there is no doubt that user-based platforms extend the logic of the outrage industry in ways that multiply the avenues and outlets for outrage. While Facebook is the most widely known version of this media form, offering interactivity while profiting from the commodification of the user's information (her market coordinates, friendship networks, shopping habits, political interests, even her zip code), the lure of interactivity has revamped older media as well, with mainstream newspapers and magazines revising their monodirectional transmission through online comment sections and other modes of user engagement. The old adage that the mall is the cathedral of secular society can be updated as the Internet becomes late capitalism's public sphere. In this environment of hyper immediacy, outrage thrives, especially under the auspices of suspicion, fear, and conspiracy. It is, as M. J. Crockett comes close to suggesting, the Internet's gasoline, lucrative to the extreme.

For Berry and Sobieraj, writing in the Obama era and with only glancing attention to the proliferation of digital media, outrage is a decided negative, one whose power, they hope, can be undermined by attention to the historical emergence of the industry and the genre conventions on which the industry turns. But as we all know, putting the genie back in the bottle, in the midst of the daily mania of the Trump–Fox News love-affair-war-dance, is probably as impossible as it feels. Certainly, any assumption that the political task is to reign in the desublimated thrills of "anti-democracy as fun," as Brown puts it, obviates two sets of questions that have important implications for how we understand the terrain of contemporary sexual politics ("Populism"). The first set concerns the widely held perception that outrage is an obstacle in contemporary political culture *no matter what*, that it is best understood as a symptom of a catastrophic disorganization of the affective, analytic, and activist components of political life and that as such we must find a way to outmaneuver it. But can we study our way out of outrage? Can we talk people out of outrage—or, more aptly, can you counter the power and ubiquity of outrage by positioning an analysis of it against it? Is there an epistemological fix to outrage, a pedagogy or mechanism through which the prerogative we give to knowledge wields the leverage necessary to imperil outrage and its effects? Can we be sure that the quickest route to a better world lies in subduing—we would be right to say sublimating—outrage and its excessive and excessively profitable affective overload?

At the root of these questions is a simple one: does outrage pose an imminent societal danger? (We'll get to the more provocative question "and if so, for whom?" shortly.) For Teddy Wayne, writing in the *New York Times*, the answer is yes, especially when it comes to social media platforms where outrage is "ultimately," he writes, "the milquetoast cousin to direct action, a way to protest by tapping and clicking rather than boycotting and marching." The problem with outrage here is that while it inflames and spreads, it also paralyzes, becoming an end run around political participation, a quick fix in a world where traditional avenues of agency have gone awry, whether through overt strategies of disenfranchisement, the fragmentation of publics into consumer markets, or the convergent consensus from both the Left and the Right that the social contract as a whole has failed. As with other arguments against outrage, this one tends to read it in symptomatic terms: it is captivating because personally cathartic, but it is born of technological alienation that makes its satisfactions contradictory and fleeting, bound not only to the libidinal pleasures of the mob, which rely on anonymity, but also to the immediacy of first-person declaration. This double bind is anything but inhibiting, which is why Wayne marshals scholars who have studied Internet outrage to rally behind the injunction, as Ryan Martin puts it, "'to calm down and think things through'" (qtd. in Wayne). The convergence of opinion in the literature on outrage leads me to wonder: is outrage really a substitution for agency, the affective ghost of the Enlightenment in our increasingly medieval times?[11] Or is outrage where agency now lives?

    This last question matters to me most because of its comportment with one of feminism's first lessons: that the distribution of affects is irreducibly gendered, pitting rationality against feeling and ascribing anger (which Sianne Ngai names, in her "bestiary of affects," the "lion" of the emotional world) to masculinity not as fault or threat but as triumph and honor (7). We are surely exhausted by the inexhaustible purchase of the same old story, its unfolding under the auspices of white supremacy, and the historical compact between white masculinity and the institutional power it ratifies: outraged white men are heroes, protectors, and social warriors while outraged women are hags, harpies, and feminazis, routinely vilified or simply ignored.[12] And outraged men of color? They tend to exit the story early, via the postslavery profit industry of mass incarceration or in state orchestrated scenes of assassination, both of which cast their narrative downfall as their own damned fault. Today, these ancient storylines are set to autoplay in the twilight of the hegemony of liberal whiteness, which is what I call white subjectivity as it has been held (at least provisionally) accountable to the history of its own privilege in the post-segregationist era. This is a version of white identity, tacitly multicultural, that was founded in disidentification if not political competition with overtly nationalist and supremacist formations of whiteness that have long practiced and preached the gospel of racial purity.[13] Its political apex is best evoked in the soothing moderation of the Obama era, which might explain why the imperative to stop-and-think has been sounded as if it bears nothing but progressive overtones. But while outrage is, at the level of the data commodity, an equal opportunity instigator, its cultural reception as political expression is an entirely different matter. In the simplest terms, the *right* to outrage—like all rights—has never been equally conferred.[14]

What must not be conceded, then, is the primacy of the ensuing question, which will help us arrive at the second meaning at stake in this introduction's title: *whose* outrage are we talking about when we worry that outrage is a prophylactic for political engagement? To query *who* is to engage a first-order feminist question, one that can rip open the insides of feminist collectives as much as generate collective stances against the differently faced enemies who line up against women, including when women victimize and exploit other women. Certainly no one who studies gender or race or the multifaceted complexity of their intersections in the United States can question the political function of outrage as a part of the visceral power of historical and ongoing activisms. This is just as true of #MeToo and the viral engine that characterizes and feeds it as it is of Black Lives Matter and the yet unnamed or distinctly local projects that are registering, from laptops as well as in the streets, their intolerance for the brutality and open predation practiced by the Trump regime in its chest-thumping restitution of the identity politics of the founders' originating declaration: that those who deserve to determine the shape of the world for everyone are rich, white, and male. In this broader context, as a response to the manic disposition of the present, outrage is nothing if not an invaluable resource for staying alert and remaining sane. Paradoxically, it may even be a kind of life preserver for optimisms to come, as it helps meet the political order of a manic *now* with a decided refusal to acclimate to current conditions: no, *not now*.

The scholars whose work appears in this special issue take their turns in wrenching from the outrage they feel toward the authoritarianism and rabid racism and misogyny of our times a range of compelling meditations on feminism, sexuality, power, and publicity. With fourteen contributions, the issue is split between two genres of academic writing: the publication-length article and the keyword essay. If read in the order in which they appear, the volume moves across three general thematics. The first concerns feminism's political and theoretical investment in the sexual politics of the contemporary moment. Here, we examine the emergence of "#MeToo" as a distinctly feminist political movement (Eva Cherniavsky), the political demand it exacts from feminists in the form of "solidarity" (Rebecca Wanzo), the contradictory inheritances it assumes from the political theory of #MeToo avatar Catharine MacKinnon (Joseph J. Fischel), and the civil war with evangelical Christianity and its theft of the figure of "mother" that any effort in the name of sexual freedoms cannot afford to ignore (Mairead Sullivan). The first thematic ends (so to speak) with a close reading of one of the most controversial #MeToo stories, that of Aziz Ansari, in order to review and revise feminist understandings of heterosexual disappointment and political desire (Andrea Long Chu).

The middle thematic of the volume is oriented toward the vicissitudes of sex in the conjuncture between perversion and pleasure. It begins with the historical constructions of the "sex offender" (Terrance Wooten) and "pedophile" (Kadji Amin) before a rather delicious dissection of the disavowed sadomasochism of MacKinnon's most influential feminist work (Samia Vasa). From here we consider the confessional risks and pleasures of "testimony" (Juana María Rodríguez) and the political necessity of refusing visibility and speech as the ascribed priorities for black feminist sexual freedom (Shoniqua Roach). The final thematic foregrounds the university and contestations over its rules of sexual engagement, moving from a keyword analysis of the double-bind of "consent" as a property-based ethics (Emily A. Owens) to the terrible privilege of expertise that protected Larry Nassar and his serial crimes for decades (Jennifer Doyle) to the controversy over the pedagogy of the "trigger warning" (Lynne Joyrich) and the unacknowledged history it shares with fan cultures. The volume closes with a consideration of the difficulties facing institutional feminism as it seeks to found and promote a university culture free of sexual harm under the historical conditions of neoliberalism (Jennifer C. Nash).

Suffice it to say that this special issue does not aim to be a comprehensive conversation about the cascade of events that comprise the contemporary terrain of sexual politics. It might be best read as an archive of emergent concerns in the affective environment of 2018, as #MeToo continued to gain political visibility and it seemed absolutely vital to gather an interdisciplinary and intergenerational array of scholars to parse the terms and engage the complexity of the long imagined return of feminism to the center of public culture. It is certainly the case that as this issue goes to press, the initial controversies that engaged us have given way to new political emergencies, as the breathless pace in which right-wing extremism

is being institutionalized continues unabated, eliciting inconsolable political outrage at its desublimated desire to govern by shoving the impunity of
white male power down everyone's throat. This issue honors that outrage
and the double temporality that ignites and justifies it: *now, not now.*

ROBYN WIEGMAN is a professor of literature and gender, sexuality, and feminist studies at
Duke University and former director of women's studies at both Duke and the University of
California, Irvine. She has published *Object Lessons* (Duke University Press, 2012), *American Anatomies: Theorizing Race and Gender* (Duke University Press, 1995), and numerous
anthologies, including *Women's Studies on Its Own* (Duke University Press, 2002) and *Feminism beside Itself* (Routledge, 1995). She is currently working on "Arguments Worth Having,"
which locates points of critical dissension in contemporary encounters between feminist,
queer, and critical race thinking.

Notes

1   While the scholarly archive on
morality discourses and their
politically conservative effects is
vast, two important edited collections provide instruction into the
key points of the discussion. See
Fahs, Dudy, and Stage; and Herdt.

2   See Jane Ward for a compelling
discussion of some of the political and personal stakes of holding
one's tongue in the name of feminist strategy. "We are whispering
to one another, *please don't muddy
the waters by talking about false
equivalences now. We are admon-
ishing each other out of fear,
please, I beg you not to distract
from this powerful wellspring of
feminist truths, this unstoppable
testimony of violation and survival, by attending to gray areas
and complexities. Not now. The
stakes are too high. This is finally
working!"*

3   For an important early discussion of the role of women's studies
analysis in addressing the current
conjuncture of "sex and power,"
see Ashwini Tambe's inquiry into
the global reach of #MeToo, the
impunity of Trump as a "trigger
provoking the fury at the heart of
[the movement]," and the dynamic
of moral panic alive in the current
moment (197, 198). Tambe's essay

also addresses how the media's
representation of #MeToo, along
with the movement's own discourses, are "out of step with currents in contemporary academic
feminism" that highlight pleasure
and healing, intersectional analysis, and a nonmoralistic relation to
transactional sex (200).

4   I am invoking the simple but brilliantly astute phrase "pleasure
and danger" here, which is drawn
from the 1982 Barnard Conference
on Sexuality and the edited collection by Carole Vance that followed
it. For context and commentary of
the conference and the feminist
sex wars more broadly, see Duggan and Hunter; Stein and Press;
and Wilson.

5   See Wiegman, "No Guarantee," for
a discussion of the way academic
feminism today functions as a
pedagogy of correction by revers-
ing its founding relationship to
movement feminism. Instead of
serving as the academic arm of the
movement, it enacts the political
agency that will revise the ways in
which the movement has failed.

6   The news outlet *Vox* kept a running list of the accused, organized
by industry, through April 2018.
See North.

7   In a related discussion about the current compact between authoritarianism and neoliberalism, see Brown, "Neoliberalism's."

8   My thinking here is inspired by Eva Cherniavsky's meditation on mania in ch. 4 of *Neocitizenship*, esp. 125–27.

9   In placing the history of morality crusades in the United States alongside the practices and ideologies of antipornography feminism, Rubin highlighted four feminist missteps: its recruitment of state regulation for censorship, best demonstrated by the legal activism of Catharine MacKinnon, its leading figure; its failure to differentiate sexual representations and fantasy worlds from real life, especially in the oft-repeated equation of lesbian sadomasochism with patriarchal sexual violence; its critique of transactional sex, which overinflated coercion while altogether dismissing consent; and its tendency to apply a feminist litmus test to erotic choices, thereby restricting the politics of sexuality to specific sex acts and/or their participants. In 2010, *GLQ* published a special issue on Rubin's work that features a retrospective discussion of her groundbreaking essay. See Rubin, "Blood." For a broad discussion of the punitive practices of the state in relation to sexuality, see Lancaster.

10   For prominent popular writing on this question, see Beck; Blanton; Gessen; Hamblin; Hempel; and Schulte.

11   I am citing Purnima Bose here, who has characterized the anti-science conservative Christian political project as the fantasy restoration of the dark ages—a characterization that I wish seemed more funny or fantastical than true.

12   Evidence for this claim can be found everywhere but let me use an example from yesterday because its significance will in no way be diminished by the temporal lag that accompanies academic publishing. On the contrary, what was on display at the Senate Judiciary Committee's second hearing on the nomination of Brett Kavanaugh on September 27, 2018 tells us everything we need to know about the implicit rules governing the affective dispensations of gender and race, organized in Manichean overdrive as masculine entitlement and feminine constraint. Kavanaugh's Trumpian display of outrage, belligerence, and accusation was deemed heroic by GOP senators and the right-wing media, while Christine Blasey Ford earned credibility through the pitch and tenor of her emotional restraint. Anger for her was not an option. See Loofbourow; and Thomas. In a slightly different trajectory of analysis, see Tolentino for a discussion of male bonding as the affective tie in both the scenes of assault described by Kavanaugh's accusers and the Senate hearing room.

13   See Wiegman, "Political."

14   Think here of the response in October 2018 to the protests that accompanied the nomination of Brett Kavanaugh to the Supreme Court—not only those that took place inside the hearing room but the many sit-ins and sound-outs in offices, corridors, elevators, civic spaces, and the streets that came to be referred to by Mitch McConnell, Paul Rand, Mitt Romney, and Trump himself, along with the Fox News chorus, as "mobs." In these terms, feminist protesters, especially those speaking as sexual assault survivors, were rendered altogether dangerous to the nation. McConnell, in a tone deafness

surprising even for him, declared, "We were literally under assault by protestors," before declaring his satisfaction that the Senate GOP "refused to be intimidated by the mob." See Olmstead.

Works Cited

Beck, Richard. "#MeToo Is Not a Witch Hunt." *Vox* 11 Jan. 2018. https://www.vox.com/identities /2017/12/21/16803206/metoo-not-sex-moral-panic.

Berry, Jeffrey M., and Sarah Sobieraj. *The Outrage Industry: Political Opinion Media and the New Incivility.* New York: Oxford UP, 2014.

Blanton, Carsie. "The Problem with Panic." *Carsie Blanton* (blog) 6 Jan. 2018. https://www .carsieblanton.com/blog/.

Brown, Wendy. "Neoliberalism's Frankenstein: Authoritarian Freedom in Twenty-first Century 'Democracies.'" *Critical Times* 1.1 (2018): 60–79.

—————. "Populism, Authoritarianism, and Making Fascism Fun Again." International Institute, University of California, San Diego. 14 Mar. 2017. https://www.youtube.com/watch ?v=CUAJ2–Z4PqI.

Cherniavsky, Eva. *Neocitizenship: Political Culture after Democracy.* New York: New York UP, 2017.

Crockett, M. J. "Moral Outrage in the Digital Age." *Nature Human Behavior* 1 (2017): 769–71.

Duggan, Lisa, and Nan D. Hunter. *Sex Wars: Sexual Dissent and Political Culture.* London: Routledge, 1995.

Fahs, Breanne, Mary L. Dudy, and Sarah Stage. "Introduction: Villains and Victims: Excavating the Moral Panics of Sexuality." *The Moral Panics of Sexuality.* Ed. Breanne Fahs, Mary L. Dudy, and Sarah Stage. London: Palgrave Macmillan, 2013. 1–23.

Foucault, Michel. *The History of Sexuality.* Vol. 1. *An Introduction.* Trans. Robert Hurley. New York: Vintage, 1978.

Gessen, Masha. "When Does a Watershed Become a Sex Panic?" *New Yorker* 14 Nov. 2017. https:// www.newyorker.com/news/our-columnists/when-does-a-watershed-become-a-sex-panic.

Hamblin, James. "This Is Not a Sex Panic." *Atlantic* 17 Jan. 2018. https://www.theatlantic.com /entertainment/archive/2018/01/this-is-not-a-sex-panic/550547/.

Hempel, Jessi. "The Problem with #MeToo and Viral Outrage." *Wired* 18 Oct. 2017. https://www .wired.com/story/the-problem-with-me-too-and-viral-outrage/.

Herdt, Gilbert, ed. *Moral Panics, Sex Panics: Fear and the Fight over Sexual Rights.* New York: New York UP, 2009.

Irvine, Janice M. "Transient Feelings and Sex Panics: The Politics of Emotion." Herdt 234–76.

Lancaster, Roger N. *Sex Panic and the Punitive State.* New York: Oxford UP, 2011.

Levine, Judith. "Will Feminism's Past Mistakes Haunt #MeToo?" *Boston Review* 8 Dec. 2017. http:// bostonreview.net/gender-sexuality/judith-levine-will-feminisms-past-mistakes-haunt-metoo.

Loofbourow, Lili. "Why Christine Blasey Ford Isn't Allowed to Be Mad." *Slate* 28 Sept. 2018. https://slate.com/news-and-politics/2018/09/brett-kavanaugh-hearing-angry-shouting.html.

Olmstead, Molly. "Trump Again Accuses Anti-Kavanaugh Protesters of Being 'Screamers.'" *Slate* 9 Oct. 2018. https://slate.com/news-and-politics/2018/10/paid-protesters-liberal-mob-kavanaugh-screamers.html.

Ngai, Sianne. *Ugly Feelings.* Cambridge, MA: Harvard UP, 2007.

North, Anna. "A Sexual Harassment Assault Allegations List." *Vox* 25 May 2018. https://www.vox.com/a/sexual-harassment-assault-allegations-list.

Rubin, Gayle. "Blood under the Bridge: Reflections on 'Thinking Sex.'" *GLQ* 17.1 (2010): 15–48.

—————. "Thinking Sex: Notes for a Radical Theory of the Politics of Sexuality." *Pleasure and Danger: Exploring Female Sexuality.* Ed. Carole S. Vance. Boston: Routledge, 1984. 267–319.

Schulte, Elizabeth. "The Myth of the '#MeToo Panic.'" *SocialistWorker.org* 19 Apr. 2018. https://socialistworker.org/2018/04/19/the-myth-of-the-metoo-panic.

Stein, Arlene, and Andrea Press. "Pleasure and Danger: Exploring Female Sexuality by Carole S. Vance." *Berkeley Journal of Sociology* 30 (1985): 205–12.

Tambe, Ashwini. "Reckoning with the Silences of #MeToo." *Feminist Studies* 44.1 (2018): 197–203.

Thomas, R. Eric. "Kavanaugh Gave a Messy, Angry Performance That Would Never Be Allowed from a Woman." *Elle* 27 Sept. 2018. https://www.elle.com/culture/career-politics/a23496358/kavanaugh-angry-opening-statement/.

Tolentino, Jia. "Brett Kavanaugh, Donald Trump, and the Things That Men Do for Other Men." *New Yorker* 26 Sept. 2018. https://www.newyorker.com/news/our-columnists/brett-kavanaugh-donald-trump-and-the-things-men-do-for-other-men.

Vance, Carole S., ed. *Pleasure and Danger: Exploring Female Sexuality.* Boston: Routledge, 1984.

Ward, Jane. "Bad Girls: On Being the Accused." *Bullybloggers* 21 Dec. 2017. https://bullybloggers.wordpress.com/2017/12/21/bad-girls-on-being-the-accused/.

Wayne, Teddy. "Clicking Their Way to Outrage." *New York Times* 3 July 2014. https://www.nytimes.com/2014/07/06/fashion/social-media-some-susceptible-to-internet-outrage.html.

Wiegman, Robyn. "No Guarantee: Feminism's Academic Affect and Political Fantasy." *Atlantis* 37.2 (2016): 83–95.

—————. "The Political Conscious: Whiteness Studies and the Paradox of Particularity." *Object Lessons.* Durham: Duke UP, 2012. 137–96.

Williams, Daniel. *God's Own Party: The Making of the Christian Right.* New York: Oxford UP, 2012.

Wilson, Elizabeth. "The Context of 'Between Pleasure and Danger': The Barnard Conference on Sexuality." *Feminist Review* 13.1 (1983): 35–41.

EVA CHERNIAVSKY

KEYWORD 1

#MeToo

*T*he past year saw the advent of a social media–based phenomenon, #MeToo, that has galvanized feminists across the political spectrum through the shared, serial revelation of sexual abuse and harassment in (and beyond) the workplace. Apart from the visceral satisfaction of seeing laid bare a culture of workplace inequity remarkable precisely for being unremarkable, because disturbingly ubiquitous and banal, #MeToo has also afforded the unusual and compelling spectacle of feminist sentiment across divisions of race, ethnicity, and class. In laying waste, seemingly overnight, to the authority of a postfeminist discourse that has saturated the public sphere for the past quarter century, #MeToo undoubtedly (re)opens promising vistas for feminist mobilization on the Left. At the same time, this keyword essay will argue that the routine characterization of #MeToo as a "movement" misrecognizes both its value and its limitations. The debates around #MeToo have largely centered on the politics of law and language. Commentators have noted the bagginess of "sexual abuse" as a category that runs together violence and intimidation with various kinds of misconduct. They have pressed the always vexing question of what constitutes consent

Volume 30, Number 1   DOI 10.1215/10407391-7481176

or worried about due process, seemingly suspended in the public outing of offenders. Others have noted the perils of a feminism aligned with the carceral state insofar as it envisions criminal prosecution of offenders as a primary mode of redress.[1] I aim to suggest that buried in these debates lies a more fundamental set of questions about the nature of activism and the contours of political practice in the present moment.

In particular, I hope to disentangle two dimensions of #MeToo that are certainly not unrelated, but are also, and importantly, *not* the same: The first concerns #MeToo as an intervention in corporate and institutional cultures where women are made systemically susceptible to sexual harassment (and worse) by men in positions of power. The second concerns #MeToo as a diagnostic of what I will call, for lack of a better phrase, the state of heterosexual culture in the u.s. today—by which I mean, more precisely, the gender politics of heterosexual relations and their attendant imaginaries.[2] Along the way, I will suggest that the folding together of these two dimensions—the apprehension of institutional power through and, indeed, *as* a series of interpersonal encounters—reveals a sense of and orientation to political action that is at once powerfully performative *and* dangerously limited. This limitation of #MeToo illuminates a central challenge for the cultivation of feminist imaginaries in neoliberal times.

By now, the doubled origin of #MeToo has been widely acknowledged and discussed. Responding to the revelations of serial abuse and rape by producer Harvey Weinstein, Hollywood actor Alyssa Milano created the hashtag, tweeting "if all the women who have been sexually harassed or assaulted wrote 'me too' as a status, we might give people a sense of the magnitude of the problem." In so doing, Milano unwittingly appropriated a formulation coined over a decade earlier by Tarana Burke, an African American community organizer working to develop services and support networks for black and brown victims of sexual abuse, especially young girls. The origin of Burke's "Me, too," as told in her own words on the website of the organization she founded and directs, Just Be, Inc., was her encounter with a thirteen-year-old girl, who confided in her about having been sexually abused by her mother's boyfriend (Burke). Interestingly—and contrary to some of the recent reporting—the origin of "Me, too" lay in Burke's *inability* to offer these words of understanding and solidarity to the girl, whom she instead cut off and referred to another female counselor.[3] Thus the (first) origin of "me, too," rested *not* in a ready identification, but in Burke's pain and distress at her own inability to perform one. Burke went on to place the "power of empathy" as the linchpin of her "Me, too" campaign, but it bears emphasis that this is an empathy in a particular context and with a particular kind of socially abjected subject: poor girls of color for whom the trauma of sexual abuse is embedded in a broader experience of social devaluation. When Burke argues for the "power of empathy," it is not a universal empathy, but a communally specific one—and it is, above all, an empathy that exacts a psychic cost.

Following the revelation that Milano's coinage amounted to an unintended appropriation, Milano and other high-profile Hollywood figures moved, to their credit, not only to acknowledge Burke's work but also to perform a public alliance with activists working on issues of gender, race, labor, and immigration. Thus, for instance, at the 75th Golden Globe Awards, organizers Burke, Rosa Clemente (hip-hop activist and 2008 Green Party vice presidential candidate), Ai-jen Poo (head of the National Domestic Workers Alliance), and Saru Jayaraman (Restaurant Opportunities Center United president) attended as the invited guests of various celebrities, including Michelle Williams, Susan Sarandon, Amy Poehler, and Meryl Streep. This careful attempt by the (largely white) cohort of media stars to honor the work of women of color organizing for women's rights in low-wage employment sectors such as the food industry, farm labor, and domestic work speaks to the now widespread feminist literacy in intersectional politics. What I would describe as the guardedly receptive response of these organizers to their interpellation within the hashtag version of Me, too, tends to signal an acknowledgment of the value of networks and exposure. Yet the apparent convergence of political projects, protesting the sexual harassment of female elites in media industries and of female subalterns in low-wage sectors, belies their fundamental asymmetry. The difference resides not only in the relative privilege and access to publicity of these two cohorts but in what that entails for the form of their mobilization. The community organizers are, precisely, *organizers.* In the sectors where they operate, giving girls or women a voice means countering the radically atomizing effects of precarity: It means carefully building contexts for people to assemble and to define their aspirations. It means canvassing, tabling, phone banking, and running meetings, over months and years. It means developing networks and a capacity for collaborative action in real time and real spaces. While the theme of women's vulnerability to male harassment and abuse is common to #MeToo and the projects of the organizers invited to the Golden Globe event, there is a world of difference between the labor of organizing people on the ground and the act of tweeting out to one's followers an offender's name. Ironically, the very presence of these organizers in the #MeToo mediascape throws into relief the contrasting character of #MeToo as a form of political mobilization that no longer operates *in the field*—within any specific industrial sector, institutional terrain, or communal framework.

My point here is not the obvious one—that #MeToo is social media based—but rather that its politics are *exclusively* realized in the production of publicity: #MeToo is an open platform for the public revelation of unchecked male privilege and abuses. It is less the means to an end (an incitement for women to organize—to assemble a "movement") than the realization of an end: an *autonomous* (extra-institutional) framework to effect the social elaboration of new, equitable norms of male conduct. The political fantasy in which it traffics is that women could, collectively (as a multiracial, multi-ethnic, economically diverse class summoned into virtual being on Twitter) delegitimate and dismantle this privilege through the *serial* exposure on a *mass* scale of the men who (ab)use it. And indeed, aside from an always intransigent Republican party, industries and corporations and institutions seem to be validating the fantasy, responding to these revelations with the removal from power or from office of the offending males. As the ranks of the exposed swell and the social capital of the violators plummets, they put all men on warning that the risks of harassing or abusing women henceforth outweigh the benefits. Social media, it seems, have liberated us from the long, slow labor of activism in the field: of organizing people in a workplace or a sector or a community to understand their conditions, claim their agency, and make effective demands on those in power—precisely the kind of labor to which organizers like Burke, Clemente, Poo, and Jayaraman have committed themselves.

In this sense, I would argue that #MeToo bears some resemblance to (and certainly, emerges out of the same political matrix as) Occupy Wall Street (ows), despite the fact that the former is a virtual mobilization while the latter involves the occupation of real spaces in real time. Both projects bypass conventional modes of political engagement, replacing demands on established power with a practice of autonomous world building. On this model, we summon the world we desire by opting to live in it *now*, whether that means planting a socialist polity in the heart of New York's financial district or performing a new norm of zero tolerance for sexual harassment and abuse and imposing it on men everywhere. Inasmuch as it restores a utopian dimension to political thought and practice, this is a valuable and compelling and perhaps a necessary model. But unlike the socialist prospect enacted by ows, the feminist prospect enacted by #MeToo is, I suspect, all too commensurate with the status quo. The fundamental limitation of the ows movement was its ephemerality—even if one might argue that it created the context for the Sanders campaign, along with a wave of Far Left candidates running for public office at the state and local levels. But the limitation of #MeToo lies in its *alignment* with a corporate-managerial culture focused on best practices, risk assessment, and individual accountability. If the private and (to some extent) public sectors have proven generally responsive to #MeToo's collective female complaint, this is not because they have been brought to heel by the power of feminist publicity, but because the very form of the complaint is calibrated to the aim of an ever more thorough and efficient management of human capital.

The very design of #MeToo, in other words, identifies the root of the problem it exposes as a structure of male privilege, expressed in the psychic organization and behavior of male subjects. It has shown little interest in how that privilege is instituted and reproduced—since the gambit is precisely that by proscribing the expression, one transforms the structures. This is the reason that #MeToo tends to make no distinction between abuses of institutionalized power (e.g., harassment by someone who controls your employment) and the exercise of what is perceived as a generalized male supremacy (controlling or disparaging behavior by any man toward any woman)—the difference, say, between Harvey Weinstein and Aziz Ansari. But that disinterest is perilous for the altogether simple reason that power expressed at the level of the subject is not constituted there. Thus, for example, in an industry where women are systematically relegated to lower-value positions or underpaid for the same labor by comparison to their male peers (which, of course, describes most industries and sectors), it seems clear that the reform of male personality *will not change* women's vulnerability to harassment, sexual or other. Its expression might require more careful management, to be sure, yet male privilege will remain perfectly alive and well. Obviously, the reverse is also true—and the creation of equitable working conditions for women does not by itself produce gender equity, without specific, concerted attention to matters of sexual culture that articulate the workplace to its broader social contexts. My point, then, is simply this: #MeToo defines as the problem a pattern of male behavior that appears to reproduce itself indifferently across varied social sites and contexts. But the fact that male supremacy is ubiquitous does *not* mean that it is monolithic. To be sure, male supremacy operates in the corporate boardroom, on the studio casting couch, on the warehouse floor, in immigrant-staffed nursing homes, and in the bedrooms of couples everywhere—but it is *not*, therefore, the *same* male supremacy. Male supremacy cannot be redressed absent confrontation with the specific institutions and organizational structures where it is reproduced. I read something akin to this analysis in Burke's tweet of February 21, 2018. "Founder is acknowledgment," she writes. "But watch carefully who are called 'leaders' of the movement. *It's as if 25+ years of on the ground movement building is not enough or maybe spending most of that time invested in the lives of Black and brown Girls isn't enough*" (my emphasis).

#MeToo represents a form of media-based activism that brackets the laborious, bottom-up work of organizing: analyzing institutional power; disseminating the analysis; forging alliances; and carefully building the conditions for the realization of political agency within defined institutional, organizational, and civic arenas. The achievement of #MeToo has been to interrupt and reverse the reign of a postfeminist common sense by enjoining a mass identification with a feminist complaint. This is no mean achievement. And yet, at the level of workplace culture, what #MeToo seems most likely to yield is *not* gender equity, but elaborated structures of surveillance and metrics of employee accountability that can serve any number of managerial aims. Here, one might recall the career of "safe spaces" on college campuses nationwide. Demanded by women and students of color as a means to make possible the discussion of sensitive political topics (creating safety for the institutionally marginalized to speak), the "safe space" has been embraced as an administrative value and is now routinely used to shut down debate (e.g., discussions of racism are disallowed when white students profess to feel unsafe). This is the common fate of the political demand transmuted into an institutional *code of conduct*. By addressing the problem of male privilege at the level of the subject, #MeToo may be dislodging a few power players and shaking up a few corporate hierarchies, but it is ultimately gifting managers with a version of feminism that remains absolutely compatible with the subordination of the workforce to continuous and proliferating forms of assessment.

As a project of institutional transformation, then, it is hard to conceive that #MeToo will fundamentally redress either cultures of gender inequity or of managerial impunity. And yet, it is precisely by centering intersubjective relations as the ground zero for the exercise of male power that #MeToo provokes this mass feminist witnessing. Simply to dismiss its subject-centered view of power is to overlook what #MeToo stands to offer, namely, a rather startling report from the field of the heterosexual imaginary. Much of the published debate on this dimension of #MeToo has moved between supporters affirming the damaging consequences of men's ongoing claim to property in women's bodies, and critics who observe how so many of the #MeToo narratives appear to erase women's sexual agency altogether, particularly by suggesting that men can be culpable for their pursuit of *consensual* relations. As Masha Gessen observes, "In the current American conversation, women are increasingly treated as children: defenseless, incapable of consent, always on the verge of being victimized. This should give us pause. Being infantilized has never worked out well for women." This should, indeed, give us pause, but perhaps the more telling point is that this narrative—which for Gessen so clearly decodes as *ideological*—feels to so many of #MeToo's supporters as *just the reverse*: as at last a confrontation with their *real conditions* of existence.

This perspective, which I half intuited from the published debates, was finally clarified for me in a classroom conversation about the charges against Aziz Ansari, in which I noted that his accuser seemed at no point to have simply called a halt to the encounter or attempted to walk away. I felt when I offered the remark that even so much as commenting on the accuser's conduct was likely to come across as a retrograde intervention, and I commented on that circumstance as well, in part to ask a question about whether there seemed to be a generational divide in responses to #MeToo. My graduate students were uniform in their view that there was nothing contradictory or surprising about the accuser's acquiescence in what she would go on to describe as an abusive encounter. One student, in particular, captured what was obviously the group sentiment when she observed that this woman may have endured a past sexual trauma and (or) have anticipated that her "no" would not be respected. Saying no is risky, this student suggested, because it creates a scenario where the man might cross the line and forcibly continue the encounter. The woman might very reasonably have decided, she explained, that going along with an unwanted encounter was more tolerable than incurring the risk of rape by the act of saying no. Acquiescence in (unwanted) sex, she argued (to the general approbation of the class), can be understood as a defense against the greater trauma of coercion.

It is one thing to say that all women—certainly all heterosexual women—are never unaware of the possibility of coercion. It is quite another to say, as did my student, that this awareness fundamentally governs their orientation to sexual contact and preempts their capacity to say (and perhaps even to know) what they want. In the end, what seems truly arresting and significant about #MeToo is the possibility that it is symptomatizing a situation, rendered so acutely in my students' identification with Ansari's accuser, in which women routinely conceive that they cannot say no and therefore, I would add, can never really mean "yes."[4] We can lose ourselves, of course, in the familiar debates about sexuality and power: What does equality mean in the context of sexual relations? Can desire ever get clear of the workings of power? Should it? Is there a difference between the imposition of power and a (consensual) restaging of power in the mode of sexual play? If consent is inevitably acquiescence in coercion, what other vistas of sexual freedom might we imagine? But doing so is to miss the vital *ethnographic* content of what #MeToo reports. #MeToo is not (and should not be) a provocation to debate all over again whether Catharine MacKinnon was right in her analysis of gender and sexuality (she wasn't), *but* rather to notice that her vision of a monolithic male power that irreducibly structures heterosexual relations appears to correspond to how many women experience sexuality in the present moment: a scene structured in and by male dominance, where the extent of women's agency lies in the management of risk. The peculiar achievement of #MeToo as an exercise in feminist world building is to expose the deeply dystopian character of lived heterosexual relations. The task for (what we used to call) sex-positive feminisms is not to refute this vision of heterosexuality (as though engaging in the normative work of theory, the question of how we *ought* to conceive heterosexuality), but to reckon with its apparent hold on the psychic life of gender.

I am deeply indebted to the members of my winter 2018 graduate seminar in feminist theory, whose conversation on #MeToo moved me well afield of my original response and, in general, broadened and deepened my understanding of the phenomenon. While I suspect that few of them would concur with the analysis I offer here, I hope they will nevertheless discern how thoroughly their perspectives have challenged and honed my own.

EVA CHERNIAVSKY is the Andrew R. Hilen Professor of American Literature and Culture at the University of Washington. She teaches and publishes in the areas of U.S. literature, visual media, and critical theory. Her most recent book, *Neocitizenship: Political Culture after Democracy* (New York University Press, 2017), explores the shifting practices and imaginaries of citizenship in the present moment through the optic of popular culture.

Notes

1 See, for example, Gessen, "Al" and "Sex"; Levine; and Ward.

2 It is notable that #MeToo not only began as the outing by women of their male harassers but has *retained* this nearly exclusive focus on male abuse of women, rather than provoke (as one assumes it might have) more diverse sorts of revelations about male harassment of other men (Kevin Spacey seems the lone exception here), or of alleged female harassers (of men or other women). This seems all the more remarkable as straight men are by no means the sole or even the primary targets against whom accusations of sexual harassment

are leveled in the workplace. As many commentators have observed, existing sexual harassment statutes are routinely used to discipline gay men and women. From this perspective, it seems plain that #MeToo is fundamentally a reckoning with the politics of heterosexuality.

3   Even the normally reliable *Guardian* gets this wrong. See Sayej.

4   Laura Kipnis makes a cognate argument in her analysis of sexual culture on college campuses. While insisting on the ways in which university administration of sexual harassment and abuse complaints has institutionalized a view of women as vulnerable and sex as injurious, she is also attuned to the ways in which this understanding is deeply embedded and reproduced in the lived forms and imaginary of hook-up culture.

Works Cited

Burke, Tarana. "The Inception." *Just Be Inc.* http://justbeinc.wixsite.com/justbeinc/the-me-too-movement-cmml (accessed 20 Sept. 2018).

Gessen, Masha. "Al Franken's Resignation and the Selective Force of #MeToo." *New Yorker* 7 Dec. 2017. https://www.newyorker.com/news/our-columnists/al-franken-resignation-and-the-selective-force-of-metoo.

——————. "Sex, Consent, and the Dangers of Misplaced Scale." *New Yorker* 27 Nov. 2017. https://www.newyorker.com/news/our-columnists/sex-consent-dangers-of-misplaced-scale.

Kipnis, Laura. *Unwanted Advances: Sexual Paranoia Comes to Campus.* New York: Harper-Collins, 2017.

Levine, Judith. "Will Feminism's Past Mistakes Haunt #MeToo?" *Boston Review* 10 Dec. 2017. http://bostonreview.net/gender-sexuality/judith-levine-will-feminisms-past-mistakes-haunt-metoo.

Sayej, Nadja. "Alyssa Milano on the #MeToo Movement: We're Not Going to Stand for It Anymore." *Guardian* 1 Dec. 2017. https://www.theguardian.om/culture/2017/dec/01/alyssa-milan-me-too-sexual-harassment-abuse.

Ward, Jane. "Bad Girls: On Being the Accused." *Where Freedom Starts: Sex, Power, Violence and #MeToo.* Verso ebooks, 2018. https://www.versobooks.com/books/2773-where-freedom-starts-sex-power-violence-metoo.

KEYWORD 2

Solidarity

A sea of knitted pink was the most prominent image at women's marches following the inauguration of a president who proudly boasted of grabbing women "by the pussy." For organizers, the Pussyhat Project was designed to be a "symbol of support and solidarity of women's rights around the globe" ("Pussyhat"). For others its meaning was more dubious. Women of color widely pointed to the irony and questionable feasibility of uniting as "women" in protests against Donald Trump, given that 52 percent of white women voted for him (Mellow 106). Other critics lambasted the hat for being "offensive to transgender women and gender nonbinary people who don't have typical female genitalia and to women of color because their genitals are more likely to be brown than pink" (Shamus). In rebuttal, the organizers stated that pink is a "female color representing caring, compassion, and love" ("Pussyhat"). Setting aside the fact that the gendered association with pink did not congeal until the second half of the twentieth century and was shorn up to sell products, the ambiguity of the pussy hat as a unifying symbol illustrates the longstanding challenge of forming solidarity as "women" (Paoletti 92).

Volume 30, Number 1   DOI 10.1215/10407391-7481190

The form of solidarity suggested by the Pussyhat Project is partially what Émile Durkheim termed a *mechanical solidarity* that springs from understanding oneself as part of a fairly undifferentiated group (81). "All women" has been an undergirding premise of the #MeToo social media movement. Affinity springs from the idea that all women have experienced some form of sexual harassment, violence, or abuse. But the Pussyhat Project should also be understood as a form of *political solidarity*, which allows people to unite under a cause or issue. Every supporter does not need to share the same identity or experience to be anti–gender violence.[1] There are multiple (often overlapping) types of solidarity. While solidarity always entails people coming together as a unit that then understands itself as having a set of "positive moral obligations" to sustain or support the issue that unites them, the conditions for forming and maintaining solidarity vary (Scholz 18–19).

Disaggregating solidarity projects can aid us in exploring what kinds of solidarity we should practice and when. One of the problems with utopian fantasies of solidarity is the idea that all right-minded people will be "in solidarity with" the person claiming injury. We are all on the side of victims of racists. We are all on the side of victims of rapists. Conflicts nevertheless emerge when people do not recognize some injuries as real or differ on the question of degree. The collapse of various injuries under the rubric of #MeToo have given rise to conflicts among feminists who disagree on the nature or extent of an injury. Author Zinzi Clemmons accused celebrated writer Junot Díaz of kissing her without her consent when she was a graduate student and writers Monica Byrne and Carmen Maria Machado alleged that he verbally abused them in public arguments with him. Díaz's feminist defenders have questioned the conflation of offenses and make a case for the possibility of repentance (Flaherty). When a woman described a date with comedian Aziz Ansari as sexual assault, some feminists affirmed her, and others termed it "bad sex" (Weiss). These conflicts demonstrate that a "reasonable woman" standard, as Jodi Dean has argued, can be just as contentious as the reasonable man standard that has governed jurisprudence (109).

I do not propose to solve these conflicts in my brief discussion of solidarity. But I would like to make a case for the specificity of the different claims grouped under the category of "sexual injury to women" in order to think with more precision about the kind of solidarity projects that are required. In the case of #MeToo, one of the most important outcomes of its recent iteration has been its elucidation of sexual harassment in the

workplace. While there has undoubtedly been political utility in acknowledging the pervasiveness of sexual assault, sexual harassment, and other
kinds of sexual injury writ large, we risk losing the lessons of what must be
remedied if injuries are homogenized.

A narrowed range of responses is another risk of homogeniz-
ing injuries. A feminist principle should be that people who come forward
to disclose that they have been sexually assaulted, harassed, or otherwise
victimized have an unassailable right to ask for the kind of support that is
best for them. They alone can know the scale of their injury. And yet, it is
also important to have what I term *scaled solidarity*: the complicated and
inevitably inadequate process of designing responses and punishments
proportionate to the injury. Acknowledging difference on every level—no
matter how challenging that can be to solidarity projects—is nonetheless
essential to long-term political success.

The origins of feminist solidarity, sometimes referred to as "sisterhood," are nineteenth-century suffragist activism and rhetoric organized
around women as an undifferentiated biological category of subjected, disenfranchised citizens. Solidarity as "women" is a utopian project that does
both affective and strategic work, which many feminists continue to utilize
well into the twentieth century even as feminists of color and some queer
theorists have pushed back against the erasure of power differentials among
women produced by universalist rhetoric. But in the nineteenth century and
today, people who have questioned the essentialist rhetoric have sometimes
been accused of being obstructive to progress (and often, disrespectful to
lionized white feminists).

Feminists of color such as bell hooks and Chandra Talpade
Mohanty have argued that we cannot and "do not need to eradicate difference
to feel solidarity" (hooks 138) and that the basis of solidarity can be "common differences" (Mohanty 503–4). Rather than see solidarity as natural and
based on biology, hooks argues that solidarity should be seen as a "revolutionary accomplishment" that women must "work and struggle to obtain"
(127). Victimization, for hooks, is a poor foundation for a politics of solidarity
because "women who are exploited and oppressed daily cannot afford to
relinquish the belief that they exercise some measure of control, however
relative, over their lives" (128). Whether or not we accept hooks's claim that
some women reject inhabiting the category of victim in self-understanding
or activism, the idea that everyone does not experience and interpret injury
in the same way has utility in exploring the diverse responses needed for
various feminist interventions.

The importance of recognizing different kinds of injury is essential to responding appropriately and sustaining solidarity-shaped political work. Different interpretations of what counts as injury and the homogenization of all injuries have, in fact, challenged solidarity around Title IX and #MeToo activism. The organizational challenge is not so much about agreeing that we are the same as about discovering remedies that speak to real differences in injury (even if injuries sometimes roughly fit into the same category of gender oppression).

Solidarity projects are often organized around identity politics. Many commentators on the Right and the (ostensible) Left blamed Hillary Clinton's defeat on such "identity politics" after the 2016 election, some focusing on feminists, people of color, and queer people as "narcissistically unaware of conditions outside of their self-defined groups, and indifferent to the tasks of reaching out to Americans in every walk of life" (Lilla). Such criticisms placed white, working-class people (often men) at the center of American life without irony, ignoring the white colonialist, racist, and sexist identity politics that have organized u.s. law and society for over four hundred years. Some liberal and Leftist critics believed addressing inequalities other than class was obstructive to solidarity because these "other issues" allegedly displaced class as a central issue and focused on "multiplying victim minorities" (Smith). And yet, the election of Donald Trump clearly mobilized white identity politics in the long tradition of white nationalist solidarity projects.

In contrast, the #MeToo social media–based social movement that re-emerged in 2017 crossed race, class, and national lines, even as affluent white women were the visible torchbearers for the movement. African American activist Tarana Burke mobilized the phrase "Me Too" in 2006 to address the ubiquity of sexual violence against girls and women, and she was particularly concerned with the silence around injury to girls and women of color. But the phrase gained new life after the multiple stories about powerful Hollywood producer Harvey Weinstein sexually harassing and assaulting women in the industry were published in the *New York Times* and *New Yorker* in October of 2017. Shortly thereafter, actress Alyssa Milano tweeted: "Me too. Suggested by a friend: 'If all the women who have been sexually assaulted wrote "Me too." as a status, we might give people a sense of the magnitude of the problem'" (Milano).

Echoing Burke's original intent, Facebook and Twitter were filled with #MeToo testimonials from people around the world, mostly stories of injuries that had not been redressed, creating an overwhelming testament to the everyday nature of sexual harassment and assault of women. Some men also spoke of injury, but the perpetrators were overwhelmingly men and the victims predominately women, indicative of a kind of MacKinnonite domination in which "the defining theme [. . .] is the male pursuit of control over women's sexuality—men not as individuals nor as biological beings, but as a gender group characterized by maleness as socially constructed, of which this pursuit is definitive" (MacKinnon 532). #MeToo is, by turns, an expression of affinity, a witnessing, and a call to arms.

As with the Pussyhat Project, #MeToo gains influence and promotes solidarity through the lack of differentiation. And yet, all the stories are not the same. The slippage between a sexist joke, a catcall, an unwanted hug at work, quid pro quo sexual harassment, and rape does the work of illustrating how sexual violence should be seen on a spectrum. #MeToo can nevertheless flatten out differences and mask the specificity of injuries. Uniting against the big "P"—Patriarchy—encourages consciousness raising but may not address how these varied injuries require different forms of redress. In other words, we can be in solidarity with each other against men guilty of sexual misconduct or assault, but that solidarity's utility in designing a path for redress can be hampered by constructing too broad a category of injury and too few options for punishment.

Burke offered a powerful intervention into silence around sexual violence. However, despite the criticism that the 2017 #MeToo moment only made the issue legible because wealthy, attractive, white women became the face of it, I think it also offers an opportunity to speak specifically to issues of women and labor and the myths around women and work that have circulated to defend the sexist status quo. The solidarity that emerged in Hollywood addressed not only psychological (and sometimes physical) harms but also economic harms produced by women's shared vulnerabilities to sexual abuse at work; as workers, women were expected to add sex work to their already delineated jobs. As Gayle Rubin reminds us in her classic essay, "The Traffic in Women," understanding the economics of gender oppression helps us understand the "exact mechanisms by which particular conventions of sexuality are produced and maintained" (47). #MeToo allows us to see these actresses as workers who experience discrimination as workers precisely *because* they are women. Pornography and modeling are the rare forms of the entertainment industry where women receive more compensation because they are women, a market enabled by women legally having the most value because of their appearance. If that is often treated as women's most powerful capital in the entertainment industry, powerful men have long understood their capital as giving them access to women's bodies as a condition of market exchange. Some critics of #MeToo have charged that its political visibility has arisen only because those giving it voice are affluent white women who function as "good victims" in discourses of injury, a discursive practice that I have discussed elsewhere (Wanzo 204–22). While Hollywood actresses seem to be poor examples of canaries in coalmines, the lack of regulation in their industry does provide a powerful example of the specific kind of injury that women disproportionately face in unchecked capitalism.

Harvey Weinstein is a perfect example of MacKinnonite male domination. There was literally no way to win within the system in which he wielded so much power. He was the head of his company; there was thus no one supervising him to whom women could appeal. As actress Ashley Judd asked derisively, "Were we supposed to call some fantasy attorney general of moviedom?" (Lockett). In this perfect system of male domination, speaking up resulted in losing work. But women who remained silent were indicted for not choosing other lines of work, for not being heroes "helping other women," even though there was no one to appeal to who could prevent someone with his power from being a perpetrator. Message boards are filled with people claiming women "knew the game," as if quid pro quo for sex is a work condition that *might* be regrettable but not untenable. Women who might have submitted to him for the chance at work could be judged for exchanging sex for opportunity. It was an open secret, and the entire industry enabled this behavior.

Weinstein has also been accused of rape, but sexual assault does not define every single interaction he had with women he injured. In every case, however, this was a story of women attempting to work and of an infrastructure in which sex work was considered a requirement not only for employment but often for the *opportunity* for employment. The acceptance of this practice as a regrettable but unavoidable part of the industry treated sexual harassment as a job hazard. I emphasize what all the women have in common not to suggest that any victim's injury holds greater or lesser value, but to zero in on a category of injury that requires specific responses.

The remedies to sexual injury in Hollywood have not taken a broad approach. Time's Up, a coalition of women in Hollywood, has been focused specifically on supporting issues of sexual injury in the workplace in Hollywood and elsewhere ("Our"). Feminists may sometimes disagree on what counts as sexual injury and may also lack solidarity on whether or not the erotic can, or should, be erased from spaces where people work.

However, feminists and nonfeminists alike should be able to build a coalition around the idea that sex acts, unwanted touching, and coerced intimate performances—including affective labor demanded from a sexually suggestive work environment—should not be a condition for employment in non-sex work industries. And those who do work in industries requiring some aspect of sex work should not perform work they have not agreed to and for which they are not compensated.

Both Gayle Rubin's and Catharine MacKinnon's Marxist analyses demonstrate the ways in which mechanical solidarity / identity affinity models can still be useful when speaking to injuries that "women" as a category might experience in specific structural contexts. In the decades since many women attached to second wave feminism did their work, many theorists have pushed back against what has been seen as essentialism, biological determinism, and totalizing frameworks. And yet, their structural accounts still have a great deal of utility for understanding how the *refusal* to recognize that such structures exist perpetuates the continued existence of those structures.

That said, one of the pitfalls of mechanical solidarity, Durkheim argues, is repressive law. He saw homogeneity as encouraging repressive juridical models when people feel connected through identity categories (57–84). In other words, the more linked a community feels because of sameness, the more undifferentiated their responses. And in the wake of not only #MeToo but a broader discussion of the range of offenses, from sexual nuisance to sexual assault, we need to construct varied responses. Mechanical / single affinity solidarity models can fail to make distinctions between injuries or to accommodate other solidarity commitments. This is why we also need a feminist scaled solidarity model.

A feminist scaled solidarity acknowledges that an end to gender oppression in all its forms is an absolute good, and everyone who experiences such oppression has a right to pursue individuated, reparative, and structural redress. But because gendered injury does not exist in isolation from other solidarity commitments, feminists must also do the difficult and inevitably inadequate work of constructing proportional responses that allow us to continue inhabiting a world in which these injuries are omnipresent. In other words, scaled solidarity takes seriously the MacKinnonite belief in the embeddedness of gendered oppression but believes that this very omnipresence mandates that everyone who commits injurious acts cannot be discarded.

Seeing all sexual injuries as the same is a feminist form of broken windows policing that does not allow us to imagine that those who commit injuries can change or be stopped from committing other acts of violence. Critiquing the feminist alliance with the state in relation to gendered violence has been a project of Incite!, which has recognized that this coalition does not always make communities stronger. A feminist scaled solidarity negotiates the competing solidarities of anti-incarceration projects and antigendered violence.

Sometimes a civic or institutional solidarity—obligations of a state or institution to its citizens—can come into conflict with best practices models for survivors. Sexual assault survivor advocates often suggest that punishment should be dictated by the survivor and be "trauma based." On the one hand, survivors must have the right to pursue the path that they deem best for their well-being; but on the other, institutions have an obligation to the safety of others, an interest in preventing recurrence, and a commitment to due process for the accused. If survivors determine punishment, it is not unlikely that people will receive dissimilar punishments for similar offenses. A feminist scaled solidarity acknowledges that the seamless interaction of the political, social, legal, and therapeutic may not always be possible, and it understands institutional limits.

If a feminist scaled solidarity is often about establishing limits, it can also be about expanding our notion of what kinds of coalitions and solutions are possible. For example, in the #LoveWithAccountability forum, filmmaker, child sexual abuse survivor, and activist Aishah Shahidah Simmons argues that we need to question the idea that we lock up all perpetrators and "throw away the key." In one forum essay, survivor Danielle Lee Moss makes a case for restorative reconciliation, which suggests to an abuser that "neither of us has to be defined by the worst thing you ever did." A scaled solidarity acknowledges that some survivors will continue to work and live with their abusers, and they *are right.* It acknowledges that some will want their abusers to be locked away forever, and they *are also right.* It acknowledges that some people commit horrific crimes and will never change, while some people commit horrific crimes and may still hold some value to their families and communities. A feminist scaled solidarity acknowledges that there is not one answer to injury, that all injuries are not the same, and that one can be in solidarity with the cause of ending gender oppression and still commit to the ethical project of constructing responses to injury that consider difference. In a world of widespread injury, feminists must have some model of response that acknowledges the impossibility of wiping all offenders from the map. A feminist scaled solidarity abandons all-or-nothing responses when it recognizes that transformation for some perpetrators might mean salvation for all of us.

REBECCA WANZO is an associate professor of women, gender, and sexuality studies at Washington University in St. Louis. Her publications include *The Suffering Will Not Be Televised: African American Women and Sentimental Political Storytelling* (State University of New York Press, 2009) and essays in edited collections and journals such as *American Literature, Camera Obscura, The Journal of Popular Culture*, and *Women & Performance*. She is currently completing *The Content of Our Caricature*, a discussion of black citizenship discourse in comics and cartoon art.

Note   1   Sally J. Scholz argues that political solidarity is always about addressing oppression, but many people in power, I would argue, form bonds of political solidarity.

Works Cited   Dean, Jodi. *Solidarity of Strangers: Feminism after Identity Politics.* Berkeley: U of California P, 1996.

Durkheim, Émile. *The Division of Labor in Society.* 1893. Trans. W. D. Hall. Ed. Steven Lukes. New York: Free Press, 2014.

Flaherty, Colleen. "Junot Díaz, Feminism, and Ethnicity." *Inside Higher Ed* 29 May 2018. https://www.insidehighered.com/news/2018/05/29/rift-among-scholars-over-treatment-junot-d%C3%ADaz-he-faces-harassment-and-misconduct.

hooks, bell. "Sisterhood: Political Solidarity between Women." *Feminist Review* 23 (1986): 125–38.

Lilla, Mark. *The Once and Future Liberal: After Identity Politics.* New York: Harper, 2017.

Lockett, Dee. "Ashley Judd Says She Finally Went on the Record about Harvey Weinstein Because 'It Was the Right Thing to Do.'" *Vulture* 6 Dec. 2017. http://www.vulture.com/2017/12/why-ashley-judd-went-on-the-record-about-harvey-weinstein.html.

MacKinnon, Catharine. "Feminism, Marxism, Method, and the State: An Agenda for Theory." *Signs* 7.3 (1982): 515–44.

Mellow, Nicole E. "Voting Behavior: Continuity and Confusion in the Electorate." *The Elections of 2016.* Ed. Michael Nelson. London: Sage, 2018. 87–112.

Milano, Alyssa (@Alyssa_Milano). "If you've been sexually harassed or assaulted write 'me too' as a reply to this tweet." *Twitter* 15 Oct. 2017, 1:21 p.m. https://twitter.com/alyssa_milano/status/919659438700670976.

Mohanty, Chandra Talpade. "'Under Western Eyes' Revisited: Feminist Solidarity through Anticapitalist Struggles." *Signs* 2 (2003): 499–535.

Moss, Danielle Lee. "Love Centered Accountability." 17 Oct. 2016. *LoveWithAccountability.* http://www.lovewithaccountability.com/lovewithaccountability-forum/2016/10/17/love-centered-accountability-by-dr-danielle-lee-moss.

Paoletti, Jo B. *Pink and Blue: Telling the Boys from the Girls in America*. Bloomington: Indiana UP, 2012.

"Pussyhat Project Global Outreach." *Pussyhat Project* 18 Feb. 2018. https://www.pussyhatproject .com/blog/2017/2/17/yziene25963eoqq26n0sv7ihp82fps.

Rubin, Gayle. "The Traffic in Women: Notes on the Political Economy of Sex." *Deviations: A Gayle Rubin Reader*. Durham: Duke UP, 2011. 33–65.

Scholz, Sally J. *Political Solidarity*. University Park: Pennsylvania State UP, 2008.

Shamus, Kristen Jordan. "Pink Pussyhats: The Reason Feminists Are Ditching Them." *Detroit Free Press* 20 Jan. 2018. https://www.freep.com/story/news/2018/01/10/pink-pussyhats -feminists-hats-womens-march/1013630001/.

Simmons, Aishah Shahidah. "Digging Up the Roots: An Introduction to the LoveWithAccount-abilility Forum." 17 Oct. 2016. http://www.lovewithaccountability.com/lovewithaccountability -forum/2016/10/17/digging-up-the-roots-an-introduction-to-the-lovewithaccountability -forum-1.

Smith, Michael K. "Class Politics: Identity Politics without the Identity." *Counterpunch* 5 Dec. 2017. https://www.counterpunch.org/2017/12/05/class-dismissed-identity-politics-without -the-identity/.

"Our Letter of Solidarity." *Time's Up*. https://www.timesupnow.com (accessed 5 Oct. 2018).

Wanzo, Rebecca. *The Suffering Will Not Be Televised: African American Women and Senti-mental Political Storytelling*. Albany: State U of New York P, 2009.

Weiss, Bari. "Asiz Ansari Is Guilty. Of Not Being a Mind Reader." *New York Times* 15 Jan. 2018. https://www.nytimes.com/2018/01/15/opinion/aziz-ansari-babe-sexual-harassment.html.

Catharine MacKinnon's Wayward Children

*I*t is hard to diagnose a sex panic when you are in one. Only with the hindsight of generational perspective, "when some of the smoke has cleared," might the nation be embarrassed by its demonization of sexual minorities (Rubin 7). Even then it is an unsure bet. Yet presentism is not all that cautions against categorizing the post-Weinstein sexual climate a tempest, for a telltale sign of sex panic is that the men targeted are otherwise minoritized figures: Jewish, black, Mediterranean, gay, pedophilic, whatever. In the current instance, it is chiefly straight white men in power who are being named and shamed as perpetrators of sexual violence, even as a few famous gay men and several celebrity men of color have been outed too.

So are we witnessing a revitalized feminism drawing attention to the pervasiveness and stubbornness of sex inequality? Or are we in a sex panic? Yes and possibly.

The first part of this essay interrogates the substance, significance, and style of feminist legal thinker Catharine MacKinnon's oeuvre. I shall argue that both the feminist dimensions of our contemporary sexual landscape (identifying, then remedying, conduct as sexually discriminating

Volume 30, Number 1   DOI 10.1215/10407391-7481204

or subordinating) and its panicked equivalences (regrouping consented-to but unwanted sex as assaultive) can be understood nontrivially but incompletely as MacKinnon's progeny. She bequeaths both political projects to feminism: two political children.

The second part of the essay tracks the rhetorical use of "children" in MacKinnon's scholarship, the textual travails of MacKinnon's little girls. *Children* perform two rhetorical functions for MacKinnon. First, the "child" (and case law pertaining to the sexual harassment and pornography of children) allows MacKinnon to draw out *innocence* as an ideological formation that mystifies the sexual subordination of women. Second, MacKinnon remodels women as children. By rendering the former always already helpless against, vulnerable to, and abused by sex, MacKinnon authorizes a politics of censorship and repression: a politics categorically opposed to pornography, prostitution, and kink, certainly, and all but categorically opposed to sex. The ways the child and its cognates affectively and schematically operate in MacKinnon's texts serve to mirror and magnify a feminist politics split, at once radical and transformative, paternalistic and panicked.

MacKinnon's quadruplets—the two political projects her writing propels along with the two girls that work their way through her prose—sustain and advance a feminism unparalleled in its capacity to identify and redress sex inequality, a feminism that also, perhaps always, maybe consequently, catastrophizes sex as presumptively nefarious, rape-like if not rape.[1]

MacKinnon's Political Children

The Good Child

All but literally might we comprehend contemporary sexual politics as the progeny of Catharine MacKinnon. One prong of those politics—let's shorthand it as "#MeToo"—is the naming, shaming, and sometimes ousting of elite, famous, power-holding men for sexually assaulting and/or harassing girls and/or women. The second prong of our sexual politics—let's shorthand it as "Title IX"—is the overhaul of university procedures and policies to address and reduce sexual violence on campus. These prongs, #MeToo and Title IX, could not exist but for the feminist lawyering and legal theorizing of MacKinnon.

Although she did not coin the term, MacKinnon "invented the legal claim for sexual harassment" (Galanes). MacKinnon's writings in the 1970s while at Yale Law School gave credence to the notion that sexual harassment is a form of unlawful sex discrimination as proscribed by Title VII of the Civil Rights Act of 1964 and Title IX of the Education Amendments of 1972. Most of us assume that the equivalence, sexual harassment = sex discrimination, needs no argument, let alone a full-fledged elaboration. It once did, however, and MacKinnon provided it in her *Sexual Harassment of Working Women* (1979) and in her briefs and advice as official and unofficial counsel for the earliest plaintiffs in sexual harassment cases. Indeed, not only the equivalence but also the commonsensicality, the *duh*ness, of the equivalence is in large part a result of MacKinnon's labor (MacKinnon, "Logic" 822). As MacKinnon put it years later, she was the first person to articulate this "big idea" that "sexual violation is at the core of sex discrimination" (MacKinnon and Suskind; but see Schultz). Sex discrimination consists not only in being fired, demoted, or disqualified from employment based on sex (the paradigmatic parallels of race-based discrimination), argued MacKinnon, but also in being subject to a sexually hostile work environment, to having employment opportunities conditioned on sex with the boss, and to being pressured on threat of termination to conform to normatively gendered comportment and sartorial styles (*Sexual*; see also Bellafante). MacKinnon was co-counsel and cowrote the brief for Mechelle Vinson, whose lawsuit against her employer led the Supreme Court to declare sexual harassment as actionable sex discrimination, even in the absence of tangible economic damages; that is, a hostile environment may be sufficient to constitute unlawful harassment (*Meritor Savings Bank v. Vinson*). MacKinnon, as a law student, also advised the plaintiffs of *Alexander v. Yale*, a 1977 court ruling that held that universities could be found in violation of Title IX for failing to systemically address sexual harassment on campuses. The decision was a watershed in the process of transforming a federal law historically enforced to equalize athletic opportunities for male and female college students into a tool compelling educational institutions to develop sexual misconduct policies, procedures, and bureaucracies (MacKinnon, "In Their Hands" 2062–63; Gersen and Suk). The regulatory expansion of Title IX under the Obama Administration got off the ground in large part because of *Alexander v. Yale*, and *Alexander v. Yale* got off the ground in large part because of MacKinnon's theory of sexual harassment as sex-based subordination (MacKinnon and Mitra). As one plaintiff recalls, "[F]ortunately, part of the manuscript of *Sexual Harassment of Working Women* was available to help us formulate our arguments" (Simon 54).

When we talk about sexual harassment like it's a bad thing and not just a regular Monday morning on the job, or when we talk about the lecherous professor as not just lecherous but violative and discriminating, we owe MacKinnon a debt of gratitude. That casting couch conditionals, exhibitionist executives, handsy newscasters, and entitled politicians can be constellated into a universe of "sexual harassment" is what vitalizes the #MeToo campaign; it allows women and the rest of us to connect the dots and name the elephants (Weinstein, Moore, Lauer, Halperin, and so on): this is sex discrimination. As MacKinnon herself comments, "Sexual harassment law [. . .] created the preconditions for this [#MeToo] moment" ("#MeToo").

We should be skeptical of Great Man Theory, of course, maybe less so when it is Great Woman Theory, but even then, we know that social movements, cultural transformations, and policy reforms materialize through combinations of coordination and happenstance never attributable solely to her or him. Regarding sexual harassment, we should be especially careful not to whiten the narrative. As MacKinnon points out, beginning in the late 1970s, black women like Eleanor Holmes Norton, Maxine Munford, Diane Williams, Paulette Barnes, Pamela Price, Sandra Bundy, and Mechelle Vinson were at the forefront of sexual harassment law as plaintiffs, attorneys, and activists ("Logic" 826; see also Baker; Lipsitz; and MacKinnon and Mitra). Law professor Anita Hill's testimony in 1991 before the Senate Judiciary Committee detailing Justice Clarence Thomas's inappropriate behavior as her employer "was like a national consciousness raising session" (MacKinnon and Suskind). So, too, has Hill been an outspoken advocate for harnessing the energies released by the rich, white celebrity women of #MeToo—itself a campaign against sexual violence first organized by black civil rights activist Tarana Burke—to call out the pervasiveness of sexual harassment across lower income and disproportionately racial minority vectors of employment (Garcia; Gonzales; Sperling). Nonetheless, MacKinnon is centrally responsible for establishing sexual harassment as both an actionable legal claim and a cognizable social malady. She formulated as a legal wrong what had until then been experienced as an institutional, injurious norm: "As women's pain broke through public silence, their resistance to sexual abuse became articulated as a deprivation of their entitlement to equality, and social movement became institutional change generating further social movement," like #MeToo and Title IX activism ("Logic" 813).

So that is one reading of MacKinnon, as feminist forebear of a contemporary movement exposing the varieties and ubiquity of sexual harassment. But the #MeToo moment has its critics. One central concern leveled at #MeToo is what we can call the problem of "lumping," the supposed equating of rape with quid pro quo sexual favors with exhibitionism with forceful kissing with aggressive flirting, and the summary dismissal or exile of the perpetrators (see, for example, Peyser; Young). For the most part, the charge of lumping, a charge MacKinnon finds "boring and predictable," detonates on itself when the very sine qua non of #MeToo is to relump, to reclassify as sex discriminatory conduct that heretofore passed as ordinary (male) behavior (Galanes).

The difficulty with the exhortation to delump is that feminist consciousness raising is about lumping (MacKinnon, *Toward* 83–105): *This thing happened to you? Well that thing happened to me.* This thing, that thing, and all the other things—privileges and practices of male entitlement—demean and subordinate women. Sexual harassment law, like consciousness raising, wills to lump. MacKinnon's project is and has always been a relumping project. One need not be raped to be sexually harassed; a whole assortment of behaviors that may not reach criminal thresholds of sexual assault are nevertheless unlawful and actionable as sexual harassment. One need not be fired, not hired, demoted, or not promoted on the basis of sex for conduct to count as sex discrimination. Sexual harassment, as developed by case law, admits all kinds of workplace and schoolhouse conduct—bullying, name-calling, and even sometimes simply sex itself—as discriminatory sex practices. Indeed, that there are two indexical forms of sexual harassment, one targeting sexual misconduct across vertical relations (quid pro quo transactions, for example, *have sex with me and I'll promote you*) and the other targeting sexual misconduct across horizontal relations (hostile environment, for example, severe and pervasive bullying), speaks to the lumping directive at the core of the law and at the core of the contemporary movement.

Consider, from MacKinnon and #MeToo perspectives, comedian Louis C. K., who is on the bad man list primarily for masturbating in front of other women comedians and associates. News reports of his alleged misconduct, if we lived in a sex-equal world (which is to say, a world-changing "if"), would not be so condemning. After all, Louis C. K. requested the affirmative consent of two women comedians before proceeding to masturbate in front of them; Louis C. K. did not masturbate in front of a woman after she denied his request; another young woman agreed to watch Louis C. K. masturbate; a woman performer listened to Louis C. K. masturbate on the phone for several minutes and did not hang up (Ryzik, Buckley, and Kantor).

In the cases documented, Louis C. K. did not physically contact, let alone penetrate, any of the complainants; he did not force himself upon them or use coercive methods; he did not condition job promotion or demotion on sex; in short, he requested consent to jerk off. Is he not the fantasy man of satirized university sexual misconduct codes?

MacKinnon's interventions offer both a vocabulary and a political analysis to identify what is wrongful about Louis C. K.'s conduct. For what morally indicts C. K.'s behavior is not consent, or rather not *nonconsent*, as if the women refused C. K.'s advances and he forced himself upon them. Rather, C. K.'s behavior is immoral, inter alia, because it is conditioned upon as it perpetuates sex inequality.

When MacKinnon writes, "[C]onsent is a pathetic standard of equal sex for a free people," what she means is: it arrives too late ("Rape" 465). She concedes that affirmative consent is a better standard from criminal sex law than silence or nonconsent (MacKinnon and Suskind), but the substitution does absolutely nothing to change a sex unequal world. A lot of sex that is consented to and agreed upon, even affirmatively, is no doubt immiserating or unpleasant, or the pleasure is one-sided (for him). It is also sex that installs inequality, affirmation that affirms sex hierarchy. From these lights, every time the young woman on the set of *The Chris Rock Show* reluctantly permitted Louis C. K. to masturbate in front of her, she ratified, to him, her subordination: *I am your cum rag*. Her yes-saying says yes to his superordination and entitlement. That problem cannot be fixed through redefining consent, consent education, or saying "yes" ever more boldly. That problem, braided from three others—enculturation (*I should demur, I should not cause a scene*), fear of repercussions (getting fired or bad-mouthed in a close-knit industry), and lack of alternatives (*where will I get a gig now?*)—is structural, which does not mean it is irresolvable. A promise of #MeToo is to lift the curtain enough times on men, on men in positions of power, on whole industries and employment vectors, on everyday practices that should never have become just-the-way-things-are, to transform the conditions of our public lives, professional possibilities, and our intimacies.

The Evil Twin

The lump-critics are not altogether wrong, however, in noticing how more and more sex across power differences—which is all sex—is perceived as suspect if not wrongful. And in this trend, too, we might see MacKinnon's political child, an evil twin.

In an interview at Harvard Law School, MacKinnon concedes that someone like Louis C. K.—brutish but not brutal, clumsily domineering but not coercive—should not be imprisoned for his behavior and that such behavior should not be considered criminal (MacKinnon and Suskind). However, once the wrong of the comedian's conduct is identified as the same kind of wrong as the wrong of rape—for rape, asserts MacKinnon, is "a crime of inequality that fundamentally includes gender" ("Rape" 436), or more simply, "rape is a crime of gender inequality" (431)—we find ourselves headed toward a cul-de-sac of sex inequality equivalencies proximate to but not identical with the cul-de-sac of all-sex-across-power-relationships-is-rape. For it is one matter to claim that a core wrong of rape is the instantiation of gender inequality. It is another matter to claim that all sex under unequal conditions, or that all sex eroticized by or partially procured through inequality, is rape. MacKinnon entertains the latter position: "Awareness of social hierarchy is absent in the criminal law of rape's treatment of force [. . .]. [F]orms of force typically correlated with male sex and gender—such as the economic dominion of employers, dominance in the patriarchal family, [. . .] *not to mention the clout of male approval and the masculine ability to affirm and confirm feminine identity*—are not regarded as forms of force at all. But they are" (*Women's* 244; emphasis added).

We are in a sex pickle nearing panic. If legal "force" includes, as it probably should, forms of conduct and exploitation of vulnerability beyond physical overpowering, but also includes, as it likely should not, "the clout of male approval"; and if rape is legally defined, as MacKinnon proposes, as "a physical invasion of a sexual nature under circumstances of threat or use of force" ("Rape" 474), then Louis C. K. *is* a rapist precisely for leveraging the young women's yearning for his attention. Even as MacKinnon qualifies that for sex to count as rape an inequality must be "exploite[d]" or "direct[ly] use[d]," she reads *exploitation* and *direct use* into any sex that is consented to but unwanted ("Rape" 474, 476; *Women's* 243–44). Indeed, such an interpretation is central to her proposal in "Rape Redefined" to excise consent altogether from rape law.

MacKinnon neither wrote nor said that all sex is rape, but sex is guilty until proven innocent ("Rape" 476). Sex is not simply one of many vectors of inequality between men and women, alongside, say, the inequalities perpetuated in employment, education, and the family. Sex—sex as in sexuality, heterosexuality, gender, and fucking—is *the* power plant of sex inequality for MacKinnon ("Feminism, Marxism, Method, and the State: An Agenda" 515).[2] "Our sexuality, meaning gender identity, is not only violable, it *is* (hence we are) our violation" ("Feminism, Marxism, Method, and the State: Toward" 656). It is this core contribution of MacKinnon's, frustrating and fascinating, unshakably true yet wildly hyperbolic, that underpins so much feminist unsureness about sex, a contribution that impels us to see the mandate of #MeToo as both the naming and shaming of bad men as well as the quarantining of every man (because every man is everyman) on the planet from school, work, and any other place girls and women exist.

While that nonexistent predicative, *all sex is rape,* is falsely attributed to caricature her argument (*Women's* 327–38), MacKinnon does insist that sex installs inequality, that sex is inequality, that sex makes inequality between the sexes, and that sex, "ordinary" sex under patriarchal conditions, produces and perpetuates patriarchy. Add to this equation her later argument that sex is rape when a woman "feels" sex as violating (*Feminism* 82) or when sex is perceived as violating from "a woman's point of view" (*Toward* 182), and the #MeToo movement and its addressees inherit another legacy of MacKinnon, another political child.[3]

When MacKinnon condemns all pornography ("Pornography, Civil"), prostitution ("Prostitution"; "Trafficking, Prostitution, and Inequality"), BDSM sex ("Feminism, Marxism, Method, and the State: Toward" 650; *Women's* 264), a whole lot of gay sex ("Road"), and a whole lot of straight sex ("Feminism, Marxism, Method, and the State: Toward"; *Women's* 129) as unequal, therefore wrongful, and possibly rape, these condemnations are fuel for the fire of sex negativity turned sex panic turned indictment of all sexual contact men initiate. Journalist Glenn Thrush was removed (later suspended) from the *New York Times* for hitting on, sometimes kissing, younger women at bars. I am not defending his conduct, but the Thrush case is an instance in which it seems to me that lumping—lumping of behaviors ("It wasn't that Thrush was offering young women a quid pro quo deal [. . .]. Thrush, just by his stature . . ."), experience ("each woman described feeling [. . .] scared, violated, ashamed, weirded out"), and penalties—may disserve #MeToo (McGann). This lumping, in which feeling "weirded out" is like feeling "violated," or in which sex secured through threat of demotion is comparable to an influential colleague moving in for the kiss, potentially undercuts the feminist aspirations of the movement. Not incidentally, this will-to-lump is in lockstep with MacKinnon's worldview, or at least one of them: that sex between people unequal to each other along some socially salient dimension is, presumptively, rape. It is the same line of thinking, seductively syllogistic and profoundly misguided, that led one journalist to claim that Louis C. K.'s *asking* a woman to show her his penis is "enough to make her feel threatened" and that his "words alone" (words, recall, seeking consent) are "a major part of his harassment" (Cauterucci). Let me reiterate that I find C. K.'s alleged behaviors not just reprehensible but sex subordinating. Nevertheless, to reclassify those behaviors as threatening and harassing is hasty, incites conservative backlash, and triggers a chain of equivalences that foments alarmism.

MacKinnon's political children grow apart, amping up sex panic and eradicating sex inequality. This split is sharpened by her rhetorical children: the "child," the "girl," and the "teenager" inhabit MacKinnon's oeuvre. They embody as they escalate an intractable ambiguity bestowed by MacKinnon to feminist politics.

MacKinnon's Rhetorical Children

The Good Child

An uninjured and even occasionally desirous girl travels across MacKinnon's scholarship. Yet MacKinnon rhetorically deploys the child and the teenager less to reclassify them as sexually agentic subjects than to shore up how the nation's sentimental attachment to their sexlessness buttresses sex inequality and leaves women unprotected by law and unprotected from men. Herewith, four examples.

1. When assessing age of consent laws, MacKinnon writes:

[T]his rule [. . .] confuses people by defining as rape some sex that some people want to have [. . .]. If the rape law worked, there would be no need for statutory rape laws. Abuse of power, access, trust, and exploitation of vulnerabilities to pressure people into sex that is not wanted for its own sake would be illegal [. . .]. Young age [. . .] is thus ossified into an absolute rule. This segregates out some of the most sympathetic cases for relative structural powerlessness in sexual interactions and leaves the rest of the victims [. . .] unprotected, their inequalities uncounted. By cushioning its excesses, this helps keeps male dominance as a social system in place. (Women's 245–46)

This is stunningly brilliant commentary, despite (actually, because of) its misreading of sex law and its empirical questionability.[4] First, MacKinnon asserts that some people, young girls no less, might want to have sex, and that that sex should not be coded as rape (this is quite a concession from a scholar made famous for defining heterosexuality as the eroticization of male dominance and female submission): "All that fumbling around might be the most equal sex they will have in their lives" ("Rape" 471). Second, MacKinnon goes after the seemingly unassailable—protecting young people from sexual advances—and deflates moralistic righteousness posing as feminist principle. Age of consent law and its legal fiction, the sexless child, legitimate extant rape law and its legal fiction, a woman who always wants it. By marking sex below age *x* as the paradigmatic form of bad, as in illegal, sex, age of consent laws function to render all that other unequal, unwanted, unwelcomed, unpleasant sex as everyday heterosex, as what sex normally is, provided the participants are adults. Our exclusionary enthrallment to preserving the fictive innocence of the fictive child serves two functions, then, both toxic: denying the sexual agency of the adolescent as well as the sexual injury of the adult woman.

2. When considering the threshold of institutional liability for sexual harassment (the "deliberate indifference" standard), MacKinnon observes dryly: "The most positive outcomes [. . .] have occurred in cases in which a teacher *had sex with* or sexually molested an underage, disabled, or boy student—or all three at once ("In Their Hands" 2079; emphasis added). As with age of consent laws, MacKinnon shores up how sexual harassment law, designed to target sex inequality, is hijacked to quell "moral outrage" (2087), leaving girls and women to fend for themselves. The conservative co-optation pivots on the sacred innocence of the child and, more pointedly, on the dominant presumption that *boys* are not for sexual use like girls and women (see also MacKinnon, "Not" 334, 339; "Pornography, Civil" 66n158). When MacKinnon describes some of the sexual harassment cases involving teenage students and older teachers, coaches, and principals, she refers to "relationships" between the parties and not (only) to "child molestation" or "abuse" ("In Their Hands" 2065, 2072, 2074–75). Note the clause "had sex with" in the above-quoted passage. This is telling, for it is not that MacKinnon sees no harm in what may have been a consensual or at least wanted relationship between a younger subordinate and older supervisor, but that the harm is the harm of sexual-harassment-as-sex-discrimination by virtue of leveraging sex out of inequality; it is decidedly not the harm of lost innocence, moralistic indignation for which MacKinnon has no patience ("Not"). MacKinnon's maneuver to demoralize the child in order to recast women's injury, a maneuver repeated in multiple locations, yields unexpected returns: her children are more consistently sexually agentic and undamaged than her women ("Rape" 471).

3. When criticizing the legal standard of "obscenity" for policing the sexual amorality of, rather than redressing the sex inequality elemental

to, pornography, MacKinnon queries the "child pornography" exemption that courts have carved out from First Amendment protection:

> *Women are known to be brutally coerced into pornographic performances. But so far it is only with children, usually male children, that courts consider that the speech of pornographers was once someone else's life [. . .]. Two boys masturbating with no showing of explicit force demonstrates the harm of child pornography [to the Supreme Court], while shoving money up a woman's vagina [. . .] raises serious questions of "regulation of 'conduct' having a communicative element." ("Not" 339, 339n56)*

Without getting into the weeds of obscenity doctrine, I understand MacKinnon's general point as this: it matters not a whit if material determined to be child pornography also carries with it expressive value; harm to the child in the production and distribution of his or her pornographic image outweighs any artistry of the image. If women are likewise harmed by pornography (and pornography, as MacKinnon defines it, harms women; *Women's* 301; *Butterfly* 29–30), why should it matter whether or not the porn has expressive value? Why should the harm to women not override pornography's otherwise First Amendment protections ("Not" 332–33n37; *Women's* 306–7)?

Meanwhile, the violated *boy* of child pornography, MacKinnon admonishes, provides the same evidence of co-optation as the violated boy of sexual harassment liability: a cultural anxiety that boys are being treated like women rather than being socialized to dominate them (*Toward* 208; "Not" 334n42). That foundational cases of child pornography and obscenity law involve depictions of boys, intimates MacKinnon, may have less to do with protecting vulnerable youth from sexual aggression than with men's discomfort at representations of their sexuality as submissive, passive, or gazed at.

4. When classifying all prostitution as sex trafficking, MacKinnon states:

> *Although no one can deny that most women enter the sex industry with previously violated childhoods, what is denied is that defending prostitution supports their continuous violation on the rationale that they are no longer little girls. What those seem to miss who care only about prostituted children [. . .] is that in the sex trade, adults and children are not two separate groups of people. They are the same group of people at two points in time. ("Trafficking, Prostitution, and Inequality" 298)*

MacKinnon undermines the good liberal's distinction between the adult prostitute and the child prostitute, as if the former exercises free choice in a commodity market like any other (but the sex worker's commodity is herself), whereas the latter is and always is a trafficked victim. The imagined difference between adults and children is one of "five underlying moral distinctions" MacKinnon identifies as structuring debates around sex work (272). For MacKinnon, the entire landscape of prostitution is so saturated by poverty, by prior and ongoing abuse of girls and women, and by nonexistent employment opportunities that the distinctions between prostitution and trafficking, adult and child, consensual and forced, indoor and outdoor, legal and illegal are all bunk, at root ideological fabrications to legitimate unwanted, abusive, commercial sex undertaken for survival.

In these four passages, MacKinnon aims to dismantle liberal and liberal feminist distinctions between choice and coercion, between expression and conduct (*Only*). Whether or not one ultimately agrees with MacKinnon that these distinctions serve to strengthen rather than undermine the market in sexual services, that is, a market predominantly in girls and women, her takedown of liberal commitments gives reason for pause. It is this sort of puncturing of common sense, a puncturing of a yesteryear liberal consensus around sex, gender difference, and inequality, that enables us to see a convergence, to observe that a core problem threads through the misconduct of the sexual "predator and jokester" alike (Berlant, "Predator"), the Roy Moores and the Al Frankens. The core problem is not the youthfulness of young girls and women, but youthfulness as a proxy for and index of the typically gendered inequality leveraged by the powerful for sex.

Embracing this rhetorical child of MacKinnon's, and embracing too her send-up of the "child" of sex law and U.S. moralism, we might reject #MeAt14, a wayward child of #MeToo. The hashtag campaign #MeAt14 arose in response to allegations leveled against then Alabama Senate candidate Roy Moore that he pursued, kissed, and molested teenage girls when he was in his thirties. The youngest of the girls was at the time fourteen years old. In the weeks leading up to Moore's election-day defeat, hundreds of women, Alabamans and non-Alabamans, celebrities and ordinary folk, posted pictures of their fourteen-year-old selves online, with the hashtag #MeAt14 and comments like, "Can't Consent at 14. Not in Alabama. Not anywhere" and "When I was 14, I got braces . . ." (Contrera). The images feature dorky kids doing dorky stuff, like homework; they are not dressed up for the school dance. The images and captions bespeak the supposed naïveté and incompetence of any and every teenage girl. National Public Radio summarized the campaign succinctly: "#MeAt14 Reminds Internet 14-Year-Olds Are Innocent, Immature, Unable to Consent" (Benderev).

MacKinnon and any MacKinnon feminist should be skeptical if not outright dismissive of such a campaign. #MeAt14 converts the phenomenon of an older man leveraging age and power to sexually assault or advance upon girls (for example, by driving a victim to a remote spot in his car to grope her) into a phenomenon of a pedophilic man who ruins innocence, the frivolous joys of childhood. What about all of Moore's alleged victims who might be seventeen, eighteen, or twenty-two?[5] Are they undeserving of sympathy or support because they are adult women? If Moore sequestered girls and young women from their communities to force himself upon them, then what difference does age difference make? On the other hand, what about fourteen-year-olds who joyfully engage in sexual activity? Refiguring ruined preadolescent and adolescent innocence as the social problem, rather than male sexual predation buttressed by male privilege and entitlement, substitutes pervasive sex inequality for sick men and cute kids. #MeToo, unlike #MeAt14, recalls that sexual manipulation, coercion, assault, and misconduct are practiced by superordinated men against subordinated girls and women of all ages. For #MeToo, as for MacKinnon, young age aggravates women's vulnerability but young age is not ipso facto vulnerability. This is the kind of distinction that might hedge against a movement like #MeToo going full throttle sex negative, sex panic, or sex terroristic. Political foci on sexual abuse, and on abuse of power for sex, rather than on sex that is intergenerational, public, kinky, or otherwise weird, holds at bay—or could hold at bay, depending on how we define *abuse, power*, and *sex*—sex panic flooding feminist politics.

The Evil Twin

MacKinnon has another rhetorical child, though, and she is seduced by the very innocence of the child and by that innocence's corresponding moralism, which she otherwise so unceremoniously rejects. For example, to demystify for her readers the adult/child distinction in sex work, she reports: "In Kolkata, scores of girls around thirteen years old line the streets of the redlight areas I visited. Once, glancing down a narrow alley, I saw a tiny naked girl of about six with her legs being spread wide, crotch out. So when, exactly, does she choose?" ("Trafficking, Prostitution, and Inequality" 280–81). It is as if MacKinnon does not trust the force of her feminist analysis (that prostitutes are abused as children; that the line separating girls from women is merely a legal fiction, a "false notion that women become equal at age 18" ["Pornography as Trafficking" 998]; that limited choices and coercive circumstances are not age-bound), and so instead must rely upon, must conjure, the little naked girl to convince by outraging her readers. This figure and its evocation—moral outrage—is exactly the figure she refuses as the indexical beneficiary of sexual harassment law and (child) pornography proscriptions, for the figure shrouds a system of group-based sex inequality with the spectacle of one child ruined.

In the lecture version of her article describing this prostituted child, MacKinnon says, "It is this [profit from sex trafficking] that makes coltish 13-year-old girls into sole meal tickets for families of five. And by the way, the girl behind that example: we got her out. [*Pause*] I just found that out" ("Trafficking, Prostitution and Inequality: A Public Lecture"; see also "Trafficking, Prostitution, and Inequality" 293–94).

Six, thirteen: her age is beside the point. The interchangeability is the point. In the article and the talk, the sexual injury of the girl child supplants sex inequality, and the remedy is now dramatized neocolonial rescue, not political economic transformations that would enable meaningful educational and employment opportunities for girls and women.

One wonders: "Got her out" where? Where does the girl live now? Did she want to be rescued? (Probably, but who knows?) Is she a student somewhere? A worker? What are the conditions of her current employment (Bernstein and Shih)? How much better or worse are those conditions than the conditions of selling sex (Nussbaum)? How did MacKinnon's materialist broadside against the gendered patterning and hierarchy of selling sex, and against the forced conditions of many women's lives parading as "choice," boil down to the figure of the brown girl child, sexualized and exposed on an Indian city street corner, awaiting her rescue from the Feminist Hero of the Global North (Kempadoo)? MacKinnon's project of demystifying sexual commerce employs the rhetorical prop—the wounded girl child—she thoroughly or almost thoroughly dispels in her discussions of pornography, rape, and even, in the very same article, prostitution. The discursive move enflames outrage and righteousness that threaten to engulf feminist movement with a reinstallation of sex moralism—the pathologizing and individualizing of sexual predators and the valorizing of supposedly woke white women who leaned in and saved the children.

Sex moralism crashes into MacKinnon's feminist analysis full force with two final, related rhetorical figurations: women as children and children as women.

Women as children. In her analyses of pornography and prostitution, MacKinnon emphasizes that women in these industries (which, for MacKinnon, are "ultimately circular," as pornography supplies the sexuality clients demand from prostitutes; "Pornography as Trafficking" 1001) enter as children and/or were sexually abused as children (995, 998). As she puts it, "[T]he fact that most women in prostitution were sexually abused as children, and most entered prostitution before they were adults, undermines the patina of freedom [. . .] that is the marketing strategy apparently needed for most customers to enjoy them" ("Prostitution" 27–28). Or: "Some of the same reasons children are granted some specific legal avenues for redress [. . .] also hold true for women's comparative social position to men" ("Pornography, Civil" 36). Or: "One woman, testifying that all the women in a group of ex-prostitutes were *brought into prostitution as children through pornography*, characterized their collective experience" (57; emphasis added).

This last act of ventriloquism is surprising hearsay from a lawyer: reporting on the reporting of another woman claiming to speak for women (see also Halley 50), a series of substitutions authorized by the specter of the abused child. Once the sexually abused child enters discourse, once she speaks in her silence for all women everywhere, who cares about evidence?

MacKinnon states directly: "women are not children" ("Pornography, Civil" 38). Yet her wholesale proscriptions against commercial sex, pornography, and BDSM sex hold traction when they do largely because she renders women so helpless and vulnerable, their lives ineluctably determined by, and continuations of, their childhood. As Katie Roiphe overstates, "[I]f you're going to claim that women have as little power and autonomy as MacKinnon claims, then they may as well be children" (148). The conversion of agentic women into injurable girls invites, as critics of #MeToo and Title IX activism forewarn, state and third party overreach. "What becomes of students so committed to their own vulnerability" asks Laura Kipnis, "conditioned to imagine they have no agency, and protected from unequal power arrangements in romantic life?"

Children as women. Having regressed women to children, MacKinnon then alchemizes children into women. The antipornography municipal ordinances she drafted with Andrea Dworkin include "the use of men, children, or transsexuals *in the place of women*" in their definitions of pornography ("Pornography, Civil" 1–2n1; emphasis added). If you are sexually subordinated, you are a "woman," regardless of your anatomy, biology, self-identification, or age (Halley 56–57). MacKinnon makes an analogous assertion in her assessment of prostitution: "[S]ome boys and men are trafficked, many of whom are prostituting as women; actually, the majority" ("Trafficking, Prostitution and Inequality: A Public Lecture"). So while MacKinnon accuses pornography of depicting women as childlike for men's arousal ("Pornography, Civil" 38n77), it is MacKinnon who insists that children are placeholders for women in sex industries, that women are harmed like girls by sex, and that women's decisions, decision-making capacities, and life chances are so thoroughly corroded by prior child sexual abuse.

Now we have a new picture of sex inequality, or the same picture from a different view. It is no longer that MacKinnon wishes to instruct her readers and audiences that the sexual abuse of children and men are distractions from or mystifications of sexual violence against women (critical presuppositions to the arguments she levels against legal definitions and prosecutions of "obscenity" and "child pornography"). Instead, children and prostituted boys—not to mention gay men ("Road") and nonhuman animals (*Women's* 91–102)—all occupy the status of "woman." They are all women, insofar as *women* designates not persons assigned female at birth, but any person, group, or population in a position of sexual submission.

Combine, then, MacKinnon's assimilation of girls, boys, male prostitutes, gay men, and animals into "women" with her argument that the difference between ordinary men and rapists is, more or less, "get[ting] caught" ("Feminism, Marxism, Method, and the State: Toward" 650), and that "normal masculinity under conditions of sex inequality is consistent with sexual predation" ("In Their Hands" 2055), and we enter sex panic. For then any sex, across any difference, installs inequality, subordinates women, and is likely rape.

MacKinnon's side constraint, "women are not children," buckles under the pressure of her totalizing critique, just as her side constraint that "inequality" must be "exploit[ed]" for sex to be rape ("Rape" 474) buckles once exploitation means "use of force" and "force" includes "the clout of male approval" (*Women's* 244), or, for that matter, "force" encompasses pornography ("Pornography as Trafficking" 996), prostitution ("Prostitution" 24–25), and sex that is consented to but unwanted as "its own reward" ("Trafficking, Prostitution, and Inequality" 281).

∎

We adopt difficult children from MacKinnon. On the one hand, her sex inequality analysis allows us to morally distinguish the actions of Louis C. K. from Roy Moore while nonetheless recognizing the actions of both as sexually subordinating women and superordinating themselves. On the other hand, when rape is itself defined as any act of sex under unequal conditions compelled by "force" so broadly defined, MacKinnon dissolves the differences we might otherwise draw between the comedian and the judge, Al Franken and Harvey Weinstein, Glenn Thrush and Matt Lauer, to see them instead as indistinguishable members of a dominant group, men, dominating girls and women.

When MacKinnon wedges a gap between children and women, when she exposes as hypocrisy the moral hand wringing over the sexualized teen against the incredulity directed at sexually violated adult women, she instigates a campaign against sexual violence and injustice that withstands metastasizing, moralizing panic. And yet, once MacKinnon reduces women to the "inner little girl" that "stands as [her] true abused self" (Berlant, "Subject" 73n44); once adult women's decisions, occupations, and situations are made explicable by their sexual abuse as children, and once MacKinnon extends the alleged harms of child pornography to the harms of all pornography everywhere and always, then any sex across power differences, all sex, is suspect. When MacKinnon makes women into children, children into women, and redefines sex-for-male-approval as "force," the brakes are off. The diagnoses and prophesies of sex panic are no longer baseless.

Many thanks to Lauren Berlant, Andrea Long Chu, Shelley Fischel, Ellen Rooney, Matthew Shafer, Igor Souza, and Robyn Wiegman. This paper benefited from the insights of Inderpal Grewal and the students in our fall 2017 lecture course, "Sex, Knowledge, and Power." I am grateful to Eliana Fischel for helping take care of our father so I could finish the article by deadline. Some of the ideas for this paper first percolate in my article, "Per Se or Power? Age and Sexual Consent" (2010), and a few passages are reprinted with permission from Screw Consent: A Better Politics of Sexual Justice, *by Joseph J. Fischel, © 2019 by the Regents of the University of California, published by the University of California Press.*

JOSEPH J. FISCHEL is an associate professor of women's, gender, and sexuality studies at Yale University and author of *Screw Consent: A Better Politics of Sexual Justice* (University of California Press, 2019). He is currently researching the life and afterlife of sodomy law in New Orleans and beyond.

Notes

1 As something of an inversion of this essay's arguments, Laura Purdy's "Shulamith Firestone's Children" claims that the radical feminist's exhortation to liberate the child from parental control is ill founded, ignoring the protection and superintendence necessary for moral cultivation.

2 See also, among others, Dworkin; Rich; and Wittig.

3 Halley delineates how MacKinnon's analysis of rape and rape law changes across her oeuvre (41–53).

4 State laws do, to varying degrees, criminalize sex across some

vertical power relationships beyond or in conjunction with age of consent statutes. Moreover, most states do not "ossif[y]" "young age" "into an absolute rule," but instead proscribe sex outside specified age spans. See Fischel, *"Per Se."*

5   As MacKinnon writes of child pornography laws, "It also seems worth observing that a law that has the abuse disappear legally when its victims get one day older is difficult to administer effectively" ("Pornography, Civil" 39n77). For MacKinnon, child pornography is materially and politically inseparable from the pornography of women.

Works Cited

Alexander v. Yale University, 459 F. Supp. 1 (D. Conn. 1977).

Baker, Carrie N. "Race, Class, and Sexual Harassment in the 1970s." *Feminist Studies* 30.1 (2004): 7–27.

Bellafante, Ginia. "Before #MeToo, There Was Catharine MacKinnon and Her Book, 'Sexual Harassment of Working Women.'" *New York Times* 19 Mar. 2018. https://www.nytimes.com /2018/03/19/books/review/metoo-workplace-sexual-harassment-catharine-mackinnon.html.

Benderev, Chris. "#MeAt14 Reminds Internet 14-Year-Olds Are Innocent, Immature, Unable to Consent." *NPR: The Two-Way* 11 Nov. 2017. https://www.npr.org/sections/thetwoway/2017 /11/11/563531559/-meat14-reminds-internet-14-year-olds-are-innocent-immature-unable -to-consent.

Berlant, Lauren. "The Predator and the Jokester." *New Inquiry* 13 Dec. 2017. https:// thenewinquiry.com/the-predator-and-the-jokester/.

───────────. "The Subject of True Feeling: Pain, Privacy, and Politics." *Cultural Pluralism, Identity Politics, and the Law.* Ed. Austin Sarat and Thomas R. Kearns. Ann Arbor: U of Michigan P, 1999. 49–84.

Bernstein, Elizabeth, and Eleanor Shih. "The Erotics of Authenticity: Sex Trafficking and 'Reality Tourism' in Thailand." *Social Politics* 21.3 (2014): 430–60.

Cauterucci, Christina. "Louis C. K.'s Public Statement Unnervingly Misunderstands the Concept of Consent." *Slate* 10 Nov. 2017. http://www.slate.com/blogs/xx_factor/2017/11/10/louis _c_k_s_masturbation_statement_unnervingly_misunderstands_the_concept.html.

Contrera, Jessica. "Women Respond to Roy Moore Allegations by Reminding the World What It Looks Like to Be 14." *Washington Post* 13 Nov. 2017. https://www.washingtonpost.com /news/arts-and-entertainment/wp/2017/11/13/women-respond-to-roy-moore-allegations-by -reminding-the-world-what-it-looks-like-to-be-14.

Dworkin, Andrea. *Intercourse.* New York: Free Press, 1987.

Fischel, Joseph J. *"Per Se* or Power? Age and Sexual Consent." *Yale Journal of Law & Feminism* 22.2 (2010): 279–341.

───────────. *Screw Consent: A Better Politics of Sexual Justice.* Berkeley: U of California P, 2019.

Galanes, Philip. "Catharine MacKinnon and Gretchen Carlson Have a Few Things to Say." *New York Times* 17 Mar. 2018. https://www.nytimes.com/2018/03/17/business/catharine -mackinnon-gretchen-carlson.html.

Garcia, Sandra E. "The Woman Who Created #MeToo Long before Hashtags." *New York Times* 20 Oct. 2017. https://www.nytimes.com/2017/10/20/us/me-too-movement-tarana-burke.html.

Gersen, Jacob, and Jeannie Suk. "The Sex Bureaucracy." *California Law Review* 104 (2016): 881–948.

Gonzales, Susan. "The Fight against Sexual Harassment Isn't Nearly Over, Says Anita Hill." *Yale Daily News* 31 Oct. 2017. https://news.yale.edu/2017/10/31/fight-against-sexual-harassment-isnt-nearly-over-says-anita-hill.

Halley, Janet. *Split Decisions: How and Why to Take a Break from Feminism.* Princeton: Princeton UP, 2006.

Kempadoo, Kamala. "The Modern-Day White (Wo)Man's Burden: Trends in Anti-Trafficking and Anti-Slavery Campaigns." *Journal of Human Trafficking* 1.1 (2015): 8–20.

Kipnis, Laura. "Sexual Paranoia Strikes Academe." *Chronicle of Higher Education* 27 Feb. 2015. https://www.chronicle.com/article/Sexual-Paranoia-Strikes/190351?cid=wcontentgrid_40_5.

Lipsitz, Raina. "Sexual Harassment Law Was Shaped by the Battles of Black Women." *Nation* 20 Oct. 2017. https://www.thenation.com/article/sexual-harassment-law-was-shaped-by-the-battles-of-black-women/.

MacKinnon, Catharine A. *Butterfly Politics.* Cambridge, MA: Belknap, 2017.

──────────. "Feminism, Marxism, Method, and the State: An Agenda for Theory." *Signs* 7.3 (1982): 515–44.

──────────. "Feminism, Marxism, Method, and the State: Toward Feminist Jurisprudence." *Signs* 8.4 (1983): 635–58.

──────────. *Feminism Unmodified: Discourses on Life and Law.* Cambridge, MA: Harvard UP, 1987.

──────────. "In Their Hands: Restoring Institutional Liability for Sexual Harassment in Education." *Yale Law Journal* 125.7 (2016): 2038–105.

──────────. "The Logic of Experience: Reflections on the Development of Sexual Harassment Law." *Georgetown Law Review* 90.3 (2002): 813–33.

──────────. "#MeToo Has Done What the Law Could Not." *New York Times* 4 Feb. 2018. https://www.nytimes.com/2018/02/04/opinion/metoo-law-legal-system.html.

──────────. "Not a Moral Issue." *Yale Law & Policy Review* 2.2 (1984): 321–45.

──────────. *Only Words.* Cambridge, MA: Harvard UP, 1996.

──────────. "Pornography as Trafficking." *Michigan Journal of International Law* 26 (2005): 993–1012.

──────────. "Pornography, Civil Rights, and Speech." *Harvard Civil Rights-Civil Liberties Law Review* 20.1 (1985): 1–70.

──────────. "Prostitution and Civil Rights." *Michigan Journal of Gender & Law* 1 (1993): 13–32.

──────────. "Rape Redefined." *Harvard Law & Policy Review* 10 (2016): 431–78.

—————————. "The Road Not Taken: Sex Equality in *Lawrence v. Texas.*" *Ohio State Law Journal* 65 (2004): 1081–94.

—————————. *Sexual Harassment of Working Women.* New Haven: Yale UP, 1979.

—————————. *Toward a Feminist Theory of the State.* Cambridge, MA: Harvard UP, 1989.

—————————. "Trafficking, Prostitution, and Inequality." *Harvard Civil Rights-Civil Liberties Law Review* 46 (2011): 271–310.

—————————. "Trafficking, Prostitution and Inequality: A Public Lecture by Catharine MacKinnon." *University of Chicago Law School* 14 Nov. 2011. https://www.law.uchicago.edu /recordings/catharine-mackinnon-trafficking-prostitution-and-inequality.

—————————. *Women's Lives, Men's Laws.* Cambridge, MA: Belknap, 2007.

MacKinnon, Catharine A., and Durba Mitra. "Ask a Feminist: Sexual Harassment in the Age of #MeToo." *Signs* (4 June 2018). http://signsjournal.org/mackinnon-metoo/.

MacKinnon, Catharine A., and Ron Suskind. "Sex, Lies, and Justice: A Conversation between MacKinnon and Ron Suskind." *Harvard Law School* 14 Apr. 2016. https://today.law.harvard .edu/hls-catharine-mackinnon-comments-state-gender-equality/.

McGann, Laura. "Exclusive: NYT White House Correspondent Glenn Thrush's History of Bad Judgment around Young Women Journalists." *Vox* 20 Nov. 2017. https://www.vox.com/policy -and-politics/2017/11/20/16678094/glenn-thrush-new-york-times.

Meritor Savings Bank v. Vinson, 477 U.S. 57 (1986).

Nussbaum, Martha C. "'Whether from Reason or Prejudice': Taking Money for Bodily Services." *Journal of Legal Studies* 27.2 (1998): 693–734.

Peyser, Andrea. "#MeToo Has Lumped Trivial in with Legitimate Sexual Assault." *New York Post* 17 Nov. 2017. https://nypost.com/2017/11/17/metoo-has-lumped-trivial-in-with-legitimate -sexual-assault/.

Purdy, Laura. "Shulamith Firestone's Children." *The Philosopher's Child: Critical Perspectives in the Western Tradition.* Ed. Susan M. Turner and Gareth B. Matthews. Rochester: U of Rochester P, 1999. 189–202.

Rich, Adrienne. "Compulsory Heterosexuality and Lesbian Existence." *Signs* 5.4 (1980): 631–60.

Roiphe, Katie. *The Morning After: Sex, Fear, and Feminism on Campus.* Boston: Little, Brown, 1993.

Rubin, Gayle S. "Thinking Sex: Notes for a Radical Theory of the Politics of Sexuality." *The Lesbian and Gay Studies Reader.* Ed. Henry Abelove, Michèle Aiana Barale, and David M. Halperin. New York: Routledge, 1993. 3–37.

Ryzik, Melena, Cara Buckley, and Jodi Kantor. "Louis C. K. Is Accused by 5 Women of Sexual Misconduct." *New York Times* 9 Nov. 2017. https://www.nytimes.com/2017/11/09/arts/television /louis-ck-sexual-misconduct.html.

Schultz, Vicki. "The Sanitized Workplace." *Yale Law Journal* 112.8 (2003): 2061–193.

Simon, Anne E. *"Alexander v. Yale University*: An Informal History." *Directions in Sexual Harassment Law.* Ed. Catharine A. MacKinnon and Reva B. Siegel. New Haven: Yale UP, 2004. 51–59.

Sperling, Nicole. "Anita Hill Schools Hollywood on Sexual Harassment." *Vanity Fair* HWD 1 Dec. 2017. https://www.vanityfair.com/hollywood/2017/12/anita-hill-schools-hollywood -sexual-harassment.

Wittig, Monique. "The Straight Mind." *Feminist Issues* 1 (1980): 103–11.

Young, Cathy. "Is 'Weinsteining' Getting Out of Hand?" *Los Angeles Times* 1 Nov. 2017. http://www.latimes.com/opinion/op-ed/la-oe-young-weinsteining-goes-too-far-20171101-story .html.

KEYWORD 3

Mother

*I*n this keyword, "mother" announces the triangulation of heteronormative "family values," reproductive regulation, and the sex panic that targets trans and gender-variant folks under the Trump administration. It has long been rumored that Mike Pence, current vice president of the United States, refers to his wife as "mother," a formulation of their relationship often heralded by the religious right and dismissed with disgust by the liberal left. As in all things in the post-truth Trump era, what matters here is not the factuality of the nickname but the *truth effect* of its symbolism and the consequences of its implementation as state policy. Behind the circus that is the Trump administration, Pence has emerged as the regulatory engine of the current political administration, and with him comes the emergence of a new melding of Reagan-influenced free market politics with evangelical religious fundamentalism. From Pence's nicknaming his wife "mother" to Ivanka's #womenwhowork as a stand-in for the monied mommy balancing act, Christian-led conservatism is taking hold through a retrenchment of heteroscripted family values by way of regulations on reproduction, gender, and sexuality against the backdrop of a supposedly antiregulatory regime.

Volume 30, Number 1   DOI 10.1215/10407391-7481218

This keyword explores how the Pence machine, as the regulatory policy driver behind the Trump administration, is rolling back rights for women and LGBTQ communities. *Mother*, in this way, names the evangelical revival of Christian conservatism, the staggering rollback of women's reproductive rights and healthcare access both nationally and globally, and the federal assaults on trans people from bathroom bills to military bans, all under the rubric of a kind of protectionist moral crusade. In this framing, through both social mores and regulatory fervor, the Pence-Trump machine argues for its place on the side of good (white) men.

Echoing legislation enacted by Pence as governor of Indiana, the new attacks on reproductive rights and protections for trans and gender nonconforming folks since January 2017 have been sweeping. On his third day in office, Trump reinstated and expanded the Mexico City policy, often referred to as the Global Gag Rule, effectively denying funding to any international aid organization—not just family planning organizations—that provide clients with information about contraception and abortion services. Foreshadowing regulations to come, the expansion of the Global Gag Rule set the stage for the Trump administration's policy of withholding of funds from the United Nations Population Fund, the largest provider of contraceptives and family planning services worldwide. The effect of these regulations is to police women's access to reproductive care while almost guaranteeing a rise in maternal mortality rates. As one of his first major moves as president, Trump's expansion of the Global Gag Rule has set the tone for policy assaults on women's lives both nationally and internationally. This tone has been borne out nationally in regulations from the rollback of birth control coverage to a healthcare proposal that would make maternity care optional, to the enactment of gag rule legislation on Title X funding.

Whereas the Trump administration has sought to ramp up sexuality regulation in the realm of reproductive freedoms, it has simultaneously rolled back protections for trans and queer folks. Within a month of his inauguration, Trump rescinded Title IX protections for trans youth, further fueling the bathroom ban fights and inciting violence against trans and gender-variant folks. As repeals of the Affordable Care Act failed to materialize, the Department of Justice refused to hear appeals against a temporary order ending enforcement of the ACA's nondiscrimination protection for transgender individuals. When the Department of Justice further reversed protections for trans individuals, most notably removing the injunction against North Carolina's public bathroom access bill (HB2), other departments fell in line. The Department of Health and Human Services removed demographic questions about LGBTQ recipients from the Center for Independent Living's Annual Report; the Department of Housing and Urban Development withdrew two emergency housing policies that provide direct benefits to LGBTQ homeless youth and adults; and the Census Bureau rejected a proposal to collect demographic information on LGBTQ people in the 2020 census. All of these policies mirror and expand the stalwart antichoice and anti-LGBTQ politics that were a hallmark of Pence's term as governor of Indiana.

From the time he entered conservative politics nearly thirty years ago, Pence has stood out as a vociferous opponent of women's reproductive rights, an opposition often couched in the moral high-groundedness of protecting and preserving what Adrienne Rich calls "the institution of motherhood." For example, in the run-up to his campaign for Congress in the late 1990s, Pence penned an op-ed incorrectly interpreting the findings of a government study in order to argue that children with two working parents will grow up emotionally stunted. Framing his response in opposition to a perceived feminist ideal of a dual working-parent household, Pence railed against "a culture that has sold the big lie that 'Mom doesn't matter'" (qtd. in Bradner). *Mom*, in this telling, stands in for a whole host of cultural codings that naturalize the heteronormative nuclear family with a social and moral ideal of the public, working father and the private, caring mother. What's more, this ideal of "mom" is the ground on which Pence, first as congressperson then as governor and now as vice president, argues for, on one hand, increased regulation both of women's bodies and in the realm of religious liberties and, on the other, decreased regulation and taxation in economic categories. In short, Pence, a supposed antiregulatory conservative, favors regulation when it can be parsed out as protective, even in the face of evidence that such regulations put women and children at (more) risk. Such regulation serves to further the retrenchment of heteroscripted family values, shoring up a brand of capitalism predicated on a gendered division of labor.

In the era of #MeToo, Pence and his religious right have emerged with a kind of told-you-so rhetoric. As the backlash takes hold, many men are claiming to follow the Pence Rule, formerly the Billy Graham Rule, which refers to Pence's refusal to dine with women or drink alcohol without his wife present. In this scenario, Karen Pence steps into the symbolic role of mother, the regulator of Pence's desires and behaviors. Such a rule reinforces the notion that men are naturally predatory and that women in public necessarily incite men's base tendencies. Mother, framed as she is with the moral certitude of the private and the hygienic function of the domestic, stands guard, her very presence being all that is necessary to keep the sinner in line.

Melania Trump forwarded this logic of maternal control of the sexual sphere, albeit with a certain resignation, in her 2016 interview with Anderson Cooper shortly after the release of the infamous "grab 'em by the pussy" tape. In one of few televised interviews she gave during the campaign, Melania explained that she often thinks of herself as mother to two boys, Donald and Barron, a statement that she has repeated several times. Such a framing shifts accountability from the wayward Trump to the scolding mother, a dismissal couched in "boys will be boys" rhetoric. Contrary to Karen Pence's regulatory status as overseer of Mike's proclivities, Melania's dismissal forgives Donald's repeated transgressions as childish play. Whereas women, and especially mothers, are often aligned with nature, it is only when reigning in men's sexuality that this alignment shifts, pushing them to the side of reason against the imagined natural impulses of male sexual desire. Trump and Pence become good guys, protectors of women, because mommy keeps one in check and scolds the other for his compulsive and repeated trespasses. The contrast between Karen Pence and Melania Trump in their divergent responses to their husbands' public sexual mores is emblematic of the dizzying contradictions of the evangelical embrace of Trump.

The hygienic value of mother is further expressed through the regulatory control enacted to curb sexual and gendered excesses in their imagined social forms. In ongoing attempts to ban transgender military personnel, for example, transgender identity is articulated as a private freedom worthy of military protection and simultaneously framed as a medical disqualification for fitness of service. The same mommy rhetoric needed to police men in social proximity to women imagines trans service members as a distracting threat to, not to mention a financial drain on, military effectiveness. Similarly, recently proposed legislation aimed at segregating prison populations according to codifications of biological sex argues that enforcing such divisions and requiring trans folks to be housed with others who share their state-designated biological sex will maintain order and cohesion.

While antitrans regulations in both the military and the prison systems stand as the most blatant examples of anti-LGBTQ legislation under the Pence-Trump machine, the passage and protection of religious freedom bills also take explicit aim at LGBTQ communities. The Pence-Trump support of widespread religious freedom bills aims to legislate anti-LGBTQ discrimination but also seeks to dissipate the work of government-led moral control over sexuality and gender. In other words, religious freedom bills off-load the work of blatant discrimination from the government to businesses and corporations. Antitrans policies in the military and in prisons repeat the limited rights of citizenship—limited by the pathologizing necessary to mark transgender as a special population category—for transgender folks while also deeming trans folks medically unfit either to fight for the country or to be protected from the gender and sexualized violences that disproportionately target trans prisoners. Religious liberties bills make possible such minimal recognition of trans lives, that is, the base acknowledgment that trans people exist, so that any denial of flourishing to trans people not captured through regulatory regimes can be enacted at the local level through intense pathologization. While mommy scolds and reigns in masculinity's "natural," and dangerously excessive, desires, so too the state acknowledges gender and sexual desires only to enact regulation to control their imagined excess.

The same cultural values that see gender segregation as commonsensical have fueled the sex panic around bathroom access and the attendant specter of sexual violence that disguises antitrans vitriol. At the center of the current sexual panic around bathroom segregation remains the innocent girl child, in whose "name as future citizen," Lauren Berlant reminds us, "state and federal governments have long policed morality around sex and other transgressive representation" (58–59). Although many men are quick to invoke their daughters as making them aware of the dangers of rape culture for women, few invoke the specter of mothers as victims of sexual violence. The specter of sexual violence that takes shape in the bathroom thus imagines the girl child as victimized and the mother as impotent witness to the crime, neither prey nor protector. Mommy reigns in her boys, but she needs the state to protect her daughters from those "men" mommy cannot properly control. Again, under the guise of protecting women and children, state regulation extends the moral superiority of the maternal.

Mother's moral superiority is stripped and she comes under the intense scrutiny of the state, however, when she is deemed, through the operations of structural racism, to be unable to provide for her own children. Indeed, when Pence claims that popular culture has decided that "Mom doesn't matter," he belies the ways in which conservative welfare policies deny recipients of state aid the structural role of "mom." As Dorothy Roberts has argued, when the political institution of motherhood meets state-based racism, women of color are denied the provenance of morality and the protections of the private sphere that frame white women's mothering. Amid the regulatory rollback of family planning funding and contraceptive availability, social security programs under the rubric of welfare are subject to increasingly stringent eligibility criteria. Trump has positioned himself as the champion of the working class and, specifically, of working families. By contrast, his policies, most clearly measured by the tone set in the first one hundred days of his administration, have effected substantial regulatory rollbacks in economic protections for workers. The working class for which Trump claims to work is implied to be white, rural, and Christian. In other words, heteronormativity is the framing that allows for the alignment of "working" and "families" that makes mom matter. Conversely, the poor and working class targeted by the regulatory rollback of social welfare programs are, as they have been at least since the Reagan years, racialized. Targeting this imagined population, Trump issued an executive order demanding more stringent work requirements for poor recipients of government social programs (United States). Increased work requirements not only serve to deny many women and families access to social services; they paradoxically indict impoverished mothers, specifically women of color, as morally irresponsible for either not working or not properly mothering (Roberts).

Pence's own mommy doctrine finds itself curiously positioned in relation to Ivanka Trump's #womenwhowork hashtivism. Whereas Pence has decried the forgetting of "mom" in the quest to "have it all," Ivanka has emerged as the twisted voice of this familiar feminist ideal. Only three months into the Trump presidency, Ivanka published a how-to book of the same title, *Women Who Work*, and simultaneously established the Ivanka M. Trump Charitable Fund to provide grant money and support for the education and empowerment of women. Within days of the book's release, Ivanka helped broker an investment of $100 million from Saudi Arabia and the United Arab Emirates for a World Bank Women's Empowerment Fund whose origin is credited to Ivanka's leadership (World Bank). In Melania's absence, Ivanka has stepped into the position of first lady, often accompanying or even standing in for Trump in national and international events. Ivanka's #womenwhowork thus takes liberal feminism to a perverse conclusion. In order for mother to have it all—the career, the kids, and the happy marriage—Ivanka's specific brand of hashtivism must occlude the necessary labor of other women, largely immigrant and working-class women, many of whom are women of color. What's more, Ivanka's ideal of women's empowerment, while deploying the optics and rhetoric of feminist commitments, is used to garner diplomatic favor while also attempting to assuage concerns about her father's misogyny.

The Pence-Trump regime has brought with it a new zeal for an old nationalism. Sexual panics and the concomitant regulation of the nation go hand in hand with the imperial project (Wieringa). Similarly, the domestic sphere, the symbolic domain of the mother, delineates and defines the nation as domestic—that is, as contained within a border against the foreign other (Kaplan). Mother, in this colonialist frame, becomes responsible not only for reproducing the nation but for regulating it as well. Thus, the expulsion of unwanted mothers, and especially the separation of mothers from children is a central indicator of nationalist xenophobia. In other words, if mother is central to the national discourse, then the punishment of "other" mothers at the border is both a literal and symbolic shoring of the nation at the border. In the current anti-immigrant fervor, the family values of immigrants are erased by the panic incited by the image of sexually violent criminals breaking through the border. Here again, the expansion of regulation takes place through the imagined protection of certain dutiful mothers and children.

The combination of economic antiregulation and increased moral regulation is a gender project for the Pence-Trump machine. This project seeks the re-entrenchment of heteronormative family values. Specifically, economic policies target and benefit men, especially as they are framed as rural, white, and working class. Moral regulations, on the other hand, target women, both in order to keep them in the mothering domain of the private sphere and as a way to maintain women's position as an underclass, already disenfranchised by neoliberalism and white supremacy. Both modes of regulation result in women's greater dependency on men and in their decreased mobility in the public sphere. The decrease in economic regulation claims to make way for a bootstraps model of class ascension while the persistence of morality regulation, fueled by unending sexual panic, assures that mommy is always barefoot and pregnant.

Many thanks to Robyn Wiegman and Amanda Apgar for their keen editorial suggestions.

MAIREAD SULLIVAN is an assistant professor of women's and gender studies at Loyola Marymount University in Los Angeles. In addition to publishing in the field of LGBTQ public health, Sullivan is the author most recently of "Kill Daddy: Reproduction, Futurity, and the Survival of the Radical Feminist" in *Women's Studies Quarterly* and "A Crisis Emerges: Lesbian Breast Cancer in the Wake of HIV/AIDS" in the *Journal of Lesbian Studies*. Sullivan is currently finishing a book on the death of the lesbian.

Works Cited
Berlant, Lauren. *The Queen of America Goes to Washington City: Essays on Sex and Citizenship.* Durham: Duke UP, 1997.

Bradner, Eric. "Pence in 1997: Working Mothers Stunt Emotional Growth of Children." CNN 2 May 2018. https://www.cnn.com/2016/07/18/politics/mike-pence-mothers-day-care/index.html.

Kaplan, Amy. "Manifest Domesticity." *American Literature* 70.3 (1998): 581–606.

Rich, Adrienne. *Of Woman Born: Motherhood as Experience and Institution.* New York: Norton, 1995.

Roberts, Dorothy. "Racism and Patriarchy in the Meaning of Motherhood." *Journal of Gender and the Law* 1.1 (1993): 1–38.

United States, Executive Office of the President [Donald Trump]. Executive order 13828: Reducing Poverty in America by Promoting Opportunity and Economic Mobility. 10 April 2018. *Federal Register*, vol. 83, no. 72, 13 Apr. 2018, pp. 15941–44. https://www.gpo.gov/fdsys/pkg/FR-2018-04-13/pdf/2018-07874.pdf.

Wieringa, Saskia Eleonora. "Postcolonial Amnesia." *Moral Panics, Sex Panics.* New York UP, 2009. 205–33.

World Bank. "New World Bank Group Facility to Enable More Than $1 Billion for Women Entrepreneurship." 7 July 2017. https://www.worldbank.org/en/news/press-release/2017/07/08/new-world-bank-group-facility-to-enable-more-than-1-billion-for-women-entrepreneurship.

The Impossibility of Feminism

*T*his essay tells a story about feminism in the United States. The story goes like this: The feminists of the late sixties and early seventies, by opening up the personal to political critique, accidentally proved feminism impossible.[1] Heterosexuality remained largely intact. Most feminists stayed with their boyfriends and kept having bad sex. It turned out that feminism was unable to deliver on its promise to radically restructure not just material institutions but relationality as such. The theories feminists produced in order to understand sex didn't actually *do* much; in fact, paradoxically, the stronger feminist theories of sex got, the less effective they became. This is a problem about which feminists since the seventies—including me and, I am assuming, you—have been in rather serious denial. I call this problem the Impossibility of Feminism.

This is a disappointing story. I know: I'm disappointed, too. In fact, I will argue that disappointment is the governing affect of feminism as a political imaginary. By this I mean simply that most feminists are mostly disappointed in feminism most of the time. Here I am led by Clare Hemmings's excellent book *Why Stories Matter*, in which she directs her attention

Volume 30, Number 1   DOI 10.1215/10407391-7481252

to feminist theory as scene of affective investments in narrative form. Histories of feminism from the seventies to the present, Hemmings argues, are written in three modes: progress, loss, and return. Motivating all three is what Hemmings describes as an "attachment to feminism's demise"—a sense that feminism, and specifically the feminism of the seventies, has been, rightly or wrongly, "surpassed" (136–37). The affective valence of this attachment can change (in progress narratives, it is celebrated; in loss narratives, mourned), but the attachment's basic structure remains the same. In this respect, progress, loss, and return are not so much three competing genres of feminist history as they are the three most common tropes within a single historiographic genre. (The proper analogy would therefore be not to comedy, tragedy, and romance, but to something like the meet cute, the big fight, and the grand gesture within the modern romantic comedy.) I'm suggesting that these stories differ in content, but not in form: in all cases, Something Went Wrong in feminism then, and in almost every case, it falls to the feminist now to Make Things Right.

This is the basic structure not just of feminist disappointment but of disappointment generally. Disappointment is not how it feels when the object of your attachment fails to give you what you want; rather, disappointment is how it feels when *you* fail to detach yourself from the disappointing object. You ought to break up, but you don't. What's disappointing, in other words, is your own optimism: your continued belief in the world's being enough for the desires that tether you to it, all evidence to the contrary. I owe this understanding of optimism to Lauren Berlant. "All attachment," she writes in *Cruel Optimism*, "is optimistic, if we describe optimism as the force that moves you out of yourself and into the world" (1). To this I add a corollary: if optimism is the fundamental orientation of all subjects to the world, then optimism's persistence is wholly independent of the capacity of any given object to meet its expectations. Disappointment, then, is the subject's rediscovery of the fact that all optimism is in the final analysis blind. So when I say that feminism is disappointing, one thing I mean is that while feminism as a concrete political project may require objects (e.g., women, sex) or institutions (e.g., the family, the workplace), feminism as a structure of desire does not depend, for its sense, force, or direction, on *anything in the world at all.*

Perhaps the most recent episode in feminist disappointment in the United States is #MeToo, a national movement against sexual assault, harassment, and abuse that has, in some cases, resulted in the firing, resignation, or public shaming of famous and powerful men. Feminist responses to #MeToo, especially within the academy, have been, as the special issue from which you are reading attests, ambivalent. In this essay, I will not weigh the movement's successes and failures; I will pretend that I am making this move out of academic principle, rather than the thrill, guilt, disgust, uneasiness, irritation, pleasure, and cruelty that #MeToo and its train of debates have aroused in me. Instead, I'm going to focus on a single #MeToo story, one that marked a turning point from the workplace to the bedroom: that is, from a focus on sexual harassment, a traditional target of liberal feminist struggle and something that more or less everyone could agree was Not So Good, to the much more contentious matter of what to do about sex as such. By reprising seventies feminists' centering of bad sex, as *the* form of women's oppression that adumbrates every other (economic, psychic, cultural, etc.), I'll suggest that this story brings into sharp relief the thing I'm calling the Impossibility of Feminism.

On January 14, 2018, the website *Babe* published a story about a woman who went on a date with the actor and comedian Aziz Ansari. In the article, a twenty-three-year-old Brooklyn-based photographer with the pseudonym Grace described her September 2017 date with Ansari, a well-known actor and comedian, as "the worst experience with a man I've ever had." According to Grace, Ansari became sexually aggressive, ignoring her requests that they slow down and pressuring her into giving him a blowjob. Grace came to consider the experience a "sexual assault." Shortly after the article ran, Ansari released a statement describing their encounter as "by all indications [. . .] completely consensual" and reaffirmed his support for #MeToo, calling it "necessary and long overdue" (qtd. in Way). The story generated tremendous controversy. Writers from the *New York Times* and the *Atlantic* to the feminist blogosphere argued over every detail. Had Grace been forced? Did the encounter constitute sexual assault? Had she already been socialized into feminine compliance? Why hadn't she made her desires clear? *Why hadn't she left?*

As *Babe* noted, the story was complicated by the public persona Ansari had been crafting for years. Aziz Ansari rose to prominence as a regular on NBC's mockumentary-style comedy series *Parks and Recreation*, where he played Tom Haverford, a self-styled entrepreneur whose boyish optimism in the face of repeated failures as a pick-up artist endeared him to fans. In one episode, after years of Tom's trying to score a date with his coworker Ann, who finds him irritating, an exasperated Ann finally agrees to a single dinner. "The four sweetest words in the English language," Tom tells the camera afterward, repeating what Ann's just told him: "You wore me down" ("Dave"). This kind of character work was no surprise to anyone familiar with Ansari's stand-up, in which Ansari frequently offered up his own middling sexual prospects as proof of a politically flattering disavowal of alpha-male swagger. Following *Parks and Recreation*, Ansari developed a reputation as both a dating guru, coauthoring the book *Modern Romance* with a New York University professor of sociology, and a television auteur, creating, writing, and starring in Netflix's *Master of None*, which television critics hailed for its representation of South Asian Americans, its critique of the television industry, and its putatively nuanced account of thirty-something heterosexual intimacy. Off camera, Ansari has publicly identified as a feminist, telling *Late Show* host Dave Letterman in 2014, "You're a feminist if you go to a Jay-Z and Beyoncé concert, and you're not like 'I feel like Beyoncé should get 23 percent less money than Jay-Z. Also, I don't think Beyoncé should have the right to vote, and why is Beyoncé singing and dancing? Shouldn't she make Jay a steak?'" (qtd. in Marcotte).

Hence the controversy of Ansari's alleged behavior, which registered among onetime fans not only as (at best) loutish and inconsiderate but also as a betrayal of the implicit terms of digitally mediated public fantasy. After all, as *Babe* itself noted, Ansari was a "certified woke bae," a title bestowed on him by fellow comic and podcaster Phoebe Robinson in a video series produced for the website *Refinery29*. A woke bae, per Robinson, is a male celebrity who is "super hot, smart af, and effecting positive change in the world." (Other recipients of the title include Jesse Williams, Mark Ruffalo, Lin-Manuel Miranda, and Justin Trudeau.) The terms "woke" (politically conscious) and "bae" (romantic partner) were first applied together to the actor Matt McGorry in a viral *Buzzfeed* post from late 2015. In one representative photo, pulled from the actor's Instagram account, a shirtless McGorry in tortoiseshell glasses poses thoughtfully with a copy of Michelle Alexander's *The New Jim Crow*. With "woke bae," the longstanding notion of the celebrity crush is reconceived as an act of political fantasy in which fans can tweak, without giving up on, the often disappointing terms of actually existing heterosexuality as conducted with actually existing men. In this fantasy, political awareness and sex appeal are not just happily coincident; rather, the love object's politicalness has entered into and helped constitute the architecture of the love relation itself.

So when female fans lusted after Ansari, the object of their desire was, in some sense, feminism itself, understood here not as a politics in the (arguably romantic) sense of direct actions carried out in the arena of history, but as an *aesthetic* tending toward certain kinds of affective production and available for attachment, pleasure, interest, habit, curation, study, and crushing. What I'm suggesting is that feminism in the twenty-first-century United States, especially on the Internet, might be best understood as a fandom. By "fandom," I mean an intimate public organized around mass sharing of a small number of love objects and, importantly, detailed knowledge about these objects ("lore") whose value is affective rather than veridical, providing practical instructions for *how to feel* about what one loves and how to synchronize one's feelings with those others.[2] To say that feminism is a fandom is to argue that popular feminist beliefs—including being "for" intersectionality, consent, body-positivity, and self-care, and "against" erasure, the gender binary, and white feminism—are held, not out of ideological orthodoxy, but primarily in order to produce belongingness as a habitable form for going about everyday life. I could mean this derogatorily, but I don't. Politics is never accessed except by way of aesthetic mediation; on the contrary, I do not think it possible to think doing politics apart from *feeling political*, and hence the aesthetic practices people use to produce this second thing.

In fact, *Babe*, which broke the Ansari story, belongs to one of Internet feminism's primary modes of affective production. I refer here to what I call the *feminist lifestyle magazine*, examples of which include *Jezebel*, *Teen Vogue*, *The Cut*, *them.*, *Bustle*, *Autostraddle*, *Rookie*, and *Refinery29*. Defining the feminist lifestyle magazine is, beneath its blending of beauty tips with current events or celebrity gossip with political analysis, a belief that *being* a feminist, in an ontologically thick way, is both possible and desirable. In tone, the genre is pedagogical, advising readers on not just how to have sex, for instance, but how to make the sex one has contribute to the fashioning of a feminist self. I choose the word *lifestyle* for two reasons: not only because it is the industry-standard label for periodicals focused on helping readers extend ordinariness, especially through reproduction of intimacy, kinship, sociality, and the body (cooking, dressing, shopping, housekeeping, childrearing, chatting, eating, relaxing, flirting, fucking), but also for its sense as a code word, within the history of feminism itself, for what the speaker regards, disapprovingly, as someone else's withdrawal from politics into the ordinary, and in particular into "culture" and "sex." Hence the specific mutation, in publications like these, of the classic "tips and tricks" listicle popularized by beauty magazines like *Cosmopolitan*: instead of "6 Sex Positions to Try If He Has a Big Penis" (Kareem), try "Your 3-Step Guide to Practicing Non-Oppressive BDSM" (Hamilton).

This is the broader context in which the Ansari story posed, once again, a question that feminists have been struggling to answer since the

seventies. Let's decide to call this the Fucking Question. The basic structure of the Fucking Question looks like this: men being, in so many words,
The Problem, how can women keep sleeping with them without Making
The Problem Worse? Here's Ti-Grace Atkinson asking it in 1970: "Since our
society has never known a time when sex in all its aspects was not exploit-
ative and relations based on sex, e.g., the male–female relationship, were
not extremely hostile, it is difficult to understand how sexual intercourse
can even be salvaged as a practice" (44–45). If seventies feminists wanted
to claim that sex was a primary site of women's political oppression, then
they would have to answer two questions: Could heterosexuality be fixed?
And if not, was lesbianism a workable alternative?

    In the remainder of this essay, I will suggest to you that the
answers to these questions were No, and No.

■

    Consider Alice Echols's influential 1989 study *Daring to Be Bad:
Radical Feminism in America 1967–1975*. Hemmings would call this book a
loss narrative: a story about how feminism was good, until it wasn't. Echols
argues that from 1967 to the early seventies, having firmly broken with the
New Left's class politics, radical feminism blossomed into a fully systematic
critique of the patriarchal sex-class system supported by direct political
actions around abortion, marriage, and child care. By 1973, however, radical feminism had been "eclipsed" by what Echols calls "cultural feminism,"
basically a countercultural movement focused on replacing "male" values
with "female" ones that effectively withdrew from politics into the domain
of lifestyle choices, lesbianism and separatism chief among them. Echols's
project is therefore to draw as clear a distinction between radical and
cultural feminism as responsibly possible. Radical feminism was social
constructionist; cultural feminism was essentialist. Radical feminists were
egalitarians; cultural feminists were female chauvinists. If radical feminists,
at times, ignored race and class, cultural feminists ignored them *more*. Most
importantly, whereas radical feminists believed the personal was political,
cultural feminists believed the political was personal.

    By now thirty years old, *Daring to Be Bad* is the first but hardly
the most nuanced history of seventies feminism, and many have taken issue
with its conclusions. Some argue that, while lesbian feminist communities
did "show signs of" cultural feminism, these trends were best understood as
strategic moves that have helped to "sustain and nourish feminist activism"
(Verta and Taylor 41). Others simply think Echols is wrong: the historian

Anne Valk argues that lesbian feminists never retreated into "lifestyle" at all, faulting *Daring to Be Bad* for failing to understand "the role that so-called cultural activities play as a part of a militant political agenda" (308). At the same time, Echols's critics tend to ratify her framing: they agree, in other words, that cultural feminism, if it existed, was definitely Bad. I take a different tack here. I am deeply suspicious of Echols's history—that is, of both what she says happened and what she says what happened meant—but I won't dispute it directly. Instead, somewhat against my better judgment, I will accept that that cultural feminism was indeed a thing, in the manner Echols describes. To make matters worse, I will assume not only that the cultural feminism of the seventies expressed the "essence" not just of the radical feminism that preceded it but of *any feminism whatsoever.* I will do this in order to elucidate a paradox: namely, that the cultural feminist critique was far more radical than anything that came before or after it, and that it was also, for this very reason, utterly unactionable. This paradox is the Impossibility of Feminism.

So: let's posit that seventies feminism begins with bad sex. As Jane Gerhard puts it in her study *Desiring Revolution,* "Much of what galled women into feminism was precisely the sense of injustice forged in and through all things sexual," including, most proximately, "the whole range of interpersonal dynamics between women and their sexual partners" (3). Bad sex is where we'll start too. Take Anne Koedt's essay "The Myth of the Vaginal Orgasm," distributed in pamphlet form in 1968 and published in the underground journal *Notes from the Second Year* in 1970. What Koedt presents in this essay is not a full-fledged political theory of sex. Relying on postwar sexologists like Alfred Kinsey, Koedt argues that the problem of female sexual unfulfillment is not mental, as claimed by the Freudians and the marriage manuals, but anatomical: the clitoris, the one and only organ of sexual climax for women, is not "stimulated sufficiently in the conventional sexual positions" (37). In this sense, the pamphlet is eminently practical; its goal is to make sex better, that is, "mutually conducive to orgasm" (38). But it is the essay's final section, in which Koedt explains what bad sex *means,* where one finds three elements that will soon prove key to the seventies feminist theory of sexuality.

The first element resides in the status of sex within the structure of Koedt's analysis. Under conditions of patriarchy, the anatomy of intercourse is endowed with allegorical—indeed, mythic—sense. The penis is "the epitome of masculinity"; the clitoris, being "almost identical" to the penis, must therefore be disavowed, and the vagina, soft and preferably shaved, must be emphasized (40). For Koedt, this is symbolic clitoridectomy, a way of "further 'feminizing' the female by removing this cardinal vestige of her masculinity" (41). In this argument, bad sex (i.e., conventional vaginal sex) is not just bad sex; it is transformed into a scene in which masculine and feminine roles are played out through reference to a governing symbolic system. Put simply, bad sex means something.

The second element can be found in Koedt's claim about the nature of male supremacy: "The essence of male chauvinism is not the practical, economic services women supply. It is the psychological superiority" (40). Note well that this is a nonmaterialist, or if you like, culturalist claim: the "essence" of patriarchy—its soul, its principle, its Idea, even—is not economic, but "psychological." Like much of seventies feminist theory, this claim reflects a deeply ambivalent relationship to the New Left from which many radical feminists, at the time of Koedt's writing, were breaking (see Echols 51–102). In contradistinction to the politico's class-based models of oppression, in which the economic is the material base on which culture may be understood to depend, a culturalist theory locates the origins of patriarchy at the seat of subjectivity itself: that is, in relations of intimacy, affect, and desire.

Hence the third notable element of Koedt's pamphlet, found in its final paragraph. Since male chauvinism is at root a kind of relationality, she reasons, clitoral orgasm is threatening to men insofar as it makes possible another, alternative set of relations. Set free by the sexual independence of the clitoris, women might decide to "seek the company of other women on a full, human basis" (41). This is the impulse that very soon will be called separatism: the thesis that feminist practice must include a withdrawal of women from men, not just economically but on the level of relating itself.

To recap: While "The Myth of the Vaginal Orgasm" does not present a fully articulated political theory of sex, it does showcase three of the most fundamental theoretical moves of seventies feminist theory in general. These are: 1) the transformation of bad sex into an allegory for women's oppression; 2) a culturalist theory of women's oppression; and as a result, 3) a political tendency toward separatism, in which lesbianism holds pride of place.

To see the first two of these moves systematized, we need only turn to Kate Millett's *Sexual Politics*, published in 1970. (Keep the lesbian separatist thesis in mind; we'll return to it soon.) A quick flip through the text reveals what the critic Georg Lukács once described as an "aspiration towards totality," a desire to relate any given phenomenon to the dynamic whole in which it is already integrated (198). Millett organizes her theory into eight sections: Ideological, Biological, Sociological, Class, Economic and Educational, Force, Anthropological, and Psychological (26–58). That every one of these sections is a case study in both the sexual and the political depends on Millett's expansive definition of both terms. First, the latter: "The term 'politics' shall refer to power-structured relationships, arrangements whereby one group of persons is controlled by another." Then, the former: "The situation between the sexes now, and throughout history, is a case of the phenomenon Max Weber defined as *herrschaft* [*sic*], a relationship of dominance and submission" (24–25), which Millett footnotes with Weber's gloss on domination as "the possibility of imposing one's will upon the behavior of other persons" (25n3). These are, I'd suggest, *the same definition*: the political, like the sexual, is fundamentally predicated on a relationship of super- and subordination. In this theory, sex is pulling double duty: it is one, albeit privileged, part in a whole with many other parts (economic, religious, psychological, artistic, etc.), while also being, as it were, the truth of that whole, which can be found expressed in any of the parts. This is what allows Millett to claim that "sexual dominion" provides our culture's "most fundamental concept of power" (25).

Millett's theory thus depends, foundationally, on massively expanding the allegorical function of bad sex: "Coitus," she writes, although it appears to be a "biological and physical activity," is in fact a "charged microcosm of the variety of attitudes and values to which culture subscribes" and may serve as "a model of sexual politics on an individual or personal plane" (23). In this move, the feminist theorist abstracts from the scene of heterosexual intercourse a portable essence that could then be identified across the spectrum of human activity. The boss making lewd comments, the congressman rattling his saber, the capitalist lowering the wage, the father reading his paper—all could be said to have something in common with the Boyfriend, in any position. This theory was therefore an attempt to distill the empirical institutions of women's oppression (the family, the market, the school, the church, the arts, the law, the state, the bedroom, the heart) to something like a formal relation or schema. Following Janet Halley (17–20), I'll call this relation "m/f," which I, like her, intend not as the equivalent of concrete oppositions like "male/female," "masculine/ feminine," or "dominant/submissive," but rather a distinct abstract *form* underlying all of those.[3]

A clarification: you may think I am mischaracterizing Millett's argument. Yes, you could object, Millett is identifying a relation, but that relation is specifically one of power, of the control of one thing by another.

This is true. But we must distinguish the content of that relation from its form.[4] You and I might well disagree about what counts as "power" or "control"–feminists have, after all, been disagreeing about this very question for a long time–while still agreeing that some kind of relation obtains between men and women, or maleness and femaleness, or the masculine and the feminine. It's the second thing I emphasize here: that the simple positing of m/f as a formal relation had significant implications for seventies feminist theory *regardless of that relation's content.* It was m/f, for instance, that served as the logical link between the two transcendentals that hovered at both ends of the scale of analysis: on the one hand, an integrated, structural whole called Patriarchy, greater than the sum of its parts and veiled from empirical observation; and on the other hand, the gnawing sense, which in the consciousness-raising groups went by the name Women's Experience, that *something was up* with how men and women behaved. This was, in fact, an aesthetic theory of patriarchy, that is, a theory of male supremacy as a set of genre conventions soliciting certain kinds of affective expectation.[5] The proof of patriarchy's reality was not to be found by sorting through anthropological works about early man or collecting statistics about rates of sexual violence, though feminists did both of these things. Patriarchy existed, quite simply, because *women could feel it.*

So what was a girl to do? If feminist theories of patriarchy in the seventies rested so strongly on the affective sense of bad sex–indeed, if the personal was political–it was inevitable that the relationship between feminist theories of sex and the sexual practices of the feminist theorist would fall under scrutiny. Was Anne Koedt having better sex? Why had Kate Millett dedicated *Sexual Politics* to her husband? The same whispers circulate today, of course: I, perhaps like you, have attended enough boozy postconference dinners and thumbed innocently to the end of enough acknowledgments to know that feminist theory has always been about who's fucking whom. Ever since the seventies, feminists have been "stranded," as Jill Johnston put it in 1973, "between their personal needs and their political persuasions" (276). Indeed, the thesis of *Lesbian Nation*, which collects and expands on columns Johnston wrote for the *Village Voice* between 1969 and 1972, is seductively simple: "The lesbian is *the* revolutionary feminist and every other feminist is a woman who wants a better deal from her old man" (156). At its heart, Johnston argues, feminism is a "massive complaint" about bad sex, and lesbian separatism is the obvious solution (166). Importantly, separatism entailed not just economic withdrawal, but withdrawal of women's most "vital energies" from the man (180).

Yet what exactly this withdrawal entailed was difficult to put your finger on. For if patriarchy was, as the culturalist theory held, not a material institution but a formal aesthetic—not a *what*, but a *how*—then lesbian separatism, too, had to include an aesthetic intervention. It is here that the lesbian separatist thesis becomes complicated by a theory of roles. Even Johnston, something of a hardliner among separatists, admits that lesbianism per se—in the simplest sense of women sleeping with women—will not be politically sufficient, thanks to the persistence of "male identification" among many dykes (154). The formal relation m/f, initially abstracted from the scene of bad heterosexual sex in order to characterize other, nonsexual spheres of activity (economy, religion, etc.), now sticks, like a criminal charge, to lesbian sexual cultures that "have aped the normative institution" (155). "The butch or diesel dyke," Johnston writes in disapproval, "is a stylistic imitation of the male whose structures she thought she had to transpose in relation to herself to obtain gratification. Likewise the femme" (176). Lesbian separatists must therefore separate not just from men but *from other lesbians*, insofar as the latter have continued to have lesbian sex without developing a corresponding aesthetics with which to have it.

The problem, in other words, was not just men, but "male style," as Robin Morgan (1973) would describe it in her divisive keynote at the Second West Coast Lesbian Conference, held at UCLA in 1973. These days, Morgan's speech is most remembered for its vicious attacks on the transsexual folk singer Beth Elliott, whose scheduled performance had been disrupted the previous evening by a small group of attendees who regarded Elliott as a man. The episode is typically cited as proof of seventies feminism's rampant transphobia, a historiographic move I find highly suspect (see Enke). I note it only to point out that Morgan's remarks on Elliott were window dressing on a larger argument about "the epidemic of male style among women" ("Lesbianism" 33). For Morgan, the issue plaguing the women's movement was "not the Lesbian-Straight Split, nor the Lesbian-Feminist Split, but the Feminist-Collaborator Split"—that is, a schism between true feminists and the practitioners of male style (33). This latter group included, by Morgan's reckoning, women working for the McGovern campaign, women against monogamy ("the anti-mono line [having] originated with men"), women who dressed in leather and ride motorcycles, women who danced to "cock rock" like the Rolling Stones, women who joined communes and got high ("the life-style cop-out"), women who organized alongside the Gay Male Alliance, lesbians who refused to organize alongside straight women, and, as always, butches, who "in escaping the patriarchally enforced role of noxious 'femininity' adopt[ed] instead the patriarch's own style, to get drunk and swagger just like one of the boys, to write of tits and ass as if a sister were no more than a collection of chicken parts" (32–33). In short, "Lesbianism," Morgan warned, quoting a comrade, "is in danger of being co-opted by Lesbians" (34).

If all this strikes you as a little absurd, it's worth recalling that the thing about the West Coast Lesbian Conference of 1973 was that no one could agree on what a lesbian was. It is hardly accidental that when "lesbian" became the preferred name for good feminist subjectivity, it also became impossible to define. Flip through the follow-up issue of the short-lived underground newspaper the *Lesbian Tide*, and you'll see what I mean. Was a lesbian just a homosexual woman? Was a lesbian the same thing as a dyke? Was it something you were, or something you did? Was it a feeling? What about all the "apolitical 'bar lesbians'" who had crashed the conference just to pick up chicks, all of those dykes who used feminism as an excuse to fuck (Forfreedom 4)? And what about Robin Morgan herself? As one skeptical participant wrote of Morgan afterwards, "It would seem hard to me to be such a man hater while living with one of the same" (Buchanan 6). Indeed, Morgan's self-identification, which came early in her remarks, had been anything but clarifying: "I identify as a Lesbian because I love the People of Women and certain individual women with my life's blood. Yes, I live with a man—as does my sister Kate Millett. Yes, I am a Mother—as is my sister Del Martin. The man is a Faggot-Effeminist, and we are together the biological as well as the nurturant parents of our child. This confuses a lot of people—it not infrequently confuses us. But there it is" ("Lesbianism" 30).

Huh.

This sounds like an impasse, because it was one. Morgan perfectly exemplified a feminist caught between the personal and the political. By arguing that the essential characteristic of the lesbian should be a repudiation of male style, she had done nothing less than to advance lesbianism as a defense of heterosexuality: role-playing butches were out, Morgan and her faggy husband were in. In so doing, she had pushed the decision to allegorize bad sex all the way to its payoff. Seventies feminist theory had proceeded, by way of abstraction, from sex, to sexuality, to relationality; now it had bottomed out, paralyzingly, in the matter of style. The Fucking Question had become a Liking Question. I'm suggesting that seventies feminism is here revealed as a *politics of taste*. This is a terrifying claim to make. It sounds as if I am saying that seventies feminists had no moral grounds on which to oppose patriarchy, or that the matter of the world-historical defeat of the female sex was on par with, for instance, one's musical preferences, or eating habits, or favorite position in bed. I might be saying those things. But I am definitely saying that seventies feminism attained a degree of radicality never before reached in the history of progressive political movements, and that it had done so by constructing a theoretical framework that hoped to intervene politically not just in policy or even in social practice but at the level of attachment as such.

And here it is that feminism discovered itself to be Impossible. The simple fact was that *most feminists liked male style,* at least sometimes, and this liking was able to withstand the most ardent ministrations of theory. The true threat of the bar butch, after all, was not that she was apolitical; it was that she was *hot.* Even Jill Johnston knew this, recounting an early experience wearing a tie in a lesbian club in London: "The tie seemed to guarantee my role as a female who would play the part of a male. [. . .] I regarded the attitude with amused toleration, thankful to be attractive to one half of the jam-packed room for inadvertently wearing the right thing" (160). As for Robin Morgan, who would later describe herself as "hopelessly heterosexual" in the seventies (*Saturday's* 340), she really did love Kenneth Pitchford, the poet she had married in 1962, and she really did love their four-year-old son, to whom she had written a sweet letter on the plane en route to the convention in Los Angeles. Things with Kenneth had been far from perfect, but "still, we hung on somehow" (*Going* 47). They'd even resolved, one cold night in December 1966, to try a separation, following a bitter period "broken only long enough to give us each a faint, desperate, renewed energy sufficient to prolong the agony still further" (47). The separation was supposed to last four months; it lasted one night. Returning to their shared apartment to collect some of her things, Morgan found that in her brief absence Pitchford had filled the house with food, wine, candles, flowers: "None of which, even so, would have tempted me. His face, his loud tears and quiet voice, the *words* he said, however, met my own longing at least halfway, and I stayed" (47).[6]

I bring this up not just because I find Morgan's writing beautiful here, which I do, but also because this Morgan, who isn't busy bashing transsexuals or hating on the Rolling Stones, knows quite intimately that "love is more complex than theory," as one of her poems puts it (*Lady* 45). For there is no political program, I submit, capable of efficaciously restructuring people's attachment to things that are bad for them—no matter how much we in the academy tell ourselves that the purpose of a liberal arts education is, as Gayatri Spivak likes to say, "ceaseless uncoercive rearrangement of desire." You simply cannot tell people how to feel, at least with the result that they start feeling the way you want them to.

What's left is force, of one kind or another. It is now a truism that, in the eighties, some feminists began lobbying the state to recognize and crack down on violence against women—paradigmatically, rape, prostitution, and pornography. It is also a truism that the unintended consequence of this turn was to whittle women down to pure victimhood while gifting the state with a plausibly progressive rationale for policing sex and sexuality, especially among already marginalized communities. I want to suggest that this shift was born in part of seventies feminists' frustration with the genuine unactionability of a culturalist theory of patriarchy. Taste is above the law. Violence isn't. Morgan foreshadowed this in 1973, referring at key moments in her speech to the recent rape and murder of a university student whom a group of men had killed "by the repeated ramming of a broom-handle into her vagina until she died of massive internal hemorrhage" ("Lesbianism" 32). *That* was real; *that* was actionable. What the exploitation of labor already was for the New Left's class-based analysis—a material base—some feminists would increasingly find in violence against women.

The work of the feminist legal theorist Catharine MacKinnon is instructive here. In 1982, MacKinnon declares in the journal *Signs*, "Sexuality is to feminism what work is to marxism ("Feminism, Marxism, Method, and the State: An Agenda" 515). Like the cultural feminists of the seventies, MacKinnon rejects an economic explanation of women's oppression for one rooted in sex, but her model is different. Sexuality, she writes, is "a social sphere of male power of which forced sex is paradigmatic" ("Feminism, Marxism, Method, and the State: Toward" 646). Rape, not bad sex, now becomes the formal paradigm for all male dominance; indeed, it appears on almost every page of her 1983 follow-up essay. Its conceptual power is so vast that MacKinnon declares, with characteristic grandiosity, "To be rap*able*, a position which is social, not biological, defines what a woman *is*" (651). Rape is not a feeling; rape is a physical act, one that could be legally defined, criminalized, prosecuted, and punished, while serving as the analogical figurehead for all forms of violence against women. By the mid-eighties, in other words, one can find a critical shift in terms from a culturalist analysis of male style to a materialist analysis of violence against women: that is, from *bad sex* to *rape*.

■

I've ended up telling my own version of a loss narrative: feminism was about bad sex, until it was about rape. But I don't want to leave you with the impression that the same critiques frequently leveraged at Catharine

MacKinnon I would also extend, as some have, to contemporary movements like #MeToo. Grace, you'll recall, eventually decided that her encounter with Aziz Ansari had been sexual assault. Like feminism, it took her a while to reach that conclusion. "It took a really long time for me to validate this as sexual assault," she told *Babe*. "I was debating if this was an awkward sexual experience or sexual assault. And that's why I confronted so many of my friends and listened to what they had to say, because I wanted validation that it was actually bad" (qtd. in Way). One reading would throw Grace under the same bus as MacKinnon: regretful over bad (albeit patriarchally conditioned) sex, Grace revised the encounter into sexual assault, casting herself as a victim in need of rescue by an overreaching state. This reading could be feminist, but certainly doesn't have to be (see Ward; Weiss).

But another reading is possible, if we assume that the language of rape and sexual assault is not overdetermined by its legal or jurisprudential senses. When Grace identifies the encounter as sexual assault, I would suggest, she is appealing in the first place not to a legal power capable of finding Ansari guilty and doling out punishment, but to something socially intelligible as a material event—he touched me without my consent—on the basically accurate intuition that a feeling of violation, taken on its own, will bear little moral or political weight in the publics to which she belongs. What I am getting at is not material reality "itself," but rather the affective charge of "materiality" as a rhetorical figure—or to put it another way, the process by which affect in want of an object draws forth (or discloses, in the Heideggerian sense) a material event as its putative cause in order to become shareable with others (see Chu). It takes effort for me to do this second reading, though I think it is important. I do not know if Grace was sexually assaulted. I am certain she had bad sex. This tells you more about me than Grace: that I can't stand the eighties feminist analysis of rape; that I am fully seduced by the seventies feminist analysis of bad sex. I *do* think male style is an epidemic. I *do* think separatism is the only answer. Each time I read Grace's story—as I have dozens of times in writing this—I want to leap through my computer screen like the sex police: *Why didn't you become a lesbian, Grace?* This was my version of the question everyone on the Internet was asking, feminist and otherwise: *Why didn't she leave?* We knew the answer, but it was so simple we were too terrified to believe it. She stayed because she wanted to. Six words in which fifty years of feminism disintegrates like sweetener into coffee.

Reading Grace's story one final time, I realize it's clear that this is what she keeps saying, over and over again. "Whoa, let's relax for a sec, let's chill," she says (qtd. in Way). Don't ruin this for me, she means. Don't make it impossible for me to stay. I still want something from you, after everything. Don't break my desire. "I don't want to feel forced because then I'll hate you, and I'd rather not hate you," she tells him. Don't make this about violence, she means. Let me believe that you're a good guy. Make yourself into something I could want. She is not destroyed; she is disappointed. But what disappoints her is not, in the last instance, the man who is failing to be what she wants. What disappoints her is the stamina of her own desire, the surprising durability of her optimism. Let me believe, she pleads with him. Let me believe that heterosexuality isn't a lost cause. Let me believe that feminism is possible. Eventually she does leave, it's true, wriggling away to call an Uber, which he insists on calling for her. "You guys are all the same," she tells him. "You guys are all the fucking same" (qtd. in Way). He asks her what she means. She means: You hurt me. She means: You disappointed me. But she also means: You're not the first man to hurt me. You're not the first man to disappoint me. And also: You won't be the last. No wonder the reporter gave her a name that meant Another Chance.

I guess what I'm saying is that feminism is disappointing the way that heterosexuality is disappointing: not because it isn't everything you'd dreamed it would be, but because the fact that it isn't doesn't make you feel any differently. That is to say that the desire for feminism, in terms of its affective structure, is less like radical separatism and more like Robin Morgan leaving her husband for one night—and then coming back. Feminism, like good sex, is probably a fantasy. By "fantasy," I mean not something that is untrue, but something you believe in not because it's true, but because you want to. That's not, in and of itself, a shortcoming. The question is never how to get rid of fantasy; the first and last fantasy, after all, is that fantasy is something you can do without. The question is how to make adjustments in fantasies without totally breaking them, or how to survive a shift from one fantasy to another, or sometimes, just how to survive the fantasy you're already in. Feminism's being impossible doesn't keep us feminists from wanting it. That's hopeful, in a disappointing kind of way, but it's the closest I'm going to get to performing the perfunctory optimism of a final paragraph. If you like, we can call it the Impossibility of Not-Feminism.

ANDREA LONG CHU is a doctoral candidate at New York University. Her work has been published in *n+1*, *Artforum*, *Bookforum*, *Boston Review*, *Women & Performance*, *TSQ*, and *Journal of Speculative Philosophy*. Her book *Females: A Concern* is under contract with Verso.

Notes

1   For convenience, in this essay I will refer to the feminism of the late sixties and early seventies as "seventies feminism."

2   For more on intimate publics and women's culture, see Berlant, *Female* 5–13.

3   *m/f* was also the name of an important British journal of feminist theory that ran from 1978 to 1986.

4   A loosely Kantian theory of form underlies this essay that I do not have the space to elaborate in detail. By "form," I mean something 1) *nonempirical*, that is, unavailable to objective observation or verification; but 2) *experienced* nonetheless. This roughly corresponds to what Kant would call an *a priori* synthetic judgment. When I say a woman is beautiful, I am referring not to any of her empirical qualities, but to *how she looks*: she has the *look* of a beautiful woman. This is a judgment about form. Form, in this theory, is the correlate of affect. Her look is made available to me not by my sense organs, but through *my feelings*: I envy her beauty, her beauty arouses me, I am ashamed of my ugliness. Forms are felt; feelings feel forms. This reciprocal process is *aesthesis*; it is what I refer to when I use the term "aesthetic" in this essay. (This may seem the most classically misogynist example I could give; I give it because, as a trans woman and a lesbian, it is something I think about every day.)

5   I follow Lauren Berlant's definition of genre: "A genre is an aesthetic structure of affective expectation, an institution or formation that absorbs all kinds of small variations or modifications while promising that the persons transacting with it will experience the pleasure of encountering what they expected, with details varying the theme. It mediates what is singular, in the details, and general about the subject" (*Female* 4).

6   Morgan and Pitchford wouldn't separate until the eighties; they wouldn't formally divorce until 1990, at which point she had—would you believe it?—taken up with a woman.

Works Cited

Atkinson, Ti-Grace. "The Institution of Sexual Intercourse." Firestone and Koedt 42–47.

Berlant, Lauren. *Cruel Optimism.* Durham: Duke UP, 2008.

——————. *The Female Complaint: The Unfinished Business of Sentimentality in American Culture.* Durham: Duke UP, 2008.

Blackmon, Michael. "Can We Talk about How Woke Matt McGorry Was in 2015?" *Buzzfeed* 16 Dec. 2015. https://www.buzzfeed.com/michaelblackmon/can-we-talk-about-how-woke-matt-mcgorry-was-in-2015?

Buchanan, Pat. "The Living Contradiction." *Lesbian Tide* 2.10–11 (1973): 6–7.

Chu, Andrea Long. "Study in Blue: Trauma, Affect, Event." *Women & Performance* 27.3 (2017): 301–15.

"Dave Returns." *Parks and Recreation*, season 4, episode 15. NBC 16 Feb. 2012. *Netflix* https://www.netflix.com/watch/70210930.

Enke, Finn. "Collective Memory and the Transfeminist 1970s: Toward a Less Plausible History." *TSQ* 5.1 (2018): 9–29.

Firestone, Shulamith, and Anne Koedt, eds. *Notes from the Second Year: Women's Liberation: Major Writings of the Radical Feminists*. New York: Radical Feminism, 1970.

Forfreedom, Ann. "Lesbos Arise!" *Lesbian Tide* 2.10–11 (1973): 4–5, 14.

Gerhard, Jane. *Desiring Revolution: Second-Wave Feminism and the Rewriting of American Sexual Thought, 1920–1982*. New York: Columbia UP, 2001.

Halley, Janet. *Split Decisions: How and Why to Take a Break from Feminism*. Princeton: Princeton UP, 2006.

Hamilton, Jill. "6 Sex Positions to Try If He Has a Big Penis." *Cosmopolitan* 29 Nov. 2017. https://www.cosmopolitan.com/sex-love/positions/news/g5270/sex-positions-if-he-has-a-big-penis/.

Johnston, Jill. *Lesbian Nation: The Feminist Solution*. New York: Simon and Schuster, 1973.

Kareem, Soha. "Your 3-Step Guide to Practicing Non-Oppressive BDSM." *Everyday Feminism* 21 Jul. 2015. https://everydayfeminism.com/2015/07/non-oppressive-bdsm/.

Koedt, Anne. "The Myth of the Vaginal Orgasm." Firestone and Koedt 37–41.

Lukács, Georg. *History and Class Consciousness: Studies in Marxist Dialectics*. Trans. Rodney Livingstone. Cambridge, MA: MIT P, 1971.

MacKinnon, Catharine A. "Feminism, Marxism, Method, and the State: An Agenda for Theory." *Signs* 7.3 (1982): 515–44.

——————. "Feminism, Marxism, Method, and the State: Toward Feminist Jurisprudence." *Signs* 8.4 (1983): 635–58.

Marcotte, Amanda. "Aziz Ansari Is Better Than Most Celebrities at Talking about Feminism." *Slate* 7 Oct. 2014. http://www.slate.com/blogs/xx_factor/2014/10/07/aziz_ansari_embraces _feminism_on_the_late_show_with_david_letterman.html.

Millett, Kate. *Sexual Politics*. Urbana: U of Illinois P, 1970.

Morgan, Robin. *Going Too Far: The Personal Chronicle of a Feminist*. New York: Random House, 1977.

——————. *Lady of the Beasts: Poems*. New York: Random House, 1976.

——————. "Lesbianism and Feminism: Synonyms or Contradictions?" *Lesbian Tide* 2.10–11 (1973): 30–34.

——————. *Saturday's Child: A Memoir*. New York: Norton, 2000.

Robinson, Phoebe. "Aziz Ansari Just Proved to Us That He Is a Woke Bae." *Refinery29* 1 Jun. 2016. https://www.refinery29.com/2016/06/112431/aziz-ansari-woke-bae-phoebe-robinson.

Spivak, Gayatri Chakravorty. "Can There Be a Feminist World?" *Public Books* 15 May 2015. http://www.publicbooks.org/can-there-be-a-feminist-world/.

Taylor, Verta, and Leila J. Rupp. "Women's Culture and Lesbian Feminist Activism: A Reconsideration of Cultural Feminism." *Signs* 19.1 (1993): 32–61.

Valk, Anne M. "Living a Feminist Lifestyle: The Intersection of Theory and Action in a Lesbian Feminist Collective." *Feminist Studies* 28.2 (2002): 303–32.

Ward, Jane. "Thinking Bad Sex." *Bullybloggers* (blog) 4 Nov. 2017. https://bullybloggers .wordpress.com/2017/11/04/thinking-bad-sex/.

Way, Katie. "I Went on a Date with Aziz Ansari. It Turned into the Worst Night of My Life." *Babe* 14 Jan. 2018. https://babe.net/2018/01/13/aziz-ansari-28355.

Weiss, Bari. "Aziz Ansari Is Guilty. Of Not Being a Mind Reader." *New York Times* 15 Jan. 2018. https://www.nytimes.com/2018/01/15/opinion/aziz-ansari-babe-sexual-harassment.html.

KEYWORD 4

Sex Offender

*T*he keyword "sex offender" conjures up two different albeit interconnected meanings and images. First, it evokes a legal category that describes individuals who have committed or been convicted of committing one or more specific sex crimes. These crimes range in degree and severity across states but predominantly reflect themes of violence, predation, and impropriety directed most often toward women and children. Individuals who have perpetrated a sex crime are understood to have committed a sexual offense and thus are sex offenders. According to the *Oxford English Dictionary*, the term *sexual offense* was originally meant to reflect a "social offense" (crime against morality) as opposed to a "criminal offense" (crime against the state). The difference between "social offense" and "criminal offense" hints at the second conjuring of the word. In popular representations and discourses, the "sex offender" is often constructed as a sexual predator, oscillating between the rapist and the child molester (Levenson et al. 142–43; Orio 249; Shelby and Hatch 404–5). This second sense of the term is less a legal category than a cultural category, one that relies on racialized discourses to define individuals as perpetrators of sexual violence, even in

Volume 30, Number 1   DOI 10.1215/10407391-7481246

the absence of legal convictions or criminal behavior. The two categories, legal and cultural, become intermeshed and overlapped within sex panics, most often seen in the interchanging of terms such as *rape, sexual assault, sexual predator, pedophile,* and *sexual harassment,* all of which have specific legal meanings even as they reflect cultural discourses. While scholars have been increasingly attentive to the adverse material consequences endured by people who have been *legally* designated as sex offenders, we should/ might also consider the implications, and dangers, of *culturally* designating people as "rapists" and "sexual predators" (i.e., sex offenders) outside of legal definitions. Making such a distinction is important because the hyperpunitive sex offender registry came to be in part through the co-constitution and circulation of these two different usages.

The sex offender became an integral part of juridical discourse in the mid-twentieth century during what scholars have referred to as the sexual psychopath era (Leon 29). Between 1937 and 1967, twenty-six states and the District of Columbia passed legislation enabling the civil commitment of sex fiends and sexual psychopaths into psychiatric institutions as an alternative to incarceration (Swanson 215). Of the twenty-six states, seventeen required that the person be convicted of some crime before being committed for treatment; the other states allowed for commitment without conviction. "Sexual psychopaths" were people who committed serious sex crimes and/or were considered to have no control over their sexual impulses and would thus inevitably, repeatedly commit an offense. The sexual psychopath was a historical invention, and the mass adoption of legislation to manage them resulted from the accumulation of new ideas and popular images proliferating in preceding decades. Notable among them were developments in American medicine and psychiatry, which began to conceptualize "sexual perversion" as a prescriptive category used to define and describe symptoms intrinsically linked to a *type of individual*: the (sexual) pervert. Largely the result of new scientific conceptualizations, the sexual criminal became an altogether distinct type of criminal, who at his core was constituted by the presence of sexual perversion, often in the form of pedophilia or homosexuality (Jenkins 15). Following the publication of Richard Freiherr von Krafft-Ebing's notorious *Psychopathia Sexualis* (1886) and amid a slew of serial murders and sex killings between 1908 and 1916, popular discourse began to reflect a growing desire for new forms of intervention for identified sexual perverts. At the heart of these calls for intervention was the call to reduce the risk of harm to children; the term *psychopath* was used to describe Nathan Leopold and Richard Loeb, the two murderers who killed a fourteen-year-old boy in Chicago during the highly publicized "crime of the century," as it would come to be described throughout the trial in 1924 (Jenkins 47; Larson 121). The conflation of "child killer" with "homicidal pervert," and the newly popularized term *psychopath,* was a cornerstone of the infamous Albert Fish trial of 1935, a case that concretized the notion that child killers were sex offenders on the basis that child killers were sexual psychopaths; Fish, a child rapist and serial child killer, was not only described as psychopathic in popular media but was also commonly referred to as "The Bogey Man," a clear reference to a menacing figure out to harm children (Jenkins 49–50). These conflations informed the sexual psychopath laws that would dominate the twentieth century. It was in the context of the proliferation of these laws that the Los Angeles Police Department established the first Bureau of Sex Offenses in 1937, which was tasked with keeping detailed records, fingerprints, and photographs of people convicted of sex crimes, including homosexuals (Lave 566).

A decade later, California created the first statewide sex offender registry, which required anyone in the state convicted of a sex crime included on a specific list to register with the local police. California's registry legitimized the category of sex offender by endowing it with significant political and juridical meanings that were first shaped by cultural norms and moral values. The increasingly moral framework used to identify sex offenders beyond the sexual psychopath standard was evidenced by the addition of "lewd vagrancy" to the list of registrable offenses just two years after the state adopted its registry. The police routinely used the lewd vagrancy statute to charge men who were cruising public spaces for sex with other men; same-sex desire became proof of a sex crime (Goluboff 166–71). In 1950, over 90 percent of registrable arrests in Los Angeles were for consensual homosexual acts, inspired no doubt by the moral and psychiatric discourses that sutured "homosexual" to "pervert," which made same-sex desire synonymous with child sexual abuse, murder, abduction, and rape (Eskridge 59–61). At its legal onset, "sex offender" (a criminal offense) often culturally signified "homosexual" (a social offense). This was further enabled by the addition of *homosexuality* to the Diagnostics and Statistical Manual of Mental Disorders (DSM) in 1952. Homosexuals, like sexual psychopaths, could be managed through the growing psychiatric apparatus. They were also often criminalized without evidence of having committed a crime. Following California, several other states began to implement registries, including Alabama, Arizona, Florida, Mississippi, Montana, Nevada, and Ohio. By the end of the 1980s, twelve states had registry laws (Velázquez 2), many of which had statutes regarding lewdness as well as antisodomy laws. The proliferation of the registry, which categorically designated people as "sex offenders," was intimately informed by cultural constructions of deviance and difference and the pathologization of social groups.

Following a wave of sex panics beginning in the 1980s, the registry became an active agent in the creation of sex offenders through the invention of new categories of offenders and the creation of a notification system. This was made possible by the rise of popular discourses about "pedophile rings" galvanized by the establishment of the controversial National Man-Boy Love Association (NAMBLA) in 1978 and by a surge of satanic ritual abuse panics sweeping the nation throughout the 1980s (Jenkins 156–59; Lancaster 46–47). One of the keystone pieces of legislation that nationally redefined the "sex offender" was the Jacob Wetterling Crimes against Children and Sexually Violent Offender Registration Act of 1994. Named after eleven-year-old Jacob Wetterling, who was abducted in 1989 and whose remains were not found until 2016, the Act required that each state create a narrowly drawn program for registering sex offenders, including life-long registration for a subgenre of offenders classified as "sexually violent predators." These were offenders who were already convicted criminals identified as having the capacity to become recidivists; either they were deemed to have a propensity to sexual violence or they already had a history of doing so. Unlike sexual psychopath laws, which used institutionalization instead of incarceration and did not necessarily require a conviction before civil commitment, sexually violent predator statutes required a prior conviction and enabled the state to civilly commit *in addition to* incarcerate. Sexually violent predator laws were used to confine offenders in a treatment facility indefinitely after they served their prison sentence (Gookin 1).

The mandated creation of the sexually violent predator category was, like all national sex offender registration laws, based on the circumstances of the case for which the law was named. Ten months prior to the abduction of Jacob Wetterling, a man had kidnapped and molested a twelve-year-old boy just outside of St. Joseph, Minnesota. During the Wetterling investigation, it was uncovered that, unbeknown to local authorities, several halfway houses in St. Joseph housed sex offenders after their release from prison (Scholle 1). The abduction of Wetterling coupled with the knowledge of nearby sex offenders, a previous incident of child sexual abuse and kidnapping, and pre-existing popular conceptualizations of child killers as sex offenders culminated in the creation of the new sex offender legislation. The Wetterling Act was adopted despite there being no evidence that the abductor had a sexually violent history or was sexually motivated. At the time it was passed, no one knew who had committed the crime and there was no body to prove that any sexual activity had occurred. There was simply a presumption that the perpetrator was guilty of both murder and sexual assault, which was sufficient to produce legislation that included a whole new category of offender. In this way, the sexually violent predator is as much a legal distinction as it is a cultural fabrication. According to legal scholar Daniel Filler, the term was originally used "as a metaphor, comparing the actions of animals that hunt and kill other animals to sexual offenders' pursuit and sexual victimization of children" (339). Shifts in the law drew on cultural discourses that posited sex offenders as habitually violent, even though research has repeatedly demonstrated that recidivism rates among this population are quite low (Ackerman and Burns 18; Bray and Sample 72–76; Greenfield 25–27).

The cultural construction of sex offenders was expanded with the adoption of Megan's Law in 1996, a federal amendment to the Wetterling Act requiring states to notify the public of sex offenders living and working within a given community. The legislation allowed individual states to determine the level of notification required based on the perception of danger posed by the offender. The motivation was to empower the general public to geospatially locate offenders so as to reduce encounters with them for the purposes of protection, a point that the parents of Megan Kanka, the seven-year-old victim after whom the law was named, claimed might have saved their daughter's life. Community notifications conscript the general public as state-like agents to participate in the policing, surveillance, and defining of sex offenders through the pretense of risk and safety management (Levenson and Cotter 49–51). Studies have shown that public access to information about sex offenders has caused individuals on the registry to be further stigmatized and ostracized. Registered offenders have reported loss of housing and employment, physical and verbal abuse, and isolation as a result of community members' knowledge of their conviction (Huebner et al. 142–48; Levenson 162; Tewksbury 74–76). According to these types of responses, "sex offender" is ontologized as a persistent and perpetual state of being, irrespective of future or ongoing offenses or any attempts at rehabilitation. In this way, the registry, as an archive of various sexual discourses, does more than just document the existence of an offender or a sexual offence; it constructs and produces the category of sex offender. In the process, the legal specificity of particular crimes and subtypes of sexual offenders was obscured and conflated into one broad, often inaccurate grouping that began to dominate popular representations in the late twentieth and early twenty-first centuries: the sexual predator.

In 2004, the American reality television series *To Catch a Predator* aired on MSNBC, introducing an accessible depiction of sexual predation into living rooms across America. As the plotline goes, a volunteer would impersonate an underage child seeking the sexual attention of adult males over the Internet. The unsuspecting "predator" would be lured into meeting the child-decoy at the decoy's house and would then be confronted by Dateline NBC correspondent and host Chris Hansen. By the third installment of the series, police were also involved. Public discourse about the show often improperly labeled the adult males "pedophiles" based on their desire to meet up with children for sexual encounters. Hansen addressed this mischaracterization in an interview, noting that *pedophilia* "has a very specific definition" that requires a clinical diagnosis based on a set of criteria listed in the DSM. And yet, while Hansen acknowledged the difference between pedophilia (a nonlegal category) and sex offender (a legal category), he failed to address the ways in which the title of the show actively obfuscated the legal criteria for what constitutes a sexual predator. In doing so, the show discouraged viewers from understanding "sexual predator" as a legal category that typically requires a prior sex crime conviction, using it instead as a cultural category to mean *anyone* with sexual intentions toward those under the age of consent.

Given the ways that legal categories are produced through shifting cultural meanings and vice versa (e.g., the conflation of *sexual predator* with *pedophile* with *homosexual*, all under the umbrella of *sex offender*), it is important to consider how these categories are also indexed by race and gender. Indeed, there has been a long, documented history of black men being falsely accused of, convicted of, and sometimes put to death for sex crimes they did not commit, evidenced by the cases of Emmett Till, the Scottsboro Boys, and the Gloveland Four, to name a few. The false accusation and its corroboration without evidence operate precisely because of the discursive field that constructs, as David Malebranche puts it, the black phallus as a walking "weapon of mass destruction" (qtd. in McCune 31). Black men are regularly understood as sexually offending the state and larger cultural sensibilities even when they have not actually committed a sex crime. This helps make sense of the disproportionate representation of black men on registries today, as their bodies have been historically marked already as "predators," a designation that can be traced back to early colonial discourses on black peril as well as to postbellum black brute caricatures that circulated throughout the nineteenth century and that would be replaced by the image of the urban thug or "super predator" of the 1990s. As sociologist Trevor Hoppe argues about the racialized and gendered politics of the current registry, having analyzed the sex offender registration data of forty-nine states between 2015 and 2013, "roughly one out of every 119 black men living in the forty-nine states analyzed were registered sex offenders—nearly 1 percent of all black men" (584). The disproportionate racialization of the category of sex offender thus makes black men's bodies continually stand in as the cultural index of predation, perversity, and violence—in short, rapists.

The prevalence of this line of thinking has fueled current sex panics about the foreign other, evident in President Trump's references to "bad hombres," who are entering the country purportedly to rape white women, a discourse that harkens back to the early 1900s when immigrants and black migrants were said to be forcing white women into "white slavery" (prostitution). The myth of the white slave led to the passing of the Mann Act in 1910 despite those fears being rooted in a white racist imagination that could not have been further from reality.

Contemporary sex panics are primed to repeat the mistakes of the past. Whereas some scholars and activists are calling for an expanded articulation of what counts as sexual assault and moving toward affirmative or enthusiastic consent, this is not without risk. Sexual assault and consent are tied to legal categories, not just to cultural discourses, and those who commit sexual assault or violate consent can be legally prosecuted and defined as sex offenders under current sex crime laws. The expansion of criminal sexual regimes has material consequences to the lives of those who are already most vulnerable to state-sanctioned violence and community policing, a concern that is exacerbated by President Trump's continual call for more "law and order" punishment. While scholars have increasingly investigated the hyperpunitive nature of the registry, particularly with the passing of the Adam Walsh Child Protection and Safety Act of 2006, it is pressing that we also examine how investments in the legal category of the sex offender can be politically fraught, because *sex offender* operates as a cultural category as well. This means that cultural interventions that look to expand the definitions of various forms of sexual violence can create new legal categories that play out in ways that undermine some of the progressive political commitments that undergird #MeToo, #TimesUp, and broader advocacy initiatives against sexual violence.

TERRANCE WOOTEN is a postdoctoral fellow at the University of California, Santa Barbara, in the Department of Black Studies. He is currently working on his first book manuscript, tentatively titled "Lurking in the Shadows of Home: Homelessness, Carcerality, and the Figure of the Sex Offender," which examines how those who have been designated "sex offenders" and are homeless in the Maryland/DC area are managed and regulated through social policies, sex offender registries, and urban and architectural design. His scholarly interests are located at the intersections of African American studies, gender and sexuality studies, studies of poverty and homelessness, and carceral studies.

Works Cited

Ackerman, Alissa R., and Marshall Burns. "Bad Data: How Government Agencies Distort Statistics on Sex-Crime Recidivism." *Justice Policy Journal* 13.1 (2016): 1–23.

Bray, Timothy, and Lisa L. Sample. "Are Sex Offenders Dangerous?" *Criminology and Public Policy* 3.1 (2003): 59–82.

Eskridge, William N. *Dishonorable Passions: Sodomy Laws in America, 1861–2003.* New York: Viking, 2008.

Filler, Daniel M. "Making the Case for Megan's Law: A Study in Legislative Rhetoric." *Indiana Law Journal* 76.2 (2001): 315–65.

Goluboff, Risa. *Vagrant Nation: Police Power, Constitutional Change, and the Making of the 1960s.* New York: Oxford UP, 2017.

Gookin, Kathy. "Comparison of State Laws Authorizing Involuntary Commitment of Sexually Violent Predators: 2006 Update, Revised." Olympia: Washington Institute for Public Policy, Doc. No. 07-08-1101, 2007.

Greenfeld, Lawrence A. "Sex Offenses and Offenders: An Analysis of Data on Rape and Sexual Assault." Washington, DC: Bureau of Justice Statistics, 1997.

Hoppe, Trevor. "Punishing Sex: Sex Offenders and the Missing Punitive Turn in Sexuality Studies." *Law & Social Inquiry* 41.3 (2016): 573–94.

Huebner, Beth M., Kimberly R. Kras, Jason Rydberg, Timothy S. Bynum, Eric Grommon, and Breanne Pleggenkuhle. "The Effect and Implications of Sex Offender Residence Restrictions." *Criminology & Public Policy* 13.1 (2014): 139–68.

Jenkins, Philip. *Moral Panic: Changing Concepts of the Child Molester in Modern America.* New Haven: Yale UP, 1998.

Lancaster, Roger N. *Sex Panic and the Punitive State.* Berkeley: U of California P, 2011.

Larson, Edward J. "An American Tragedy: Retelling the Leopold-Loeb Story in Popular Culture." *American Journal of Legal History* 50.2 (2010): 119–56.

Lave, Tamara Rice. "Only Yesterday: The Rise and Fall of Twentieth-Century Sexual Psychopath Laws." *Louisiana Law Review* 69.3 (2009): 549–91.

Leon, Chrysanthi. *Sex Fiends, Perverts, and Pedophiles: Understanding Sex Crime Policy in America.* New York: New York UP, 2011.

Levenson, Jill S. "Collateral Consequences of Sex Offender Residence Restrictions." *Criminal Justice Studies* 21.2 (2008): 153–66.

Levenson, Jill S., and Leo P. Cotter. "The Effect of Megan's Law on Sex Offender Reintegration." *Journal of Contemporary Criminal Justice* 21.1 (2005): 49–66.

Levenson, Jill S., Yolanda N. Brannon, Timothy Fortney, and Juanita Baker. "Public Perceptions about Sex Offenders and Community Protection Policies." *Analyses of Social Issues and Public Policy* 7.1 (2007): 137–61.

McCune, Jeffrey Q. *Sexual Discretion: Black Masculinity and the Politics of Passing.* Chicago: U of Chicago P, 2014.

Orio, Scott De. "The Creation of the Modern Sex Offender." *The War on Sex.* Ed. Trevor Hoppe and David M. Halperin. Durham: Duke UP, 2017. 247–67.

Scholle, Alan. "Sex Offender Registration." FBI *Law Enforcement Bulletin* 69.7 (2000): 17–24.

Shelby, Renee Marie, and Anthony Ryan Hatch. "Obscuring Sexual Crime: Examining Media Representations of Sexual Violence in Megan's Law." *Criminal Justice Studies* 27.4 (2014): 402–18.

Swanson, Alan H. "Sexual Psychopath Statutes: Summary and Analysis." *Journal of Criminal Law, Criminology, and Police Science* 51.2 (1960): 215–35.

Tewksbury, Richard. "Collateral Consequences of Sex Offender Registration." *Journal of Contemporary Criminal Justice* 21.1 (2005): 67–81.

Velázquez, Tracy. "The Pursuit of Safety: Sex Offender Policy in the United States." New York: Vera Institute of Justice, 2008.

KEYWORD 5

Pedophile

On October 29, 2017, actor Anthony Rapp alleged that Kevin Spacey had made a drunken pass at him when the younger actor was only fourteen. When Spacey replied on Twitter by combining an apology with a coming-out statement, the response of gay and gay-friendly commentators was overwhelmingly condemnatory. Spacey's Twitter post led to a bad case of what Eve Kosofsky Sedgwick termed "paranoid reading." Under the principle that there should be no bad surprises, paranoid reading anticipates the worst. Preempting any possible conflation between homosexuality, sexual predation, and pedophilia on the part of conservatives, gay and gay-friendly commentators (Coates; Madison) rushed to accuse Spacey of this very conflation. In the *New Yorker*, Michael Schulman criticized Spacey for "muddying the waters" between sexual assault, pedophilia, and being an out, proud gay man. Clearly, Spacey touched the nerve center of a fear common to many gays and lesbians—that we will be returned to the dark time in which, in the minds of many straights as well as some unfortunate self-hating homosexuals, homosexuality was synonymous with sexual predation and child sexual abuse. Though paranoid reading aims to preempt

Volume 30, Number 1   DOI 10.1215/10407391-7481260

bad surprises, it does have its consequences. As Joseph Fischel points out, the effect of gay commentary on Spacey was to evoke the very specter of the gay pedophile commentators were attempting to ward off. As a series of men—now numbering thirty—began to come forth with new charges against Spacey, one issue was clarified: Spacey was a serial sexual harasser, not very different from the scores of powerful heterosexual men accused of serial sexual harassment and assault under the auspices of the #MeToo campaign. But was he a pedophile?

The next month, a series of women—now numbering eight—began to come forward with accusations of sexual misconduct and assault against the notoriously racist, homophobic, and transphobic Republican Roy Moore, as he ran for (and eventually lost) an Alabama Senate seat. A lurid portrait emerged of Moore as a thirty-something district attorney lurking at high schools and at the local mall where he would hit on teenage girls, whom he sometimes dated. As with Spacey, the accusations varied, from sexual assault, to pushing an underage date beyond her comfort zone, to groping an adult woman in the workplace. Media reports, however, focused less on the allegations of overt harassment and assault than on the shocking image of a lecherous grown man lusting after young girls. News outlets obsessively referred to Moore as an "accused pedophile," despite the fact that pedophilia is not a crime; child sexual abuse and child pornography are, and the hashtags #RoyMoorePedophile and #RoyMooreChildMolester trended on Twitter. Meanwhile, Moore supporters, given the mic by a fascinated press, told a queer story, one in which it was perfectly normal for teenage girls to date thirty-something men. As one white male supporter put it, "Forty years ago in Alabama, there's a lotta mamas and daddies that would be thrilled that their fourteen-year-old was getting hit on by a district attorney" ("Why"). On *Democracy Now*'s December 11, 2017, daily show, Peter Montgomery argued that Moore's continued support among his Christian Conservative constituents was not just another example of conservative religious sexual hypocrisy. Instead, it reflected the backward and antifeminist norms of a Christian conservative "subculture" obsessed with the virginity of women and intent on maintaining patriarchal authority—two objectives that marriage between mature men and extremely young brides had long been intended to secure.

On the surface of it, the response of gay and gay-friendly commentators to Spacey and of Christian conservatives to Moore could hardly present a starker contrast: outraged denunciation of the conflation of homosexuality and pedophilia, on the one hand, and calm assertions, on the other, that should the accusations against Moore be proven true, they would be examples not of pedophilia, but of perfectly ordinary heterosexual dating customs. One could hardly have invented a better allegory of the differential cultural threat of gay versus straight sex with minors. As attested by the fact that some of the girls' parents knew and approved of them dating Moore, straight men pursuing teenage girls is understood, in some quarters at least, as part of the natural order of things. If Moore exposes the uneasy open secret of straight adult men's attraction to teenage girls, Spacey exemplifies the cultural taboo on acknowledging a similarly normal version of homosexuality inclusive of attraction to teenage youths. The moment this possibility arises, the accused must be sacrificially pilloried (Fischel) lest any straights "get the wrong idea," namely, that homosexuality and intergenerational sex might *not* be mutually exclusive. This essay explores what acknowledging the unacknowledgeable—an *unexceptional* intergenerational homosexuality—would mean for thinking sexual justice in the #MeToo moment.

Pederasty, History, Temporality

If reactions differed, the *explanations* commentators ventured for Moore's and Spacey's pursuit of teens ran parallel. In both cases, commentators invoked historical and cultural backwardness as an explanation, if not an excuse, for their pursuit of young people. Left-leaning commentators like Montgomery made Moore signify the outdated sexual mores of a perverse Christian conservative subculture that conspires to give young girls to older men in order to perpetuate an authoritarian and patriarchal social structure in which women's sexual autonomy and desire matter not, but their ability to be pure virgin wives and self-sacrificing mothers matters a great deal. Meanwhile, gay-affirmative commentators painted Spacey as a self-hating, secretive, old-school closet case—all because (regardless of the fact that everyone in Hollywood seems to have either known or supposed that he was gay) he neglected to officially come out of the closet until forced to do so by Rapp's accusation. The lone article that dares admit, "The truth is that many young gay men have positive, formative relationships with older men at the beginning of their sexual lives," ends squarely on the note of blame (Schulman). Schulman contends that, unlike the oppressed gay men of the past, Spacey had the opportunity to come out in a public act of gay affirmation. "For whatever reasons," Schulman laments, "Spacey chose not to take that route, and he wound up getting pushed out in a way that feels dispiritingly retro." He ends by suggesting that the fact of being closeted led Spacey in some of the same "wild directions" of gay men in the past. These directions, we must surmise, included groping men, exposing one's genitalia, and coming on to boys—more or less desperate pre-Stonewall cruising attempts sadly out of date in the world of public, normalized, civil homosexuality that gay activists worked so hard to build. Spacey is to be resented, in short, for ungratefully failing to embrace the brave new gay world and, in fact, thrusting it dispiritingly backward into the old mores of harmful, because clandestine and desperate, "wild" attempts at sex.

I find the "old-school closet case" explanation for Spacey's behavior wrongheaded and the parallel Christian conservative subculture explanation for Moore's continued support only slightly more illuminating. It is no coincidence, in either case, that commentators invoke "backwardness" to explain the pursuit of underage teens. As my book *Disturbing Attachments: Genet, Modern Pederasty, and Queer History* (2017) demonstrates, age-differentiated male-male sex, what I term "pederasty," has been persistently cast as a backward, and in some cases, Ancient Greek anachronism—out of place in any time and without any meaningful connection to contemporaneous social structure and mores. The book uncovers the lineaments of the common and even dominant practice of twentieth-century pederasty, as well as some marginalized traditions for thinking it. Modern pederasty, I contend, is neither inexplicable nor a desperate response to homophobic oppression. It is not the case that, once liberated from the shadows and accorded a deserved public legitimacy, homosexuality shed its pre-Stonewall distortions—including sex for pay, sex with minors, public sex, and clandestine sexual overtures now legible as harassment—to reveal itself as a paragon of egalitarian sexual ethics. To the contrary, the gay liberation and early gay civil rights moment of the 1970s and 1980s in Euro-North America played an active role in transforming homosexuality itself. Writing, in broad historical perspective, of the emergence of what we now know as "modern" male homosexuality, David Halperin summarizes, "Homosexual relations cease to be compulsorily structured by a polarization of identities and roles (active/passive, insertive/receptive, masculine/feminine, or man/boy). Exclusive, lifelong, companionate, romantic, and mutual homosexual love becomes possible for both partners" (133–34). Indeed, the body of historical and anthropological scholarship on male homosexuality is more likely to describe sex orchestrated by polarized sexual positions, gender roles, or generations (as well as class, race, and "trade" economies) than the vision of mutual attraction between two of a kind that "homosexuality" calls to mind today.

How did the definitional center of same-sex sexuality shift so consequentially? Movements for gay civil rights were one important node in this genealogy. Insofar as they sought rights and recognition from a heteronormative culture, gay rights movements in France and the United States worked actively to shift the definition of homosexuality, and the sex and relationship norms of gay culture, into line with dominant social ideals. Legitimate male homosexuality worthy of civil rights had to be cleansed of effeminacy and transgender expression, public sex, and, perhaps most urgently, pederasty. In the United States, according to Regina Kunzel, "the transformation of a movement for sexual liberation into a movement for civil rights, requiring in turn a respectable homosexual subject deserving of such rights, ultimately led to an effort to remove the 'pedophile' from the category homosexual" (216). But, "pedophile" was by no means a universally recognized, transhistorical category. According to Gillian Harkins, "In 1978, the idea that all adults who have sex with children are paedophiles and that all paedophiles are moral predators, was barely emerging. Only a decade later, all adults who have sex with children would become popularly (and at times legally) defined as paedophiles, all paedophiles would be depicted as predatory and 'children' considered naturally vulnerable might be as old as eighteen" (103). The emergence of the "pedophile" as a prominent social category in the late 1970s and 1980s, the pedophile "sex panics"—which disproportionately targeted gays and lesbians—that raged in this same period, and the mobilization of a gay civil rights movement seeking mainstream legitimacy all conspired to redefine homosexuality as presumptively same(ish)-age as well as same-sex.

Pederasty, as well as traditions of intergenerational lesbian relationships, hardly stood a chance against the demonizing popular redefinition of any sexual relationship with a minor as monstrous pedophilia. Our current moment, in which the historical practice of intergenerational same-sex relationships has been all but forgotten and is practically impossible to speak of publicly, is the aftermath of this history. The speed with which commentators rushed to brand Spacey a "pedophile" and assert the incompatibility of "pedophilia" and homosexuality testifies to the contemporary certainty that there never was an intergenerational homosexuality, that the gay pedophile was entirely a homophobic invention, and/or that pre-Stonewall oppression might explain away the intergenerational gay and lesbian relationships of the past.

Sex and Power

But, readers might object, why am I invoking intergenerational homosexual relationships when the real issue at stake is sexual assault and the abuse of power? By using the case of Spacey to correct the record on pederasty, am I not giving fuel to the idea that gay men are pedophiles—or rather, *pederasts*—and that pederasts are, inevitably, sexual predators?

While it *is* risky to bring up pederasty in tandem with the Spacey case, to do so sheds light on a zone of opacity within the current movement, under the banner of the #MeToo campaign, to expose incidents of sexual harassment and assault and to hold their perpetrators accountable. This is the issue of the intimacy of sex and power. In line with the popular feminist slogan, "rape is about power, not sex," many feminist accounts have sought to distance these abuses, many of which occurred on the job, from sex proper. By this same logic, calling the sexual harassment or assault of minors "pedophilia" in a well-meaning effort to foment indignation against them is politically counterproductive, since it focuses attention on sexuality rather than abuse. As Rachel Hope Cleaves and Nicholas Syrett point out, if Moore were a pedophile, he ought to seek treatment. Indeed, both Spacey and Harvey Weinstein have sought to preempt consequences for their actions by checking into The Meadows, a facility that treats "sex addiction." However, the feminist demand, Cleaves and Syrett argue, is not treatment, but justice, accountability, and more broadly, a transformation of the institutional cultures that facilitate and cover up sexual abuse. Likewise, in an interview, Dr. Joye Swan counters the notion that men like Weinstein are "sex addicts" by asserting, "Weinstein doesn't love sex—he loves power and intimidation [. . .]: He's just another man who craves using his 'extraordinary power' to hurt women" (Solis).

Certainly, Weinstein loves power, but it is also significant that one of the primary vehicles through which he exercises power over women is *sex*. This is also why Spacey *had to* come out as gay in his apology to Rapp. Sex and sexuality are not immaterial to instances of sexual abuse. What the wave of recent revelations of sexual abuse by men in positions of power demonstrates is that *power is sexy*. In private conversations, feminist friends have wondered, with genuine incomprehension, how college-aged men could want to have sex with passed out, unresponsive women and whether men are so deluded as to expect women to respond with desire when they show them their penises in the workplace or so clueless as to mistake shocked and numbed nonresponse for aroused assent. The deplorable truth is that, under the current state of U.S. sexual norms, for many men a) reciprocity is not necessary for satisfying sex; and b) nonconsent can itself be a turn-on. Sexual arousal, for many American men, is compatible with the exercise of power and the humiliation of others (Ward). This includes power to transgress professional norms by walking around in an open bathrobe, power to make subordinate women feel uncomfortable or afraid, and power to force a subordinate to accept an unwanted sexual interaction. We might rehear the popular feminist mantra, "rape is not about sex, it is about power," differently, then, not as a statement of fact, but as an activist rewriting of reality that seeks to conjure into being a new sexual order, one in which sex is not about power and power is not sexualized.

But while the injunction to separate sex from abuses of power has crucial political goals, it does little to help us understand or address our current sexual order. This is a sexual order, which many feminist, race, and queer theorists seek to address, in which power and vulnerability structure our most intimate fantasies and pleasures. For it is far too simplistic to think that men *alone* find power sexy. As Maggie Nelson writes, there is "no control group" for American women who reach maturity without exposure to eroticized cultural narratives of female sexual violation (66). How, then, can their sexual beings *not* be formed in some complex relation to the erotics of vulnerability, violation, and nonconsent? Nelson's own response is sexual masochism. Indeed, since the feminist "sex wars" of the 1980s, sex-positive and queer feminists have heralded consensual BDSM as a means of responsibly finding pleasure within scenarios that might include sexual humiliation, staged nonconsent, and age play. Likewise, a growing cluster of black feminists are acknowledging that racialized sexuality can function not only as a site of injury but also a source of "ecstasy" (Nash) and of pleasurable abjection (Scott). We might understand *both* the choice to practice loving and gentle same-age vanilla sex *and* the decision to delve into the darkest BDSM or race play scenarios as responses to a sexual order shot through with power and danger. Such a sexual order gives rise to serial institutionally sanctioned assault and abuse as well as kinky, responsible queer pleasures, to racial pornotroping and racial "ecstasy" (Nash) alike.

In *Disturbing Attachments*, I use the concept of *pederastic modernity* to draw out the complexities of a modern social order riven with inequalities that animate erotic life. The eroticization and sexual exploitation of trans and cis women, of workplace hierarchies, of the undocumented, and of people of color are part and parcel of this modern sexual order. If I refer to it as "pederastic," it is to challenge the presupposition that, as the expression of premodern, illiberal, and hierarchically stratified social orders, pederasty has no place in the "modern West." This presupposition does more to buttress Euro-North American imperial power through the fiction of modern Western sexual egalitarianism than to actually bring an egalitarian sexual and social order into being. As perhaps *the* form of sexuality most conspicuously animated by social inequality, modern pederasty reveals the sheer *pervasiveness* and *normalcy* of the entanglement of sex and power across Euro-North America. Moore's and Spacey's sexual pressuring and, at times, assault of teens is *not* of a different order than the scores of cases of important men sexually harassing and assaulting adult subordinates. It is not shocking that a culture that eroticizes power in its manifold guises should also feed the eroticization of all positions of subordination, including youth. The task at hand is to transform our social and sexual worlds in ways that enhance sexual agency, particularly for the more vulnerable, without, for that matter, describing sex in a way that impossibly cleanses it of all relations of power. The challenge is to do so without exceptionalizing sex with minors or making it the scapegoat for sexuality's responsiveness to power more generally.

KADJI AMIN is assistant professor of women's, gender, and sexuality studies at Emory University. Previously, he was a Mellon Postdoctoral Fellow in "Sex" at the University of Pennsylvania Humanities Forum (2015–16) and a faculty fellow at the Humanities Institute at Stony Brook (2015). He is the author of *Disturbing Attachments: Genet, Modern Pederasty, and Queer History* (Duke University Press, 2017) and is working on a second book project that traces critical genealogies of key ways in which "transgender" is being institutionalized in the Global North.

Works Cited   Amin, Kadji. *Disturbing Attachments: Genet, Modern Pederasty, and Queer History.* Durham: Duke UP, 2017.

Cleaves, Rachel Hope, and Nicholas Syrett. "Roy Moore Is Not a Pedophile." *Washington Post* 19 Nov. 2017. https://www.washingtonpost.com/opinions/roy-moore-is-not-a-pedophile/2017/11/19/1a9ae238-cb21-11e7-aa96-54417592cf72_story.html.

Coates, Tyler. "Kevin Spacey's Misguided Apology for Sexual Misconduct Is Awkward and Irresponsible." *Esquire* 30 Oct. 2017. http://www.esquire.com/entertainment/movies/a13117025/kevin-spacey-coming-out-anthony-rapp/.

Fischel, Joseph. "How Calling Kevin Spacey a Pedophile Hurts the Gay Community." *Slate* 1 Nov. 2017. http://www.slate.com/blogs/outward/2017/11/01/how_calling_kevin_spacey_a_pedophile_hurts_the_gay_community.html.

Halperin, David. *How to Do the History of Homosexuality.* Chicago: U of Chicago P, 2002.

Harkins, Gillian. "Foucault, the Family, and the Cold Monster of Neoliberalism." *Foucault, the Family, and Politics.* Ed. Robbie Duschinsky and Leon Antonio Rocha. New York: Palgrave Macmillan, 2012. 82–117.

Kunzel, Regina. *Criminal Intimacy: Prison and the Uneven History of Modern American Sexuality.* Chicago: U of Chicago P, 2008.

Madison, Ira, III. "How Kevin Spacey's 'Coming Out' Grossly Conflates Pedophilia and Homosexuality." *Daily Beast* 30 Oct. 2017. https://www.thedailybeast.com/how-kevin-spaceys-coming-out-grossly-conflates-pedophilia-and-homosexuality.

Nash, Jennifer C. *The Black Body in Ecstasy: Reading Race, Reading Pornography.* Durham: Duke UP, 2014.

Nelson, Maggie. *The Argonauts.* Minneapolis: Graywolf, 2015.

Schulman, Michael. "Kevin Spacey Muddies the Waters." *New Yorker* 30 Oct. 2017. https://www.newyorker.com/culture/cultural-comment/kevin-spacey-muddies-the-waters.

Scott, Darieck. *Extravagant Abjection: Blackness, Power, and Sexuality in the African American Literary Imagination.* New York: New York UP, 2010.

Sedgwick, Eve Kosofsky. "Paranoid Reading and Reparative Reading, or, You're So Paranoid, You Probably Think This Essay Is about You." *Touching Feeling: Affect, Pedagogy, Performativity.* Durham: Duke UP, 2003. 123–52.

Solis, Marie. "Harvey Weinstein's Sex Addiction Is Not a Real Thing, Experts Say." *Newsweek* 12 Oct. 2017. http://www.newsweek.com/harvey-weinstein-isnt-sex-addict-because-sex-addiction-isnt-real-experts-say-682853.

Ward, Jane. *Not Gay: Sex between Straight White Men.* New York: New York UP, 2015.

"Why These Alabama Voters Are Sticking by Roy Moore." *Vice News* 9 Dec. 2017. https://news.vice.com/en_us/article/j5ddvk/why-these-alabama-voters-are-sticking-by-roy-moore.

Toward an s/m Theory of MacKinnon

Participants typically agreed on an ethic of openness, honesty, and self-awareness. [. . .] What brought women to these groups is difficult to distinguish from what happened once they were there.
—MacKinnon

[Marxism and feminism] exist to argue, respectively, that the relations in which many work and few gain, in which some dominate and others are subordinated, in which some fuck and others get fucked and *everybody knows* what those words mean, are the prime moment of politics.
—MacKinnon; my emphasis

*M*acKinnon backs her reader, you, into a corner.[1] The corner becomes the universe, all the more infinite and vast in its finitude and closeddoorness. The MacKinnonian camera is positioned exactly below that which is fucking you.[2] You recognize yourself as a heterosexual woman in that moment because MacKinnon doesn't recognize you if you're anything else. Are you behind the camera? Are you being made to hold it? Are you floating above the scene, detached from your body? Are you there at all? Difficult to know what is happening. According to MacKinnon, though, *everybody knows*. Can you think a world that is not this universe of a corner? Is there an outside at all? You can't make out if you're inside and feeling good about your powerlessness, or if you're able to reflect on how thoroughly bad you feel. Is this pleasure? You are in the middle of something without knowing how you would like it to end, or proceed. You may not complain because MacKinnon is staging this whole scene for *your* benefit, so that you can finally *know* what the world is about. It is about sex.[3]

Catharine MacKinnon's radical feminist work on sexuality has been critiqued by queer, sex-positive feminists for her disinvestment in

Volume 30, Number 1   DOI 10.1215/10407391-7481274

women's sexual pleasure and her watertight positions on the meanings and effects of pornography.[4] She is also widely recognized and cited for her clear articulation of the constitutive relationship between everyday sexuality and sexual violence.[5] Almost everyone agrees that MacKinnon's political vision is more oriented toward ending the culture of sexual violence than cultivating cultures of good, consensual, pleasurable sex within what she sees as the absolutely violent conditions of capitalist patriarchy. Unlike most sexual violence feminisms that pay attention to both ends of this political vision—good sex *and* no rape—MacKinnon appears to be willing ultimately to sacrifice sex for feminism. In what follows, I offer a reading of *Toward a Feminist Theory of the State*[6] to suggest that the MacKinnonian end of sexuality is, alas,[7] composed of endlessly more sex.

I consider select parts of the book to argue that MacKinnon ends up repeating what she claims to end: the sadomasochistic blur of sexuality and violence. In effect, she sets up an s/m scene of and for feminism. This is not a new claim;[8] however, I offer a psychoanalytic reading of the very switchy form of this sadomasochism and its relationship to the exquisite, self-flagellating reading pleasures of her text. Whether you agree with her or not, you cannot stop reading her, can you. The unique value of MacKinnon's feminism is to be located not in its foreclosures of sexual pleasure and consent, but in her anguish that pleasure persists in an oblique relation to anything that forecloses it. Her vehement critique of sexuality unfurls for you as a fervent s/m textuality. My reading takes this instance of repetition as *the* question of sexuality and violence that all sexual violence feminism finds itself encountering and crashing against, over and over. While MacKinnon would want to cast this as ideology—we reproduce that which has already destroyed us—I read this production of self-destructive pleasure as the very terrain on which sexuality—and her s/m textuality—unfolds. I suggest that the MacKinnonian subject is not only ideologically compromised but also internally riven, like you: s/he[9] wants what s/he does not want, s/he does not know what s/he wants, s/he does not want what s/he knows s/he wants, s/he does not know where pleasure begins and (if) pain ends: s/he is a psychoanalytic subject.

MacKinnon makes and unmakes her feminist subject/reader by activating an s/m economy of inflicting and enduring pain. If nothing else, this at least reveals the devastating investment in sex that lies at the heart of MacKinnon's politics. MacKinnon, I argue, does not reduce the sexual to fucking and subordination in the domain of reality, but in fact explodes the scope of the sexual within feminist politics. The blurring of content and tone, reality and consciousness, feminine pain and feminist pleasure is much more the stuff of sex in MacKinnon than has been recognized in feminist scholarship. This is not to say that her argument is flawed; on the contrary, the operations of her textuality only intensify the stakes, thereby implicating feminism right alongside patriarchal cultures in the deadly life of pleasure. Complex configurations of forceful desire proliferate within all feminisms that claim to want to end sexual violence. MacKinnon, however, allows her own political desire to unfold *as* a play of violence. She presents us with the truth of sexuality, but only as it exists in a scene: complete, powerful, and imbued with real desire, but only as long as the scene lasts—not that it ever ends.

Setting Up a Scene:
What's s/m Got to Do with the Revolution?

Sexuality is not confined to that which is done as pleasure in bed or as an ostensible reproductive act; it does not refer exclusively to genital contact or arousal or sensation, or narrowly to sex-desire or libido or eros. Sexuality is conceived as a far broader social phenomenon, as nothing less than the *dynamic of sex* as social hierarchy, its pleasure the experience of power in its gendered form.
—MacKinnon; my emphasis

Is women's sexuality its absence?
—MacKinnon

In *Toward a Feminist Theory of the State*, MacKinnon argues that sexuality is violent—femininity is essentially masochistic and masculinity is essentially sadistic—and that this constitutive overlap is both the result and the basis of patriarchy. It is not biological sex that produces gender. For MacKinnon, the feminine and the masculine positions of power in sexuality—you are a man if you dominate/fuck, you are a woman if you submit/are fucked—inaugurates the irredeemably hierarchical socio-cultural codes of gender.[10] Femininity is constituted in and through powerlessness. The eroticization of masculine domination is sex. This eroticization is deadly, for it makes women (and men) mistake rape for sex, domination for love. As such, there is no field of power that is not eroticized when it comes to the relations between men and women. MacKinnon uses the term *fucking* to elide the distinction between sex and rape, love and violation (251). In this top-down structure of power, pleasure is not unreal, but it is ideological. This means that for anyone, especially women, to feel pleasure is to be compromised, or entirely given over to the terms of the ruling class. The more women feel good about sex, the more complicit they are in sexual hierarchies. According to MacKinnon, femininity is pure masochism, and *that* is bad for women. The social and the sexual are so seamlessly sutured that women simply reproduce the same power equations in the workplace, in the market, in the bedroom, with their children, among themselves, even in their own heads, even if they happen to be lesbians. Feminism, for MacKinnon, is revolutionary because it is able to engage the very terms on which sexuality is propped up, and this engagement in itself is disruptive of the near total metaphysical perfection of the sexual system. It is the task of feminist politics to put an end to this crucial alliance between sex and violence, even if it means putting an end to sex as we know it. MacKinnon takes the structuralism of her account to its logical extreme in her discussion of law: injury to one woman is injury to all women, it is possible to know in advance what will constitute this structural harm to women, and adjudication is possible when it comes to violence against women. On the one hand, heterosexuality renders women completely powerless; on the other, legal reform will bring them to serious power.

MacKinnon has been critiqued for both her articulation of the problem, sexuality, and the proposed solution, feminist jurisprudence. In between is the process of consciousness raising, which I will come back to in the next section. For now, I want to focus on the *dynamic* between feminine powerlessness and feminist powerfulness. According to Wendy Brown, this is the distinctiveness of the "rhetorical structure" of MacKinnon's work (79). In Brown's view, MacKinnon channels a late modern anxiety and political despair through her "theoretical closures and political foreclosures" (91). Brown argues that MacKinnon incites "libidinal excitation" and taps and reworks "pornographic guilt" (91), only to "manipulate" (95) her readers into settling for a conservatism about pornography and sexuality without changing anything about them. In effect, MacKinnon creates a picture that is historically inaccurate, politically useless, and textually irresponsible for it rehearses and exploits "a powerful underground (pornographic) code of gender and sexuality" (91) that it claims to denounce. The powerlessness, says Brown, is all laid out only so that MacKinnon can rally her readers toward a "solution" that does not even begin to address the problem that MacKinnon herself posits. Brown argues that MacKinnon suspends "us" "in a complex pornographic experience in which MacKinnon is both purveyor and object of desire and her analysis is proffered as substitute for the sex she abuses us for wanting" (91).

Brown's reading raises several questions for me. Is the movement between femininity and feminism a onetime event in the MacKinnonian text? Does the reader start with misery and get manipulated into feeling powerful? Does s/he begin with nothing/patriarchy and end with everything/something/law? What does it mean for MacKinnon to be both purveyor and object? Though Brown presents this "both"-ness as a severely controlled environment for readers, I am struck by the possibilities of identificatory movements that this may open up. In her discussion of Freud's case study of a patient he calls Dora, Parveen Adams argues that it is not clear if Dora identifies only with her father, and therefore with masculinity. Adams calls attention to the constant movement of Dora's positions in fantasy and in dreams: "[S]he oscillates between a masculine and a feminine position" (13).[11] Adams reminds her readers that for Freud, "a sadist is always also a masochist," an exhibitionist is also a voyeur (13).[12] Drawing on Adams's work, Lalitha Gopalan analyses a number of Indian films of the eighties and nineties in which women protagonists avenge sexual violence by castrating or mutilating or brutally killing their rapists. Gopalan argues that the identification structures of these cinematic texts allow the spectator to swing from masochistic viewing positions to sadistic viewing positions and back, and back, hence the term sadomasochism. In Gopalan's complex and layered reading of these films, it is this constant sadomasochistic movement in viewing positions that produces the cinematic pleasures of these films (42–45). I use the term *sadomasochism* to characterize the reading pleasures of MacKinnon in a similar way.

Just as MacKinnon wants to preserve masculinity and femininity as altogether separate ways of being in the world, many readers of MacKinnon[13] posit powerlessness and powerfulness as two entirely different textual positions. This separation, however, holds up neither in the (psychic) world nor in the MacKinnonian text. Powerlessness is not where it all begins in MacKinnon, and power is certainly not where anything ends. There is neither a beginning nor an end in sight. There is, on the contrary, a constant shuttling, a switching between positions of powerlessness and powerfulness. Power itself is not available in any position. What you, as a reader, have access to is either a lack or an excess. Or both.[14] If MacKinnon is both purveyor and object, the reader is both object and purveyor, feminine and feminist too. Or neither.[15] What's more, you keep oscillating, for the suspension is pendular. It is this experience of switching from a masochistic position to a sadistic one, and back, and back, which becomes the formal, dynamic structure of your participation in the text. It is because of this constant movement in reading positions that the reader is implicated in the movement of power and pleasure of the text; no reader can claim innocence of, or complete mastery over, this dynamic.[16]

Almost every paragraph of the book consistently articulates what it considers to be the impossibility of women's sexuality: "Top-down relations feel sexual" (147). "[W]omen notice that sexual harassment looks a great deal like ordinary heterosexual initiation under conditions of gender inequality" (112). "The moment women 'have' it—'have sex' in the dual gender/sexuality sense—it is lost as theirs. To have it is to have it taken away" (172–73). Several readers, most notably Brown and Janet Halley (57), have persuasively argued that MacKinnon's insistence on women's powerlessness installs injury as the essence of femininity. Nonetheless, it is remarkable that MacKinnon makes this "injury" available for circulation between text and reader. You're injured: here, revolution; so, injured? REVOLUTION; so, so injured: "Women's situation offers no outside to stand on or gaze at, no inside to escape to, too much urgency to wait, no place else to go, and nothing to use but the twisted tools that have been shoved down our throats. There is no Archimedean point—or, men are their own Archimedean point, which makes it not very Archimedean. If feminism is revolutionary, this is why" (MacKinnon 116–17).

Feminist jurisprudence is certainly offered as a way out by Mac-Kinnon, but in itself, legal reform functions like a part of the same impossible equation between constitution and liberation. "Can such a state be made to serve the interests of those upon whose powerlessness its power is erected?" (161). If the state is "male," how can it speak for women? MacKinnon issues recurrent warnings that the state can never be the outside to women's oppression and sexual violence. For Halley, this is an internal contradiction that undermines MacKinnon's radical critique of sexuality (41–58). This contradiction, though, could also be read as a fantastic and nonlogical dimension of the text. On the one hand, MacKinnon thinks that being inside is a trap and having proof of an outside could mean that you may be able to get out. On the other, you, the woman who seeks consciousness,[17] the activist who has emerged out of the consciousness-raising effort,[18] and the theorist,[19] everyone is inside. Reality is inside consciousness, which is inside reality.[20] Both Drucilla Cornell (128) and Brown (91) refer to this reading experience of being inside a text that offers its readers both the hope of a way out and the dreadful horror of there being no outside, but neither accounts for the intense engagement that this doubleness produces.

Law, especially in the form of the state, can, of course, be interpreted as the sign of an outside that MacKinnon channels as a way out.

However, for MacKinnon, all manifestations of the socio-political world are simply equivalent at the level of form: literature, cinema, sexual relation- ships, law, politics are all representations of sexuality. They may not rep- resent sexuality in the same way, they may have differing purchases on the socio-political world, but they all have the same *function* in MacKinnon's textual universe. The law is not special;[21] it is not liberatory, just as cinema or literature cannot be. The law is a fantasy of the way out. Law is the pro- jection of an outside on the screen that is the closed door of this text. *This* is law's work in the dynamic of sex in MacKinnon's s/m textuality. Thus, the political rallying for feminist jurisprudence does not disrupt feminine powerlessness, but provides an anchoring point for the switch to feminist powerfulness. Against this backdrop of the movement of power and pain and the dynamic of sex, it is not consciousness that needs to be raised, but reality.

(If) You Don't Know What You Know: Reality-Raising and Consciousness

Where does consciousness come from?
—MacKinnon

[F]eminist theory probes hidden mean- ings in ordinariness and proceeds as if the truth of women's condition is acces- sible to women's collective inquiry.
—MacKinnon

In MacKinnon's textual universe, the only way for women to fight their own constitution as women is to uncover, bit by bit, the itinerary and the mass nature of their production. Accessing each other's truths as structural rather than individual will allow women to apprehend their own roles in the heterosexual system. Women will come into consciousness of their selves; neither the self nor the consciousness precedes this moment of communal confrontation. Though MacKinnon often presents these claims as undeniable facts, she is decidedly skeptical of objectivity.[22] One of her quar- rels with Marxism is that its focus on the real is seriously obfuscatory on the question of sexuality. It is Marxism, according to MacKinnon, that does not let women realize that there is a fundamental alliance between "the parasite of a parasite," that is, the bourgeois woman, and "the slave of a slave," that is, the proletarian woman (9). As such, what a particular theory or structure assumes as the "real" is often a mechanism of maintaining the status quo. MacKinnon doesn't reject this mode of politics; she embraces it to a point of implosion. In the introduction to *Toward the Feminist Theory of the State*, for example, MacKinnon describes as "epic theory" her attempt to provide "a symbolic picture of an ordered whole" that is "systematically deranged" (x). She presents *her* real as the domain of pervasive sexual violence, of "rape, battery, sexual harassment, sexual abuse of children, prostitution and pornography" (127). There is almost too much of *this* reality in MacKinnon's text. She undoes her own near constant usage of the verb "is" by insisting that aperspectivalism is anything but the route to objective truth. Reality is an epistemological difficulty for her feminism.

In most of her theoretical work, MacKinnon is engaged with sexual politics at the level of epistemology (ix): how do we know what we know about sex, how do we know this is pleasure, or pain, how do we know this is rape, how do we separate consent from a patriarchal understanding of feminine sexuality—if at all? Even as MacKinnon answers all of her own questions, she maintains that there is no neutral place from which one can gather data and come at proper knowledge; consciousness is as ideologically compromised as reality. More, consciousness is as painful as reality. She argues persuasively that consciousness raising is not about the discovery of a real "real," but about the making of something new, about a different use of the same tools that make women women.[23] Consciousness raising is not a fact-finding mission, but a full-fledged epistemological undertaking with no guarantees.

It is nearly impossible, after all of these critiques of realism, to take MacKinnon's own enunciations of the real as literal descriptions of the world.[24] Her text *stages* the real as a question of politics, not of empirically verifiable truths. Male power, she says, is as much a myth as it is real (100). The staging of that which is deemed to be real, and the realness of the staging, come together to create a dizzying circuit that is fundamental to the s/m textuality of *Toward a Feminist Theory of the State*. These gestures establish MacKinnon's reality as a production of her own complex textual universe. MacKinnon doesn't simply swap the content of what gets to count as real; she asks us to think about what the real counts for in our politics. For my reading, the important question is not what is true in the reality that MacKinnon posits, but if true, what is the nature of "if" in MacKinnon's feminism? MacKinnon makes it possible to read "is" and "if" together not for the sake of truth, but for the sake of politics.

MacKinnon recognizes the contingent nature of theoretical formulations only to stake *everything* on a particular theoretical formulation. Consequently, the (masochistic) tone of this text is *do* or *die*. She is totally committed to the scene, to the interests of women. There is no escape valve of contingency or humility; there is no admission of the possibility of being wrong. This is why it is so hard to resist the spectacle of the text, regardless of whether one agrees with the content of these so-called interests of (heterosexual) women. There's no cultural feminist ethic here of convincing the reader that the text is right. There's no liberal feminist conviction here that there may be many truths. There's only the authoritative institution of a universe, a tight political economy of gestures and images, a complex set of stakes, and the sustained, delicious, longed-for calls to action. MacKinnon denies all truth except the force of this political desire, all affect except the feminist anguish of being unable to distinguish between rape and sex, and all sexual fantasies except the heady fantasy of rising to total feminist power from utter powerlessness in capitalist patriarchies *and* back, and around, and if.

MacKinnon honors both the epistemological difficulty and the political necessity of feminism: she asserts that we do not—may never—know if what we know is knowledge, and she insists we work toward true knowledge, for there is nothing else to do.[25] MacKinnon maintains simultaneously the desire implicated in reality and the reality of desire; she brings them into contact with each other; the distinctions blur. On the one hand, you get a political program, the desire for a new reality, as a response to the terrible reality of the desire for femininity/masochism; on the other, you get an anguish, unassimilable to the political program, the recognition that the feminist and the feminine are inextricably implicated in the reality that you want to change.[26] There is an atmosphere of indistinguishability in the text between consciousness and reality, pain and pleasure, sexuality and violence. MacKinnon wants neither: neither objectivity nor subjectivity, neither femininity nor domination, neither sexuality nor violence. *She wants both.* The sadomasochism, thus, transacts "both" in every form. Caught not only between feminine powerlessness and feminist powerfulness, the reader switches between every dualism posited in the text: "subject and object, person and thing, dominant and subordinate, 'fuckor and fuckee'" (Brown 88).

Feminine powerlessness and feminist powerfulness have the same driving force: anguish. However, the other side of anguish is not pleasure. The chapter called "Sexuality," for example, is all about sexual violence. This does not (only) mean that sexuality is inseparable and indistinguishable from sexual violence. Something unbearable—MacKinnon circumscribes this as sexual violence—drives feminism *and* sexuality, but their pleasures do not neutralize the anguish that precedes, and exceeds, them. Something does not add up. Perhaps the self-abnegating intensity of

MacKinnon's knowingness is a powerful measure of what cannot be known: of sex, of violence, of feminism, of reality, of consciousness, of her own textuality.[27] Unlike most of her readers, I think that there is fundamental *unknowingness* at the heart of MacKinnon's feminism; there is suspension, oscillation, a dynamic, and you don't know where you are.

Have Feminism, Not / Which Is / Which Can't Be / Without Sex

The battery cycle accords with the rhythms of heterosexual sex. The rhythm of lesbian sadomasochism is the same.
—MacKinnon

A minute-by-minute moving picture is created of women *becoming, refusing, sustaining* their condition.
—MacKinnon; my emphasis

While tracking a number of surprising resonances between MacKinnon and Lacanian psychoanalytic theory, Cornell points out that MacKinnon does not write in psychoanalytic terms: "MacKinnon completely externalizes the power of desire because she pays no attention to the unconscious. As a result, her analysis of feminine desire, and desire more generally, is overly simplistic. Desire, for MacKinnon, is expressed by women in one way, because male power makes it so. Certainly, if psychoanalytic theory has taught us anything, it has taught us that the relationship between desire and politics is extremely complicated and, indeed, much more complicated than MacKinnon herself would have it" (134). While this is all true,[28] Mac-Kinnon is unexpectedly more productive through a psychoanalytic reading. For if the MacKinnonian subject is staked out in her own annihilation and in deep anguish about her liberation, this is territory that is almost unreadable outside of psychoanalysis. Instead of reading MacKinnon only literally, why not affirm her affirmations, blindly follow her blindfolded arguments, read seriously her very serious pronouncements, enter her reality through the closed door?[29] Neither ironic irreverence nor undying devotion, this reading aspires to both.

According to MacKinnon, masochism is so bad that there is no option for feminism but to invoke urgent, reparative measures in the form of legal redress. And yet, MacKinnon's descriptions of masochism invoke a response in the very register of the sexual that she seeks to destroy. She asks, "Why is hierarchy sexy?" (136). She scoffs at "the excitement at reduction of a person to a thing" (130). She declares with as much contempt as is textually possible: "Man fucks woman; subject verb object" (124). How impossible to not read this sex-negative feminism as a defiant reproduction of the sexual. How impossible to not read this militant feminism as a fantasy of power, forced, in spite of itself, to contend with masochism as a condition of experiencing the social. How impossible to not admit shamefully that the sex ed teacher may have only ended up producing a sex fantasy of prohibition, chastity, and modesty. MacKinnon argues that "male sexual desire is [. . .] simultaneously created and serviced, never satisfied once and for all, while male force is romanticized, even sacralized, potentiated and naturalized, by being submerged into sex itself" (137). What, however, of the desire that MacKinnon's own text creates and services, never satisfied with itself or with its heterosexually feminine reader? You are wrong, masochism is bad, you are so bad, masochism is so wrong, it goes on and on, MacKinnon does, thereby elevating *and* reducing her own feminism to an utterly delightful single-mindedness.

For Brown, this is one of the fundamental problems with MacKinnon: the reader cannot help but be exploited and activated sexually by MacKinnon's rehearsal of the "code" (91) that she herself claims to critique. Brown's explicitly stated mission is to figure out why MacKinnon is successful, why "students" (91) hold on to her analysis in spite of its weaknesses. But how is this characterization of the reader any different from MacKinnon's lament that women want what they should not want? MacKinnon is relentlessly critical of women who seem to want to maintain the status quo of patriarchy at home and in the workplace and in the parliament and in their bedrooms. Why, cries MacKinnon, do these women want to harm themselves to the point of annihilation? Unwittingly, perhaps, Brown echoes MacKinnon's outraged bewilderment: why do you want it when it is so bad for you? I believe that both MacKinnon and Brown are onto something crucial: the subject/reader may have a complex relationship to that which is deemed harmful, painful, or simply not politically useful.[30]

For MacKinnon, the axes of pleasure and politics seem to be in an oblique relation. What feels good is what needs to be disrupted by politics so that we can end the oppression and the subordination of women. MacKinnon wants to align this oblique relation; she wants politics to guide your experience of pleasure. For example, it is not enough to say that lesbian sadomasochists engage in s/m sexuality because they like it; MacKinnon wants you to explain how you can possibly justify engaging in violence—the forceful sex that women are taught to want—by citing pleasure. I want—if only temporarily—to wrest these axes apart and argue for a pleasure that is not only politically harmful but pleasurable *because* it cannot be aligned with a political program. Such a pleasure may generate its own politics,[31] but MacKinnon forecloses this possibility altogether by fantasizing an s/m scene about the end of masochistic fantasies. Surprisingly, MacKinnon's critics engage in a somewhat parallel exercise when they read her only to ask if and how she is useful to feminism. This insistence on political utility forecloses the very possibility of a reading pleasure that does not—and cannot—contribute to politics.[32] In this foreclosure, many critics of MacKinnon may inadvertently be allied with her in her anguish that pleasure persists, that it may be politically harmful, and that that's probably why one wants it.

MacKinnon's feminism, like any other politics of sexuality, is forced to contend with the specter of becoming part of the very scene of sexuality it critiques. In my reading, the sadomasochism of her textuality does not consist in MacKinnon bullying the reader to give up on feminine powerlessness and embrace feminist power, but in the doubling of pleasure: inhabiting both sides of power-ness in an endless loop. This is probably why most readers of MacKinnon report intense engagements with the text, whether they are laudatory or critical. Thus, it is not enough to say that MacKinnon is pornographic or that she "fucks her audiences" (Cornell qtd. in Brown 91), for these assessments do not account for the depth of your reading experience.[33] The s/m textuality of MacKinnon undoes its own radical feminist critique of sexuality by amplifying and aggravating pleasure in the name of ending it. MacKinnon engages the terms of power not outside of sex, but as sex, continues to name violence as violence but also delivers it as an experience of masochism (which is also a version of sadism).

That MacKinnon addresses herself mostly to heterosexual women only augments your already considerable painful pleasure. As MacKinnon's reader, you have to *play* at "becoming, refusing, sustaining" (89) the heterosexually feminine reader that you are not and cannot be. Her heterosexism has you slightly giddy, for it means that she can be read only if you are willing to perform the role of a heterosexual woman who would engage in a play of power and pain with her. It turns out that *Toward a Feminist Theory of the State* is quintessentially—wait for it—a lesbian s/m text! Heterosexuality as role-play is available to people of all sexualities, of course, but it may be particularly violent and/or/but meaningful and/or/but pleasurable for a lesbian sadomasochist. I am arguing that the MacKinnonian text may be special to you in a similar way, not in spite of its heterosexism, but *because* of it. You have to admit, then, that if there's a sadist (which is also a kind of masochist) in the text, it is you, reader, it is also you.

I want to stay with MacKinnon's contentions that sexual pleasure is disturbingly proximate to the pleasure of committing violence and that the question of sexual violence often takes away from the pervasiveness of violence in the everyday of the sexual.[34] This is a "powerless" political position to be in, and yet, MacKinnon inspires, in spite of herself, taking one's submission to its extreme—not to accept that law is a way out, nor to accept that consciousness is a way out, but to see this very corner of a universe as a place made within law and within consciousness. An s/m scene, as opposed to a scene of rape, is always legally instituted between the participants, even when one does not know why one does it or where it would lead; verbal or unspoken, it is an evolving contract. The scene stages law and consciousness as much as it stages wishes and fantasies, without necessarily resolving or bypassing the political difficulty of wanting to hurt and be hurt in sex. The scene, instead, allows for a pleasurable, but perhaps politically useless, experience of this difficulty by repeating it.[35] It is in this impossible psychic space between acting out a fantasy and believing it in reality, between hurting and hurting, that MacKinnon helps you experience and stay with the most unbearable of truth possibilities: that sex may never be able to offer pleasure that is not also some kind of violence. MacKinnon's s/m practices allow us to appreciate the full horror of this predicament: not that of (heterosexual or lesbian and/or sadomasochistic) women, but of feminism.

A "pornographic" feminism against pornography, the invention of a lesbian s/m textuality to critique lesbian sadomasochism, a political call to arms against violent pleasures in the affective register of a crime of passion: how can you be indifferent to the devastating romance of MacKinnon's tribute to the entanglement of feminism and sexuality? If Brown is right, if MacKinnon does indeed offer up feminism for the sex you shouldn't want, her feminism is simply the sublimated form of sexuality. *Feminism is sex too*, MacKinnon wants you (not) to know. And therefore, feminism is subject to the same questions, the same critiques, the same unraveling that MacKinnon administers to sexuality: what feels good and bad and why do you still want it and why can't you not want it and how should you want what you can't yet want?

MacKinnon teaches us, in spite of herself, to view sexual violence as that which can perhaps be read through but *not* resolved by feminist politics. The best feminism can possibly do—and must continue doing à la MacKinnon—is to stage and repeat the very *real* violence of sexuality: the rape fantasies, the abusive situation you just could not bear to leave, the sex that felt like rape, the rape that felt like some kind of sex, the awful delights, the sighs of despair, the useless pain, all the wrong words, all the impossible pleasures, the lovely fantasy of peaceful, benign, democratic love that you did not get to live out and never will, and not for lack of trying. Feminisms that disavow this insidious and self-destructive entanglement with sexuality, feminisms that wish to purge either the world of sex or sexuality of violence, are having the same (bad) dream; it can't be done. We have on our hands a very compromising situation, for MacKinnon is with you in the corner, reader; she has been there all along.

I am grateful to Dr. Elizabeth Wilson for her careful, supportive feedback on this paper and all her immensely stabilizing guidance. Thanks also to Dr. Lynne Huffer for her enthusiastic and encouraging comments on the very first draft of this adventure. And thanks finally to Dr. Robyn Wiegman, whose detailed engagement really helped me get my act together.

SAMIA VASA is a doctoral candidate in women's, gender, and sexuality studies at Emory University. Her doctoral research project, tentatively titled "Repeating the Unreadable: Sexual Violence, Radical Feminism, and Psychoanalysis," conducts psychoanalytic, literary, and queer-negative readings of Catharine MacKinnon, Andrea Dworkin, and the Gujarat riots of 2002.

Notes

1   By "MacKinnon," I mean the text of *Toward a Feminist Theory of the State*, not the woman, the lawyer, or the activist.

2   This image was inspired by Lalitha Gopalan's discussion of women avenging sexual violence in Indian cinema of the eighties and nineties.

3   MacKinnon is mostly engaged with heterosexuality in her theoretical and legal work, though she often refers to it as "sexuality." When confronted with the question of gay or lesbian or any other kind of sexuality, MacKinnon has been known to subject them to the logic of heterosexuality. Janet Halley has powerfully demonstrated the homophobia and misogyny of such a stance in her analysis of a U.S. Supreme Court case, *Oncale v. Sundowner Offshore Services* (1998) (54–57, 290–303). Adrienne Rich, on the other hand, finds MacKinnon productive for antihomophobic work because she helps apprehend "the nature and extent of heterosexual pressures" (643). For the purposes of this paper, I take it for granted that MacKinnon's descriptions of heterosexuality have something to contribute to descriptions of sexuality in general. While the essentialism and inaccurate generalizations in her work have been very usefully critiqued, I adopt a universalizing approach (Sedgwick 3) here: I argue that the heterosexuality of and in her formulations has been sexuality all along. Leo Bersani exemplifies this approach to MacKinnon's work.

4   See, for example, Adams; Brown; Butler; Cornell; Franke; Halley; Marasco; Rubin; and Walters for their insightful and critical readings of MacKinnon.

5   This is something the contemporary #MeToo movement is also invested in navigating and theorizing.

6   Published in 1989, this book runs through the many themes and questions that MacKinnon addressed in her theoretical, legal, and activist work over a period of two decades. As such, it is an uneven text. This paper does not claim to account for the multiple, sometimes conflicting, ideas in the book; however, the fact that this text is not a consistent, cohesive, ordered whole contributes to, rather than undermining, my reading.

All the page citations of MacKinnon in the body of the paper, as well as the notes, refer to *Toward the Feminist Theory of the State*.

7   The "big secret about sex," according to Leo Bersani, is that "most people don't like it" (197).

8   Wendy Brown argues that MacKinnon's descriptions of domination and submission fold back into her own style of writing (90). Drucilla Cornell points out, "In MacKinnon's world of 'fuckees' and 'fuckors,' an obviously heterosexual social reality, the only possible alternative to being a 'fuckee' is to be a 'fuckor.' The sado-masochistic system of gender identity is, as a result, confirmed at the same time that it is supposedly being rejected" (152).

Parveen Adams and Mark Cousins, in their analysis of MacKinnon's *Only Words*, claim that MacKinnon's text is sadistic and the reader is in the position of masochistic violation (63). Others, like Halley (363) and Linda Williams (18), cite sadomasochistic sexuality and a complex understanding of masochistic pleasure as the *counterpoint* to MacKinnon's analysis of sexuality. Adams even argues that lesbian sadomasochistic practices are, in fact, a disruption of sexuality in general and of heterosexuality in particular (27–48).

9   I use "s/he" to emphasize the role-play quality of the gender of MacKinnon's subject/reader. It does not matter who you are—or who you would like to be—as long as you can occupy the position of a heterosexual woman to unlock the textual movements of her argument.

10   For MacKinnon, in fact, it is sexuality that is the "linchpin of gender inequality" (113). She argues that sexuality is a "form of power" and that it is gender that embodies this power, "not the reverse" (113).

11   Surprisingly, the chapters on Freud's Dora and a critique of MacKinnon are part of the same book by Adams.

12   In "Instincts and Their Vicissitudes," Freud argues that one of the vicissitudes that instincts undergo is a reversal into the opposite. He offers sadism-masochism and scopophilia-exhibitionism as examples of such a reversal in which the *aims* of the instincts are affected: "The active aim (to torture, to look at) is replaced by the passive aim (to be tortured, to be looked at)" (127). Further, "The enjoyment of pain would thus be an aim which was originally masochistic, but which can only become an instinctual aim in someone who was originally sadistic" (129).

13   See, in particular, Brown; and Cornell.

14   MacKinnon uses the term *power* in a non-Foucauldian sense. Men, the state, pornography are all exceedingly, unfailingly powerful; women and porn actors are unfailingly and utterly powerless—either surplus or lack on each side.

15   Though Adams cites the oscillation of Dora's identification as evidence of her wanting to be in the desiring

positions of both man and woman, Rose points out that this oscillation also signals the impossibility of being either: "This can be referred directly back to the case of Dora, woman as object and subject of desire—the impossibility of either position, for if object of desire then whose desire, and if subject of desire then its own impossibility, the impossibility of subject and desire (the one implying the fading of the other)" (47).

16   As Shoshana Felman says about the controversy after the publication of Henry James's *The Turn of the Screw*: "*[W]e are forced to participate in the scandal,* [. . .] the reader's innocence cannot remain intact; there is no such thing as an innocent reader of this text. In other words, the scandal is not simply *in* the text, it resides in *our relation to the text,* in the text's *effect on us,* its readers; what is outrageous in the text is not simply that *of which* the text is speaking, but that which makes it speak *to us*" (144).

17   MacKinnon plays with the play-acting nature of political action: "Women can act because they have been acting all along" (102).

18   MacKinnon challenges the distinction between theorizing and consciousness raising by arguing that neither allows for an escape from reality: "In contrast to science, consciousness raising does not devalue the roots of social experience as it uncovers them, nor does it set up rules for certainty. It allows *a critical embrace* of who one has been made by society rather than demanding a removal of all that one is before one can understand one's situation. [. . .] It also makes everyone a theorist" (102; my emphasis).

19   MacKinnon argues for the immanence of theorizing in relation to

the "inside" of women's oppression: "This posture places the theorist inside the world and the work, not above or outside them—which, to be frank, is where the theorist has been all along" (xvi).

20   MacKinnon's consciousness seeks to be conscious of itself, her reality seeks to be real to itself: "The pursuit of the truth of women's reality is the process of consciousness; the life situation of consciousness, its determination articulated in the minutiae of everyday existence, is what feminist consciousness seeks to be conscious of" (39).

21   This is not to deny that MacKinnon's legal career and her antipornography feminism, in particular, have not made use of law as precisely a way out of the so-called reality of women's subordination. My point is that law functions differently in her s/m textuality.

22   Knowledge is literary and relational: "An epistemology is *a story* of a relation between knower and known" (MacKinnon 96; my emphasis).

23   Consider this passionate articulation of the convoluted, almost dead-ended nature of creating a new world for women:

>   *Feminism affirms women's point of view, in large part, by revealing, criticizing, and explaining its impossibility. This is not a dialectical paradox. It is a methodological expression of women's situation, in which the struggle for consciousness is a struggle for world: for a sexuality, a history, a culture, a community, a form of power, an experience of the sacred. If women had consciousness or world, sex inequality would be harmless, or all women would be feminist. Yet women have something of both, or there would be no such thing as feminism. Why can women know that this—life*

*as we have known it—is not all,
not enough, not ours, not just?*
(MacKinnon 115)

24   Halley points out that although
      MacKinnon began her career with
      a radical position—we do not know,
      we cannot know, we seek women's
      point of view—she later modified
      her stance: *we* speak from the
      point of view of women, and from
      our point of view, injury to one
      woman is injury to all women
      everywhere. Halley argues that
      MacKinnon started with express-
      ing a painful desire to know
      reality but ended up claiming to
      know the painful reality of desire
      (41–57). In my reading, this is not
      simply a one-way movement from
      desire to reality.

25   Women are both totally identified
      with their conditions and com-
      pletely alienated from them: "Real-
      izing that women largely recog-
      nize themselves in sex-stereotyped
      terms, really do feel the needs they
      have been encouraged to feel, do
      feel fulfilled in the expected ways,
      often actually choose what has
      been prescribed, makes possible
      the realization that women at the
      same time do not recognize them-
      selves in, do not feel, and have not
      chosen this place" (MacKinnon
      102).

26   Consider, for example, this com-
      plex, admittedly self-contradictory
      formulation: "Women's complicity
      in their condition does not contra-
      dict its fundamental unacceptabil-
      ity if women have little choice but
      to become persons who then freely
      choose women's roles. For this rea-
      son, the reality of women's oppres-
      sion is, finally, neither demon-
      strable nor refutable empirically"
      (MacKinnon 124).

27   An example of MacKinnon's
      unknowingness can be found
      toward the end of the chapter
      titled "Sexuality": "The feminist

psychic universe certainly recognizes that people do not always
know what they want, have hidden
desires and inaccessible needs,
lack awareness of motivation, have
contorted and opaque interactions,
and have an interest in obscuring what is really going on. But
this does not essentially conceal
that what women really want is
more sex. It is true, as Freudians
have persuasively observed, that
*many things are sexual that do
not present themselves as such.* But
in ways Freud never dreamed"
(MacKinnon 152; my emphasis). It
is difficult to read such statements
about Freud without a sense of
irony given that the formal contradictions of sexuality are the very
object of psychoanalysis.

28   Adams and Cousins also point out
      that "[t]he term 'representation'
      seems to irritate her almost as
      much as 'fantasy'" (Adams 60).

29   MacKinnon herself advocates
      such double negative affirma-
      tions: "Women experienced the
      walls that have contained them
      as walls—and sometimes walked
      through them" (91).

30   In fact, as Bersani puts it, sexual-
      ity is nothing but an intensely
      pleasurable, self-shattering rela-
      tionship to pain: "Freud keeps
      returning to a line of speculation
      in which the sexual emerges as the
      jouissance of exploded limits, as
      the ecstatic suffering into which
      the human organism momentarily
      plunges when it is 'pressed' beyond
      a certain threshold of endurance.
      Sexuality, at least in the mode in
      which it is constituted, may be a
      tautology for masochism" (217).
      MacKinnon and Brown recognize
      these masochistic tendencies in
      women and readers only to reject
      them as politically useless, or even
      harmful.

31 Bersani articulates the difference between rooting for a politically acceptable form of sexual pleasure versus reading sexuality as its own mode of politics as "the question not of the reflection or expression of politics in sex, but rather of the extremely obscure process by which sexual pleasure *generates* politics" (208).

32 While criticizing MacKinnon and Andrea Dworkin's "pastoralizing, redemptive intentions," Bersani argues that their "indictment of sex—their refusal to prettify it, to romanticize it, to maintain that fucking has anything to do with community or love—has had the immensely desirable effect of publicizing, of lucidly laying out for us, the inestimable value of sex as—at least in certain of its ineradicable aspects—anticommunal, antiegalitarian, antinurturing, antiloving" (215). I am attempting, on the contrary, to argue that MacKinnon's redemptive intentions, if any, are precisely the site of a repetition of what she wants to redeem, or end: sex. As such, the place of negativity in her work may be located not just in her critique of sexuality but also in her s/m textuality/feminism.

33 Not that I think that pornographic materials or getting fucked cannot be deep (reading) experiences, but I am assuming that Brown and Cornell use the terms *pornographic* and *fuck* in this context to imply something that is not exactly deep or profound.

34 Rose offers a much more productive psychoanalytic formulation of these insights:

> [A]s feminism turns to questions of censorship, violence and sado-masochism, psychoanalysis hands back to it a fundamental violence of the psychic realm— hands back to it, therefore, nothing less than the difficulty of sexuality itself. For if psychic life has its own violence; if there is an aggression in the very movement of the drives; if sexual difference, because of the forcing it requires, leaves the subject divided against the sexual other as well as herself or himself; if the earliest instances of female sexuality contain a difficulty not solely explicable in terms of the violent repudiation with which the little girl leaves them behind [. . .] then there can be no analysis for women which sees violence solely as accident, imposition, or external event. (16)

35 In her brief discussion of the dissolution of the *école freudienne* by Lacan in 1980, Rose ponders the relationship between psychoanalysis, femininity, and institutionality in the responses of two women analysts, Michèle Montrelay and Marie-Christine Hamon. For Montrelay, Rose notes, "the only way to deal with that crisis is to continue to *be* an analyst, that is, to continue to create a space in which the problem of identification and its laws, in all their force and impossibility, can repeatedly be experienced" (5).

Works Cited

Adams, Parveen. *The Emptiness of the Image: Psychoanalysis and Sexual Differences*. New York: Routledge, 1996.

Adams, Parveen, and Mark Cousins. "The Truth on Assault." *The Emptiness of the Image*. New York: Routledge, 2015. 57–69.

Bersani, Leo. "Is the Rectum a Grave?" *October* 43 (1987): 197–222.

Brown, Wendy. "The Mirror of Pornography." *States of Injury: Power and Freedom in Late Modernity*. Princeton: Princeton UP, 1995. 77–95.

Butler, Judith. "Against Proper Objects." Introduction. *More Gender Trouble: Feminist Meets Queer Theory*. Spec. issue of *differences* 6.2–3 (1994): 1–26.

Cornell, Drucilla. "Feminism Always Modified: The Affirmation of Feminine Difference Rethought." *Beyond Accommodation: Ethical Feminism, Deconstruction and the Law*. New York: Routledge, 1991. 119–64.

Felman, Shoshana. *Writing and Madness: (Literature / Philosophy / Psychoanalysis)*. Trans. Martha Noel Evans. Stanford: Stanford UP, 2003.

Franke, Katherine. "Theorizing Yes: An Essay on Feminism, Law, and Desire." *Columbia Law Review* 101 (2001): 181–208.

Freud, Sigmund. "Fragment of an Analysis of a Case of Hysteria." 1901. *The Standard Edition of the Complete Psychological Works of Sigmund Freud*. Trans. and ed. James Strachey. Vol. 7. London: Hogarth, 1953. 7–122. 24 vols. 1953–74.

——————. "Instincts and Their Vicissitudes." 1915. *The Standard Edition*. Vol. 14. 1957. 117–40.

Gopalan, Lalitha. "Avenging Women in Indian Cinema." *Cinema of Interruptions: Action Genres in Contemporary Indian Cinema*. London: British Film Institute, 2002. 34–62.

Halley, Janet. *Split Feminisms: How and Why to Take a Break from Feminism*. Princeton: Princeton UP, 2006.

MacKinnon, Catharine. *Only Words*. Cambridge, MA: Harvard UP, 1993.

——————. *Toward a Feminist Theory of the State*. Cambridge, MA: Harvard UP, 1989.

Marasco, Robyn. "'Already the Effect of the Whip': Critical Theory and the Feminine Ideal." *Feminist Theory and the Frankfurt School*. Spec. issue of *differences* 17.1 (2006): 88–115.

Rich, Adrienne. "Compulsory Heterosexuality and Lesbian Existence." *Signs* 5.4 (1980): 631–60.

Rose, Jacqueline. *Sexuality in the Field of Vision*. 1986. Calcutta: Seagull, 2005.

Rubin, Gayle. "Thinking Sex: Notes for a Radical Theory of the Politics of Sexuality." *Deviations*. Durham: Duke UP, 2011. 137–81.

Scott, Joan Wallach. *The Fantasy of Feminist History*. Durham: Duke UP, 2011.

Sedgwick, Eve Kosofsky. "Axiomatic." *Epistemology of the Closet*. Berkeley: U of California P, 1990. 1–63.

Walters, Suzanna Danuta. "Introduction: The Dangers of a Metaphor—Beyond the Battlefield in the Sex Wars." *Signs* 42.1 (2016): 1–9.

Williams, Linda. *Hardcore: Power, Pleasure, and the "Frenzy of the Visible."* Berkeley: U of California P, 1989.

KEYWORD 6

Testimony

*T*he #MeToo moment has brought us to a reckoning with testimony. In legal discourse, testimony, already tethered to racialized and
gendered notions of rationality and consent, is part of a larger evidentiary
process used to establish a set of facts. Judges and jurors are presented with
evidence and asked to adjudicate a set of claims, positioning individual
testimony within the larger context of other truth claims and interpretive
framings. The veracity and value assigned to testimony, however, has always
been predicated on who we are and how we are positioned in regimes of
power. Because we must present ourselves to a law formed through colonial
occupation, enslavement, and patriarchal control, the testimony of those
who "speak from the position of the not supposed to speak," to borrow
from Fred Moten, has always been suspect, when it has been allowed at all
(217). Outside of law, these same marginalized subjects have long turned to
extrajuridical forms of testimony, using personal narratives to make public
claims for collective human rights and recognition. These traditions have
included the slave narratives of the African diaspora, the Latin American

Volume 30, Number 1   DOI 10.1215/10407391-7481288

tradition of *testimonio*, and the feminist tradition of using autobiography to theorize the messy conditions of our lives.

Social media, however, has changed almost everything we associate with testimony. Platforms like Facebook, Twitter, and Instagram determine the speed, scope, audience, and rhetorical contours of testimonial claims and the structures of available response. Once testimonies leave us, they get taken up and circulated by others, flung with care or abandoned to those far away and nearest to us, in the service of promoting both individual claims for redress and larger political demands for justice. We see how they land in the form of Likes, Comments, Retweets, because we are always being invited to Share. These forms of engagement on social media are seen as a way of offering our support for those that have been harmed, a kind of digital solidarity that can travel the world in a manner of minutes. Just as law determines what is admissible as a speech act that can enter into the public record, technology itself informs the linguistic possibilities of these affective responses. Today, emojis, memes, and character limits are used to impart shape to our engagement with the trauma of another, another who becomes increasingly removed from the scene of testimony. Once testimony enters the digital sphere, judgment is intended to be swift, rendered not by a judge, a jury, or an individual reader, but by a hive-mind of shared publics and the imagined possibilities of a shared politics. While law and autobiographical narrative rely on a slow deliberate use of evidence and rhetorical logic to build a compelling elucidation of a series of events, #MeToo carries the force of judgment, absent narrative complexity or calls for sustained interpretive analysis.

The feminist injunction to "believe women" is predicated on the assumption that the very act of testimony serves as evidence of the violence it speaks. This claim to the transparency and self-evidentiary claims of experience and the quick turn to punitive forms of justice should give us pause. Even as we understand how social media performs another proximity to the "real" through the imagined immediacy of an ever urgent present, like law, literature, and other forms of representation and self-representation, the testimonies that circulate around #MeToo are mediated by the social and political context in which they are delivered and received, molded through the very contours of language. When we narrate our experiences, particularly when what is being narrated is sex, violence, and the machinations of power, our testimony is received by diverse audiences with disparate frames of legibility that interpret these terms through their own archives of sexual and social experiences, breaking apart the imagined sameness of #MeToo.

In its public appeals, #MeToo functions as a form of collective and public recognition that depends on our willingness to *not* read for difference, subtlety, or nuance. Yet, as scholars we have long understood that recognition always takes place within a field of legibility that is always partial and contingent, producing both an absence and an excess of interpretation. In her foundational essay, "The Evidence of Experience," Joan Scott warns us about assuming an underlying transparency in the recounting of experience. Her concern is that "[q]uestions about the constructed nature of experience, about how subjects are constituted as different in the first place, about how one's vision is structured—about language (or discourse) and history—are left aside" (399). What gets left aside in the discussions of #MeToo are precisely these more difficult underlying assumptions that construct our understanding of harm, violence, and, indeed, of justice (399).

In *Giving an Account of Oneself,* Judith Butler wades through the treacherous terrain of language that circulates around forms of self-representation. In recounting the various ways that a subject enters into discourse, Butler writes, "[T]he very terms by which we give an account, by which we make ourselves intelligible to ourselves and to others, are not of our making. They are social in character, and they establish social norms, a domain of unfreedom and substitutability within which our 'singular' stories are told" (21). In the #MeToo movement, the terms invoked—*victim, abuse, power*—are decidedly social, steeped in both complicated legal implications and varied social and cultural norms. Yet very often in the spaces of social media, terms such as *sexual violence* are vacated of these nuances, deployed to register unwelcome verbal sexual advances, the forcible violation of one's corporeal edges, and the kinds of sustained, systemic sexual assaults associated with colonialism and slavery. While each kind of violation evidences harm, the extent and impact of these violations are decidedly different.

When these "singular stories" spring into the space of public discourse, each encounter forms a new moment of potential collective recognition and validation. In fact, the very syntax of #MeToo is predicated on a structure of sameness in search of recognition or substitutability. Discursively, it affirms that whatever violation happened to the one giving testimony is the same as the one who echoes back, #MeToo. It is precisely this collective chorus of #MeToo that has been effective in exposing the pervasiveness of diverse forms of sexual violation; the systemic ways gendered and sexual violence gets silenced, dismissed, or condoned; and the racialized historical antecedents that frame these contemporary acts of gendered violation. But that chorus and the cumulative psychic harm it carries has also been activated to make demands for punitive action that can erase the complexity and nuance of specific events and individual actors in the service of larger, more compelling, and more expedient political agendas. While appeals for revenge and retribution for sexual assault have historically been organized around the protection of white female innocence and vulnerability, the same logic of punitive justice is at times selectively extended to nonwhite women and others, particularly when the accused perpetrator fits available scripts of pathologized racialized masculinity. Even as the originating narrators and narratives that have circulated around the hashtag have varied widely, the judgments offered have been disturbingly consistent: abusers need to pay, if not with juridical intervention, then with swift, speedy, and relentless public censure. "Abusers," for surely by now they have become a genus, need to be exiled from our screens, our syllabi, our consumptive practices, and our communities.

These calls for "justice" are rarely interrogated. Within the #MeToo movement, we have seen how quickly testimony gets activated to demand punishment and more vigilant forms of state protection. At times, these calls go further to offer preventative measures that are perceived to offer protections against future harms, generally in the form of increased sexual prohibitions and surveillance offered under the guise of making potentially vulnerable parties "safer." Yet, as people of color and stigmatized sexual minorities, many of us know all too well how demands for enhanced systems of sexual surveillance and control in the service of "safety" have been used against us. The sexuality of black and brown people of all genders has long been positioned as inherently dangerous in ways that have authorized debasing forms of state surveillance, criminalization, and punishment for perceived deviance from middle-class norms of white sexual comportment. We queers have our own visceral history of "sex panics," of being marked as sexually deviant, hunted down, exposed, publicly ridiculed, and expelled from civil society. Furthermore, many queers and other people of color have known up close the punitive impulses of the carceral state and carceral feminism, whose only form of redress is dehumanization, incarceration, and exile. These corrective disciplinary measures foreclose social investments in probing the traumas around which harm festers or developing more sustainable forms of reparative justice. They are organized instead around creating a world in which only the unwounded are allowed to flourish.

In communities marked by the generational violences of settler colonialism, police occupation, state-enforced poverty, domestic abuse, and immigrant despair, wounding abounds. These hurts are harder to name. Sometimes, even when the weight of evidence makes a compelling case for injury, different publics shaped by generation, social position, proximity, and personal experience can interpret the extent, impact, and possibility for redress of that injury quite differently. We have already witnessed how some cases, inside and outside of the academy, have divided diverse feminist and progressive communities, when, having been invited to sign on, share, or echo the response and judgment of those in our social spheres (digital and otherwise) failure to comply or, worse, open disagreement gets registered as betrayal. Even as these fissures reveal the varied ways that sexual and social experiences can impact our worldview, they also expose the very different visions of justice that undergird discussions of gendered violence and social harm.

At this historical juncture, we would do well to interrogate our individual attachments—political and psychic—in the testimony and circulation of another's harm and our collective investments in public forms of punishment that erase possibilities for redemption, reparations, or amends, punishments that are always inflected through race, class, and social position. In his account of queer Latino *testimonio*, Arnaldo Cruz-Malavé probes how the desires of readers, for either connection or distance, are implicated in interpretive accounts of narrative scenes of violation and trauma. He suggests, "If we gazed on that scene and searched there for the marked subject's ontological difference or 'truth,' [. . .] we would end up not engaging with an interlocutor, but creating a subjected subject instead—a subject-for-us, that is, for us to know, to conquer, to possess" (113). Here, Cruz-Malavé asks us to interrogate the affective attachments to mastery and judgment that we bring to bear on the testimony of another. His words highlight the need to situate traumatized subjects within the fields of power that generate the conditions for trauma. But he also reminds us of the multiple ways that testimony can be instrumentalized in relation to readers' desires for recognition, for difference, or for politics. Like other forms of testimony, #MeToo uses individual stories to make larger shared political claims, and while it is this move toward collective forms of representation that creates the conditions for mobilizing publics hailed by that injury, it is also what erases the particularities of difference that define each new #MeToo moment.

As politically engaged publics, we would all do well to slow down our consumptive and reactive practices, to be careful and cautious readers willing to situate each new testimony within its own complicated context and geopolitical field of reception. Reading for difference and recognizing how we might also read differently requires that we think more honestly about our own desires and investments in the dispersal of testimonies of harm and in the social demands we make in their name, to think about how the dynamics of power, proximity, and precarity establish each of us as different kinds of vulnerable subjects. Too many of us have our own memories of #MeToo moments, small injustices and cruel violations; flashbacks poised to trigger a visceral response upon witnessing the testimony of another. Each of us brings our own histories of violence, of sex, of community to our encounters with the testimony of another. Harm, like pleasure, is corporeal. It can become lodged in our bodies, it can linger or evaporate, it can scar. Yet, we cannot assume that sharing the "same" experience or identity will amount to sharing the same political strategies and goals. The shape, force, and direction of how we might be activated by the testimony of another can never be fully knowable or predicable.

A harder question becomes what to make of those shades of difference, particularly and especially when the testimony that is being delivered is one not of violence, but of pleasure. Like experiences of sexual violence, representations of what might constitute sexual pleasure are never unmediated or transparent, but emerge within an ever changing interpretive field of intelligibility shaped by social forces but unique to each of us. How can we use this moment to listen with care to the complexities of claims of violence, as well as to the articulations of difficult pleasures, constrained enactments of agency, and the narrative refusals of facile tropes of female victimization that also surround accounts of sexual experience? Being vulnerable also means being vulnerable to one another, opening ourselves up to critique and censure because we have failed to fulfill someone else's demands for representation, for solidarity, or for political action. If we understand experience and the testimony that aims to represent it as both "always already an interpretation, and something that needs to be interpreted," it becomes easier to understand how political disagreements can arise about what might constitute sexual violence or sexual pleasure as both predictable and necessary (Scott 412). That as political activists, as scholars, as feminists, or as survivors of sexual assaults we might disagree on the interpretation or implications of corporeal experiences or the imagined strategies for addressing social harms seems the most basic foundation upon which to situate constructive dialogue and community engagement toward a world filled with less harm and greater care. And if we can understand how our vulnerability to abuse is shaped by currents of power and privilege, let us also ponder the ways that possibilities for joy, sexual and otherwise, are also conditioned by these same forces. Let us not only linger on what might constitute injury; let us also dwell on what might constitute justice. Let us talk freely and openly about how to flirt, fuck, and feel passionately in a world seething with pain and suffering in order to imagine a sexual politics that reaches for a capacious justice that does more than merely punish and prohibit, a justice where pleasure might also thrive.

JUANA MARÍA RODRÍGUEZ is a professor of ethnic studies, performance studies, and gender and women's studies at the University of California, Berkeley, and the author of *Sexual Futures, Queer Gestures, and Other Latina Longings* (New York University Press, 2014) and *Queer Latinidad: Identity Practices, Discursive Spaces* (New York University Press, 2003). She is currently working on a book on visual culture and Latina sexual labor and coediting a special issue of *TSQ* called *Trans Studies en las Américas*.

Works Cited

Butler, Judith. *Giving an Account of Oneself.* Fordham UP, 2005.

Cruz-Malavé, Arnaldo. *Queer Latino Testimonio, Keith Haring, and Juanito Xtravaganza: Hard Tails.* Palgrave Macmillan, 2007.

Moten, Fred. "Preface for a Solo by Miles Davis." *Women & Performance* 17.2 (2007): 217–46.

Scott, Joan W. "The Evidence of Experience." *The Lesbian and Gay Studies Reader.* Ed. Henry Abelove, Michèle Aina Barale, and David Halperin. New York: Routledge, 1993. 397–415.

SHONIQUA ROACH

Black Sex in the Quiet

*W*hile black feminism has been interrupting the perennial feminist pleasure/danger binary since its inception, contemporary black feminist discourses must still rely on the binary to do the narrative work of locating black injury and its redress.[1] Specifically, black feminist discourses on sexual pleasure and sexual violence are often positioned as oppositional.[2] Black sexual pleasure feminists seek to theoretically center the erotic freedoms black women ostensibly enjoy and deploy in spite of an antiblack public sphere and dominant visual field (Cruz; Lindsey and Johnson; Morgan; Nash). In contrast, "vanguard" black feminists—that is, Audre Lorde, bell hooks, Patricia Hill Collins, and so on—insist that black female visibility in the public sphere does not necessarily shift or challenge the racialized sexual stereotypes that continue to justify material violence against black women. Both discourses (black feminist denunciation of silence and embrace of publicity), however, inadvertently (re)produce a bind of black sexual freedom—a pattern in black feminist storytelling—that potentially reinforces black women's fungibility and limits black feminist imaginings of erotic freedom.[3]

Volume 30, Number 1   DOI 10.1215/10407391-7481302

© 2019 by Brown University and d i f f e r e n c e s : A Journal of Feminist Cultural Studies

Contemporary black feminist and queer critics maintain an investment in publicity as a conduit for pleasure, through which they seek some semblance of black women's sexual freedom. Specifically, black feminists use publicity as a governing frame for both injury and its redress, generating cultures of exposure and confession and obscuring the extent to which publicity continues to be predicated on whiteness as property right and blackness as fungible (Hartman; Spillers).[4] When I refer to the *fungibility* of black femininity, I mean black women's material and discursive elasticity. Saidiya Hartman elucidates: the "fungibility of the commodity [black chattel] makes the captive body an abstract and empty vessel vulnerable to the projection of others' feelings, ideas, desires, and values; and, as property, the dispossessed body of the enslaved is the surrogate for the master's body since it guarantees his disembodied universality and acts as the sign of his power and dominion" (21). Here, Hartman explicates how black bodies functioned as repositories for antebellum white ideals and desires and as vessels through which whiteness and white agendas were shored up, which they have continued to do. Hartman is in conversation with black feminist work on how the structural positionality of the black feminine constitutes a "demonic ground" upon which Western epistemologies construct notions of difference through binary oppositions such as blackness and whiteness, masculinity and femininity, publicity and privacy (McKittrick; Wynter). If black femininity is the ground upon which the white public as such has been constructed and recognized, then the appearance of black female subjectivity in public (and/or private) is always already a violent enterprise: the violent extraction of black female labor and the symbolic deployment of black female sex and sexuality are the conditions of possibility for any conception of the public sphere *and* black women's appearances within it.

My own investment in highlighting the precarity of publicity, then, is rooted in twin desires to articulate the tenuousness of *both* the private and public spheres for black sexual freedom and to illuminate the ways a black feminist insistence on publicity misses the structural positionality of black femininity as fungible public property—as the "principal point of passage between the human and nonhuman world" (Spillers, "Interstices" 155). By inadvertently valorizing publicity and denouncing silence and its associated terms, black feminists have mistaken what Sylvia Wynter characterizes as the "map for the territory" ("On How"). In Wynter's formulation, black studies critics have been so keen on contesting black subjugation that we have inadvertently advocated for inclusion into a notion of what it means to be human that, by design, excludes blackness. In conversation with Wynter's metaphor, I contend that black feminist critics have mistaken the map for the territory when we have called for moves to publicity that, on some level, presume that visibility in and of itself is sufficient to address and redress the symbolic position of black femininity as always already a condition of "unredressed injury" (Hartman 80). This condition of "unredressed injury" cannot and will not be addressed by breaking (sexual) silence, confessing our stories in public, or staking claim to pleasure in the public sphere. This is not a denial of the importance of such acts, but rather a challenge to the implicit presumption, and sometimes explicit assertion, that breaking the silence is the logical conclusion, end goal, and answer to the historical and ongoing discursive and material violence that was foundational to the very constitution of black female subjectivity (Adrienne Davis; Hartman; Spillers, "Mama's").

  In this essay, I elaborate the ways in which some black feminist critics advocate black sexual freedom, while inadvertently (re)producing "controlling images"—or "single stories"—about what black sexual freedom is and can look like (Nash, "Strange").[5] I reread black feminist engagements with silence and the constellation of terms that vibrate around it: invisibility, interiority, domesticity, privacy. In so doing, I both demonstrate black feminism's precarious relationship to silence and indicate the ways in which that contention with silence has spurred a fraught move toward confession and publicity. I argue that this form of black feminist storytelling—which I characterize as a bind of black sexual freedom—generates a culture of confession and exposure that reinforces black female fungibility under the guise of sexual liberation and limits alternative conceptions of black erotic freedom.[6] Indeed, given that both silence and publicity are fraught spaces for black sexual injury and its redress, I posit that a discursive and material space like what Kevin Quashie theorizes as "the quiet" offers black women *and* the black feminist imagination alternative ways of reading, rehearsing, and enacting black erotic freedom. I extend Quashie's conceptualization of the quiet to develop my own formulation of "black sex in the quiet," a hermeneutic that acknowledges the ways in which black fungibility renders every space precarious yet mines the various ways that black subjects carve out imaginaries of black intimacy and black erotic freedom otherwise.

  I start by reading prototypical black feminist discussions of silence to demonstrate the ways that vanguard black feminist scholars Audre Lorde and Evelynn Hammonds theorize the limits of silence and the stakes of publicity. I argue that these feminists ground and inform a long black feminist tradition that predicates sexual freedom on a disavowal of silence and embrace of publicity. In the second part of the essay, I examine the various ways that contemporary black feminists take up this black feminist tradition and inadvertently (re)produce the bind of black sexual freedom. I then move to expand Quashie's notion of "the quiet" to conceptualize an alternative reading practice—black sex in the quiet—that illuminates underexplored imaginaries of black intimacy. Finally, I use black sex in the quiet to read neo-soul artist Erykah Badu's music video "Other Side of the Game"—an ostensible scene of black cis heteronormative domesticity—for quiet articulations of black erotic freedom. Through the use of this reading practice, I aim to locate fresh possibilities for black erotic freedom. Indeed, black sex in the quiet wrestles with the ways in which the structural positionality of black femininity renders publicity precarious for black women and foregrounds the ways in which black female subjects articulate their desires for erotic freedom in heterogeneous sites and under various social and political constraints. In examining black feminist discourse on silence and publicity, black sex in the quiet charts multitudinous possibilities for black eroticism and encourages a reckoning with the various structures of power and visibility that make it (im)possible for black women to locate both injury and its redress.

"And there are so many silences to be broken"

A glance at the black feminist archive reveals the extent to which black feminists have historically posited a distinction between silence and liberated sexual subjectivity, locating *publicity* and associated terms such as *visibility, speech, redress*, and *liberation*, among others, as the necessary preconditions for black sexual freedom. Lorde's seminal 1977 "The Transformation of Silence into Language and Action" epitomizes this black feminist tradition. We can begin with the title of the piece, which positions silence as in need of transformation and unqualified to enunciate black sexual freedom for black lesbians like Lorde who inhabited particular feminist publics. Lorde's title renders silence an insufficient strategy for black feminists and reinforces binaries between silence and speech, privacy and publicity, passivity and activity, subjection and liberation. This sets up an antagonistic relationship in which silence is an impediment to black sexual freedom and publicity is the paradigmatic pathway to it.

Lorde further drives home this notion of silence as antagonistic to black sexual freedom when she declares that her silence "has not protected her" and that it presumably will not protect other black lesbian feminists either. She argues that if she had been born "mute" or if she "had maintained an oath of silence her whole life long for safety, [she] would still have suffered, and [she] would still die" (12). Lorde thus offers her essay as a radical attempt to "break that silence, and bridge some of those differences between [women]" (15). For Lorde, it is not difference that "immobilizes" women, but rather silence (22).

I do not discount the specificity of the social, political, and personal context in which Lorde wrote and gave her speech—on a lesbian literature panel at the Modern Language Association conference in 1977, a time when black lesbians and queer women of color were struggling to find their places within various single-issue-based movements for sociopolitical change. Lorde spoke in conversation with other black lesbian feminists, including members of the Combahee River Collective, who marked white lesbian separatist politics as unsustainable for black lesbians both because they needed to fight alongside black heterosexual comrades for racial justice and because of intersecting oppressions that negated the utility of single-axis approaches to their lived realities and material conditions (Combahee). Lorde's remarks thus speak to a particular kind of silence about black lesbian life, engendered in part by racialized homophobia within various communities. As a result, Lorde appealed to a particular kind of feminist public, not the public sphere in general.

In examining Lorde's work with the notion of silence, then, I would clarify that she made a discursive contribution to a deep-rooted black feminist rhetorical tradition that eschews silence in favor of publicity. Black feminist critics informed by this tradition often conflate silence with invisibility, domesticity, privacy, and subjection. In contrast, they associate publicity with visibility, speech, publicity, and liberation. Such associations foreclose critical examinations of those black private spaces and hidden erotic geographies that in practice lubricate the production and articulation of nominally liberated black sexual subjectivities in public. One need only consider black feminism's transhistorical celebration of blues women as radical sexual subjects to see such a pattern, in part because of blues women's robust relationships to publicity (Carby; Davis; Pough). When discussing the political utility of black women's blues music, for instance, Angela Davis contends that the music distinguishes "menacing problems [. . .] from the isolated individual experience and restructure[s them] as problems shared by the community. As shared problems, threats can be met and addressed within a public and collective context" (33). But this celebration of blues women's public discourse is compromised by Davis's subsequent statement that black women were unable to address issues such as intracommunal sexual violence because racism had "so thoroughly influenced" the discourse on rape "that intraracial rape could not be named" (34). That black blues women's public discourse was limited to particular issues and circulated in a public sphere hostile to black communities does not negate the importance of their work, but it does illuminate the limits of publicity for black women.

In spite of the limits of publicity, black feminists continue to devalue silence and its associated terms. For instance, though Hammonds describes silence as an outcome, on one hand, of state-sanctioned infringements on black erotic life and, on the other, of the individual and communal strategies of sexual protection that black women had historically cultivated in response to discursive and material sexual violence, she ultimately concludes that silence inhibits black sexual freedom.[7] In two of her most widely cited essays, "Black (W)holes and the Geometry of Black Female Sexuality" and "Toward a Genealogy of Black Female Sexuality: The Problematic of Silence," Hammonds addresses the many institutional factors that inhibit black feminist discourse on sexual agency, pleasure, and exploration and implores black feminists to apprehend the complex sources and detrimental effects of a politics of sexual silence in black communities. In "Black (W)holes," specifically, she takes a then-emergent queer studies project to task for both theorizing sexuality from a standpoint presuming "whiteness as the normative state of existence" and consequently blaming racialized subjects for racialized sexual silence, rather than state-sanctioned processes of racialized gendered sexual pathologization. She writes: "But the issue of silence about so-called deviant sexuality in public discourse and its submersion in private spaces for people of color is never addressed in theorizing about the canonical categories of lesbian and gay studies in the reader. More important, public discourse on the sexuality of particular racial and ethnic groups is shaped by processes that pathologize those groups, which in turn produce the submersion of sexuality and the attendant silence(s)" (128). Hammonds's take on racialized sexual silence is productive here in that she implicitly marks sexual silence and submersion as effects of both processes of erotic violence and racialized sexual agency, however limited. I want to underscore silence as a mode of black sexual articulation without overstating the existence of possibilities for racialized sexual agency, especially in light of Hammonds's contention "that the silence about sexuality on the part of black women academics [and racialized sexual subjects generally] is no more a 'choice' than was the silence practiced by early twentieth-century black women. This production of silence instead of speech is an effect of the institutions such as the academy which are engaged in the commodification of otherness" (135). Notwithstanding the blurry line that Hammonds establishes between consent and coercion relative to articulations of black sexual agency, such black feminist emphases on the limitations of silence as a tool have foreclosed considerations of silence's utility for black subjects who do not have access to sexual freedom that is not structured by antiblackness. My claim here runs counter to Hammonds's later suggestion that "the practice of a politics of silence belies the power of such a stance for social change" (136). I respond to that provocation by querying the extent to which a radical *public* politics of sexuality has produced sociopolitical change.

In "Toward a Genealogy of Black Female Sexuality," Hammonds both elaborates and complicates her understanding of silence as antithetical to black sexual freedom. She contends that black feminists often describe "Black women's sexuality [. . .] in metaphors of speechlessness, space, or vision; as a void or empty space that is simultaneously ever-visible (exposed) and invisible, where black women's bodies are always already colonized," and she suggests that the "most enduring and problematic aspect of this 'politics of silence' is that in choosing silence, black women have lost the ability to articulate any conception of their sexuality" (94, 97). Yet, she destabilizes her assertion when she concedes that, given that black women and black feminist theorists produce silence about sexuality, the "silence itself suggests that black women do have some degree of agency" (102).

Notably, despite the complexity of Hammonds's take on silence, scholars often take up her work in ways that reinforce an unqualified black feminist denunciation of silence and valorization of publicity. This resonates with the ways in which feminist and queer theorists flatten Lorde's complex stances on various analytics and archives, from silence to the erotic to pornography.[8] Notwithstanding Lorde's and Hammonds's complicated and changing considerations of both silence and publicity, they ground a contemporary mode of black feminist storytelling wherein the black feminist attainment of sexual freedom rests on a public denunciation of silence and valorization of publicity. This generates a culture wherein black feminists must expose the locus of sexual injury—often vanguard black feminist attachments to danger and injury—and declare their commitments to pleasure and/as sexual freedom. Black feminist critics find they must predicate sexual freedom on publicity in a public sphere constituted in part by black women's fungibility (Spillers).

The Bind of Black Sexual Freedom

Black feminism has been "trickster-troping," "longing," and "searching for climax" since its inception, despite ongoing claims alleging its sexual conservatism (Stallings; Rose; Lindsey and Johnson). It has been especially keen on "moving towards a politics of pleasure" since the publication of "Black (W)holes" in 1994.[9] There, Hammonds remarks that black feminist writers have emphasized "the restrictive, repressive, and dangerous aspects of black female sexuality" while underanalyzing "pleasure, exploration, and agency" (134). Her article, among others, is consistently cited when black feminists disavow silence and embrace publicity.[10] In this way, it functions as a critical conduit, a kind of rite of passage, between black feminist camps presumably preoccupied with silence and those devoted to sexual freedom. This citational practice parallels what Joan Morgan astutely characterizes as the "unwritten mandate that any black feminist work that explores the erotic engage Lorde's 'Uses of the Erotic: The Erotic as Power'" (39).

Black feminists cite "Black (W)holes" to invoke a genealogy of black female sexuality studies. They also cite it to validate their condemnation of, or move away from, a "politics of silence," which is sometimes erroneously characterized as a politics of respectability. They rhetorically reproduce its narrative logics, which generates a black feminist culture of exposure and confession. This culture of exposure and confession is premised on the exposure of a wound: silence, or a historical black feminist investment in silence and/or respectability, and a declaration to black women's liberation, which is embodied by a public commitment to pleasure.

These narrative logics are ubiquitous in contemporary black feminist work but are perhaps best exemplified in Joan Morgan's 2015 essay "Why We Get Off: Moving towards a Black Feminist Politics of Pleasure." I spotlight this essay not only because it proffers an incisive read on the field, but because Morgan explicitly characterizes it as an "origins tale" about her journey to a "black feminist politics of pleasure" (36). Morgan's piece is self-consciously invested in outlining impediments to developing a black feminist politics of pleasure and nonetheless staking a claim to black sexual freedom. Two pages into the essay, Morgan observes that "more than two decades ago, Evelyn M. Hammonds famously implored black feminist thought to move from a 'politics of silence' about black women's sexuality to a politics of articulation" (37). Morgan moves on to claim that "reverberations of Hammonds' dissatisfaction can be found well into the twenty-first century, revealing a growing frustration by new millennium feminist thinkers whose salient critiques argue that black female sexuality in feminist scholarship remains comparatively under-theorized, stubbornly heteronormative and still too comfortably reliant on a 'politics of silence'" (38). This analysis exposes the wound: an ongoing black feminist investment in silence. And it prefigures Morgan's public confessional commitment to pleasure, which is figured as the precursor to black women's liberation. Morgan explains one page later: "I position, quite deliberately, 'Pleasure Politics' as a liberatory, black feminist project" (39). In this way, a politics of silence becomes that which we have to move explicitly beyond to acquire pleasure, which will presumably reinvigorate black feminism and facilitate black sexual freedom.

Morgan's is an important project that claims black women's "verb" and articulation (Hammonds, "Black"; Spillers, "Interstices"). At the same time, it misses Hammonds's ambivalence about silence and bypasses an opportunity to examine publicity as a site that both "criminalizes blackness" and renders black female bodies fungible (Browne; Hartman). This exemplifies how this particular mode of black feminist storytelling circumvents a discussion of the ways that publicity hinges on black women's fungibility and limits black feminism's capacity to imagine alternative material and discursive approaches to black erotic freedom that would not entail such a swift dismissal of the potential of silence.

This mode of black feminist storytelling relies on the often occluded history of black women's discursive elasticity in the public sphere, not only missing a critique of black women's fungibility but also infringing on black feminist articulations of black erotic agency, however limited. Black feminists from Ann duCille to Jennifer C. Nash have cautioned against master narratives of black sexual freedom and "controlling images" of black female sexuality (see also Collins). In *The Coupling Convention: Sex, Text, and Tradition in Black Women's Fiction*, for instance, duCille cites some of the problems that arise when black critics mobilize the "master narrative of the blues as sexual signifier" (70–71). DuCille admonishes the black feminist tendency to view blues artists as genuine and as more honest than contemporaneous middle-class black women writers, a group critics described as conservative and conformist (71). She argues that critics have therefore "miss[ed] the finer points" of these artists' social critiques and reified hegemonic notions of a monolithic blackness. In this context, duCille notes that this monolithic blackness is always "southern," "rural," and "sexually uninhibited" (71), prompting her to revise the black feminist assessment of middle-class black women writers' sexual politics. In the end, duCille does not claim that middle-class black women writers are more liberated than blues women, but contends, rather, that the structural position of black female sexuality renders every site precarious.

DuCille's discussion of the inextricable links between black feminist archives and theories has significant implications for the ways we engage with the black feminist theoretical archive. The association with silence, for example, dismissively renders some black feminists antiplea-sure feminists (Morgan), while those who are against silence are swiftly characterized as pleasure feminists invested in a liberatory project. While the latter label has emerged in response to the persistent objectification and condemnation of black feminist and queer critical production on black sexuality, the label gets taken up in ways that pit black feminists against each other, flattens work that theorizes the complex nature of publicity and privacy for black women, and papers over "alternative genealogies of black feminism" and other epistemological possibilities for theorizing black erotic freedom (Stallings 60). My critique here resonates with Morgan's generative discussion of the ways in which black feminists often desexualize Lorde's conception of the erotic by presuming it is about spirituality rather than "honest bodies that like to also *fuck*" (40).

Nash's work on black feminism's antipornography stance becomes instructive here. In "Strange Bedfellows," she observes that vari-ous feminists leverage Sarah Baartman's story to "demonstrate the dangers of the dominant visual field for black female subjects," which, Nash argues, precludes a deep consideration of "the messy heterogeneity of black female sexuality" (51; 70). Attentive to the ways that black feminists evoked this story under the guise of "racial progressivism," Nash cautions against allowing "even seemingly progressive stories [to] become 'controlling images,' limit-ing the black feminist imagination" (70). My explication of the way in which contemporary modes of black feminist storytelling produce a bind of black sexual freedom heeds this warning.

It is not my goal to valorize one material or discursive site over and against another, but rather to deeply assess what different sites and forms yield for different black women's actual and imagined erotic freedoms. Rather than silence *or* publicity, then, I am invested in a reading practice of black sex in the quiet that seeks a smaller, *quieter* critical relation to the ways in which black subjects articulate, in various "scenes of subjection," their desires for intimacy, respite, and sanctuary (Hartman).

Black Sex in the Quiet

Despite the mobilization of Lorde and Hammonds in ways that (re)produce a mode of black feminist storytelling that generates a bind of black sexual freedom, both have consistently articulated the bind of black feminist thought: both Lorde and Hammonds silence and publicity are risky. Thus, rather than taking a side in what is ultimately not an unequivocally emancipatory choice, I turn to the quiet to explore alternative imaginaries that exist in the public performance of black life.

Black feminist thought has been reticent about sounding the quiet, and, when it has approached it, it has failed to harness the power of the quiet as metaphor for black intimacy. For example, black feminist scholar Luisah Teish's 1980 essay "A Quiet Subversion" uses "quiet" as a metaphor to capture pornography's ostensibly covert exploitation of black communities. She claims that black feminists have failed to address pornography's purportedly harmful impact on black communities because it occupies the position of "low man on the totem pole" of black feminist priorities.[11] She argues: "In comparison with pressing issues such as South African liberation, infant mortality, and the slow death of affirmative action, pornography may seem a 'low man' on the totem pole of Black feminists' priorities. But just as right-wing moves like the Bakke decision and anti-abortion laws serve to reverse the gains of the civil rights struggle, the media are quietly pressing forth dangerous images of Black women, a reverse of our *cultural* development and self-image" (Teish 115). Unlike my conception of the quiet, Teish views the quiet as an undetectable yet insidious force on black communities. In contrast to Teish's conception of the quiet, and much more in line with the way in which I am formulating it, Quashie's *The Sovereignty of Quiet: Beyond Resistance in Black Culture* describes the quiet as a "a metaphor for the full range of one's inner life—one's desires, ambitions, hungers, vulnerabilities, fears [. . .] which is not apolitical or without social value, but neither is it determined entirely by publicness" (6). Quashie differentiates the quiet from silence, despite its conflation in everyday discourse. He argues that "for the idea of quiet to be useful here, it will need to be understood as a quality or sensibility of being, as a manner of expression" (21). Quashie leverages the notion of quiet to locate alternative possibilities for theorizing blackness beyond the discursive frames of publicness, expressiveness, and resistance. Working toward a concept of interiority that "can support representations of blackness that are irreverent, messy, complicated—representations that have greater human texture and specificity than the broad caption resistance can offer," Quashie offers the quiet as a site and reading practice that is neither wholly emancipatory nor completely undermined by the fact of black abjection (23).

Fungible black female flesh rendered sex—black sex—surplus matter that could never be fully knowable as anything but raw potential. Black sex augments "the quiet's" ability to cultivate intimate, unknowable space for always already hypervisible black corporealities and socialities. If the quiet is a metaphor for circumspect black life, black intimacy, black unknowability, then black sex is the paragon of the quiet and its condition of possibility. In other words, black sex is what makes possible the quiet. Black sex in the quiet thus characterizes those black matters, black socialities, black "situations," black sexual sanctuaries—black lives that could never be fully known and thus could never be fully fungible.

Black sex in the quiet functions as a reading practice, a mode of reading for black intimacies forged in the space of the public. It offers one way of accounting for those black intimacies that blur the boundaries between the private and the public, silence and publicity. Black sex in the quiet is not silence. It is a different sensibility and approach to reading black intimacies that are carved out in the space of the public, despite the fungibility of black female sexuality and against the assumption of publicity as a space for black liberation.

We can use black sex in the quiet to read the musical repertoires of neo-soul women, specifically Erykah Badu. These repertoires have historically been dismissed as too sexually conservative for a black feminist sexual liberation project and too respectable to be considered erotically transgressive. But black sex in the quiet as a reading practice illuminates fresh possibilities for theorizing and analyzing black sexualities and erotics in neo-soul. Trademarked by former Motown record producer Kedar Massenburg, neo-soul names a popular musical genre that combines the lyrical, sonic, and formal elements of soul and R&B music, among other genres. It has been credited with celebrating themes of black family and unity, and incorporating, if not creating, Afrocentric cosmologies. Neo-soul incited quite a stir when it hit the black popular musical scene in the mid-to-late 1990s. Popular music critics lauded it for "reinvent[ing] a classic tradition" while "keeping it real for black audiences" (Samuels). They juxtaposed it with the musical and visual practices of a commodified hip-hop culture, lionizing neo-soul for cultivating a platform for so-called real artists to create "conscious-driven songs" (Billboard). For critics, these songs engaged "events going on around you or about relationships" as opposed to hip-hop songs that purportedly centered on "shaking one's booty or just talking about sex" (Billboard).

Although neo-soul's popular uptake historically risked reinforc-ing a heteronormative black middle-class agenda promoting "family" values and "quality" relationships, I argue that neo-soul also functions as a "quiet" genre, appearing conformist on the public surface, not operating in literal silence, yet quietly exploring nonhierarchical organizations of black inti-mate life that make it a particularly ripe site for the enactment of alternative "black freedom dreams" (David, *Mama's*; Kelley). Frequently dubbed the "queen of neo-soul," Badu can be read as a case study that elucidates the her-meneutic power of black sex in the quiet. Her 1997 debut album *Baduizm* is often credited with inaugurating the neo-soul movement, and her performa-tive persona is often acclaimed for offering new representational possibilities for black women (King; Lordi). The little scholarship that exists on Badu has largely celebrated her embodied abilities both to oppose black female "excess flesh" enactments and to circumvent the historic counterpoint to black female hypersexuality: dissemblance or asexual maternity (Fleet-wood). Indeed, Badu routinely dons gargantuan, colorful head wraps, jumbo afro wigs, form-fitting cotton skirt and dress wraps replete with Afrocentric prints, silver bracelets and necklaces, and the occasional Ankh-shaped ring. As critics have spelled out, Badu's embodiment of an "Afrocentric new age goddess" persona "has helped to redefine the stereotypically deviant, hypersexed black female body" (Jason King 230). For critics such as black cultural theorists Marlo David and Jason King, Badu has reterritorialized the black female body "as nurturing, creative, and sacred" (King 230). This reconfiguration is particularly apparent in Badu's music video "Other Side of the Game."

Of course, Badu is a popular singer and her work participates in commodified culture. But negotiating as/with the commodity form is an ongoing process for black women whose condition of possibility is fungi-bility. Different embodied strategies may yield different outcomes but will never fully resolve black women's fungibility, the structural position of black female sex and sexuality.

"Other Side of the Game" archives the anguish of a pregnant young woman in a relationship with a man who works in the illicit economy. Although the young woman is deeply satisfied in and with her relationship, she fears that her partner's work will eventually infringe on the safety, livelihood, and general well-being of her and the baby she and her part-ner are expecting. Captured with a hand-held camera that dramatizes the everydayness of the scene and scenario, which suggests a documentary, the video images Badu as its protagonist and her (then real-life partner) Andre

3000, of the hip-hop musical duo Outkast, as the source of her angst. The video both captures their mundane creation and inhabitation of the intimate life world of their visually pro-black living space and blurs the boundaries between Badu's so-called private and public lives by quietly documenting the performed intimate life of her and her fictive/then real-life partner.

When the song begins, Badu lays out her predicament:

> *Now me and baby got this situation*
> *Brotha got this complex occupation*
> *And it ain't that he don't have education*
> *Cause I was right there at his graduation.*

His "complex" occupation is dealing drugs, and it provides for their sustenance and survival, yet Badu fears the consequences. The beeping of her partner's pager, a metaphoric gesture to his "complex occupation," dramatizes her fears. The pager literally threatens to interrupt the flow of what appears to be a playful and well-choreographed morning routine. Her partner has run a shower, but when the beeping pager slices the diegetic sound of the video—a sonic function that ruptures the imagined divide between and among spectator, performer, and performance—he runs to respond to the page instead of getting in.

As he attends to his business, the diegetic sound returns and the camera re-engages a forlorn-looking Badu, who begins to open curtains, flooding the room with light as she insists that "[she] ain't saying that this life don't work / But it's [her] and baby that he hurts / Cause [she] tell[s] him right he thinks [she's] wrong / But [she] loves him strong." Her life with her partner is a positive one, yet she fears the potential ramifications of his work on the domestic conditions that they have apparently so carefully curated. Her acknowledgment of his "education" and "graduation" signals an awareness of the structural conditions that compel black men to pursue work in the public sphere that "ain't honest" in spite of educational attainment. Notably, Badu neither uncritically condemns nor acquiesces to such conditions, but instead demonstrates that such conditions necessitate quiet, critical contemplation, rather than the public debates and violent condemnation that black work in the illicit economy typically occasions.

Once he completes his call, he kisses her and joins her in the task of opening curtains, helping her to clean and primp the space. Their movement vocabulary and amiable engagement exemplifies black sex in the quiet. Their intimacy is represented as circumspect and camouflaged, clearly present but not sexually explicit. This undermines the fungibility of the black subject by sharing a glimpse of black intimate life that is not immediately generalizable by a viewer, remaining idiosyncratic even in its emphatic publicness. It is thus not fully available for appropriation and expropriation.

In the next shot, Badu covertly alerts Andre 3000 to police presence outside of their building. He saunters to the door to collect a presumably illegal package from the police, which he hands off to her. Black sex in the quiet facilitates a nuanced read of this scene, indexing the state's complex relationship to Badu's erotic life. On the one hand, Badu publicly embodies a critique of the state as an agent of personal responsibility politics and arbiter of black freedom. On the other hand, the state has a direct and illegal role in shaping the intimate life that she hopes to maintain with her partner. On the third hand, the police do not want their role here to be made public. This dilemma points to what black studies scholar Richard Iton characterizes as the "perpetual instability of radical black freedom projects" (197). In his landmark study of post–civil rights era black popular cultural performance, *In Search of the Black Fantastic,* he identifies "black fantastic" performances as those that generate "imperfect and in-process notions of autonomy" (16). For Iton, these performances rehearse alternative ways of seeing and being in an era "characterized by the dismissal of any possibilities beyond the already existing" (17). Extending Iton's assessment of "in process black radical freedom projects," I contend that while Badu's performances of black sex in the quiet do not necessarily transcend state power, she does offer alternative ways of working in, on, and through state power, as performance theorist José Esteban Muñoz might put it.

Following the exchange of the package, Badu holds down the space as her partner puts aside his work, kisses her belly, and embraces her as the diegetic track slowly fades into Badu's more upbeat "Rim Shot." The shot of Andre 3000 kissing Badu's belly, along with the video's lyrical and visual focus on a presumably heterosexual family unit, may risk an uncritical investment in heteronormativity. As Jason King notes, Badu's musical and visual depictions of heterosexual domesticity may signal what Paul Gilroy has called a "revolutionary conservatism" (Gilroy qtd. in King 230). While such concerns resurrect the age-old question of whether black heterosexuality and/or domesticity can ever be written off as unequivocally heteronormative, black sex in the quiet demonstrates that heterosexuality may be represented without imposing heternormativity.

We can use black sex in the quiet to understand how Badu's own investments in blurring the boundaries between her public and private lives have facilitated textured, specific, unknowable spaces in which to cultivate black intimacies that are decidedly far from heteronormative. For instance, in her music, she consistently defines her own black heterosexual pairings as "situations" rather than relationships or marriages. Using black sex in the quiet as a hermeneutic uncovers the ways that "situations" pose a challenge to state and religious powers that do not sanction these situations. Badu's situations publicly resist publicity, deconstructing the public/private binary. There are no public rituals to constitute these situations; they are specific and messy, and the state—or even the public—are not called upon to approve or dissolve them. They resist a certain kind of fungibility.

Badu's "situations" signal black units that are contextual rather than predetermined, flexible rather than set in stone. Such a notion is fortified by Badu and her critics' consistent blurring of the boundaries between her private and public lives. For example, critics have overwhelmingly denounced Badu's high-profile relationships with black men in the music industry, including Common, The D.O.C., and Jay Electronica, as well as Andre 3000. They have been particularly critical of the fact that she now has "3 Kids & 3 Baby Daddy's [*sic*] All by Rappers," as one celebrity blog eloquently put it ("Erykah"). Badu has consistently denounced these critics of her erotic and reproductive choices, such as when she invited her "haters" to "kiss her placenta" (Sista). Badu transports her conception of relationships as "situations" to her private life. There, "situations" require careful, nonhierarchical negotiations. And her lovers are her "brothers," with whom she creates life and from whom she parts when the situations no longer feed her psychically, emotionally, or erotically (Sista).

Although popular and academic critics alike have historically linked neo-soul work to a black heterosexual, middle-class respectability politics, reading Badu through the lens of black sex in the quiet demonstrates the necessity for more nuanced understandings of what constitute black sexual freedom and subjection, queerness and normativity, publicity and privacy. Here, I am in conversation with black feminist theorist Erica Edwards who, in "Sex after the Black Normal," argues that shifting state agendas and attendant representations of black female sexuality disrupt black feminist and queer of color grammars such as respectability, disrespectability, normativity, and non-normativity. I join Edwards in contending that we cannot understand what is liberatory or antiliberatory about any given performance of black female sexuality without situating such performances in relation to the fact of black female fungibility and the deployment of black female sex and sexuality under particular social, political, and economic regimes.

Indeed, in the time/space of the mid-to-late 1990s, Badu's performance of black intimacy stood in sharp contrast to performances of black women's sexuality that reinforced a neoliberal politics of personal responsibility masquerading as sexually liberated and free (Brooks; David, *Mama's*).

Black Erotic Freedom Otherwise

I have argued that a black feminist mode of storytelling, predicated on the denunciation of silence and valorization of publicity, has foreclosed possibilities for apprehending black erotic freedom otherwise. I mined a canonical and contemporary black feminist archive to show how this mode of black feminist storytelling produces a bind of black sexual freedom that potentially reinforces the fungibility of black women. Given the fraught natures of both publicity and silence for black female subjects, I conceptualized "black sex in the quiet" as a reading practice capable of attuning us to alternative elaborations of black sexualities and imaginings of black erotic freedom otherwise. I then used Erykah Badu's music video "Other Side of the Game" as a case study that exemplifies the ways that black sex in the quiet enables an understanding of the possibilities that exist when black women, black feminists, assume a quieter, critical relation to publicity, which is always already a scene of subjection for black subjects.

Black sex in the quiet as a reading practice mines the potential of both silence and publicity without missing the ways in which black subjects, particularly black women, are routinely subjected to what Simone Browne describes as a "scrutinizing surveillance" (156). Black sex in the quiet seeks not to reinscribe domesticity as the domain of cis women, nor dismiss gendered divisions of labor within the domestic sphere. Instead, black sex in the quiet locates alternative imaginaries of black erotic freedom. Black sex in the quiet thus pushes contemporary habits of thought within feminist studies by demonstrating the multifaceted ways that black female subjects conjure alternative imaginaries of black intimacy in the face of the fungibility of black erotic life.

I would like to thank the differences *editors and the reviewers for their generous engagement and feedback. I would also like to thank Jennifer C. Nash, Robyn Wiegman, V Varun Chaudhry, Marlo D. David, Samantha Pinto, and E. Patrick Johnson for their intellectual labor and useful suggestions on various drafts of this article.*

SHONIQUA ROACH is an assistant professor of black feminist theory in the Department of Women's, Gender, and Sexuality Studies at the University of Oregon, where her research and teaching focuses on black feminism, black sexuality studies, and black literary and visual cultures. She is currently working on her book manuscript, provisionally titled "Black Sexual Sanctuaries," which explores the possibilities for black women's sexual citizenship and erotic freedom within domains often overlooked or dismissed, including privacy and domesticity. Her work appears or is forthcoming in the *Journal of Popular Music Studies, Women & Performance, Feminist Theory, Signs,* and the *Journal of American Culture.*

Notes

1   By way of example, Hortense Spillers's foundational essay "Interstices: A Small Drama of Words" appeared in Carol Vance's groundbreaking edited volume *Pleasure and Danger: Exploring Female Sexuality.*

2   My conception of black feminism is U.S. based and particular. I create this category to stage a dialogue about contemporary U.S.-based black feminist denunciations of silence and valorizations of publicity. I do not presume to speak for the whole black feminist project, nor am I invested in perpetuating a singular racial narrative of black feminism. I am consciously excluding diasporic black feminisms, which have historically articulated different relationships to silence and publicity, relationships that are shaped by processes of imperialism, class, language, ethnicity, sexuality, and so on. Makeda Silvera's "Man Royals and Sodomites," M. Jacqui Alexander's work on "the sacred," Gloria Wekker's exploration of Afro-Surinamese women's "mati work," and Omise'eke Natasha Tinsley's theorization of the "black queer Atlantic" are exemplary here.

3   Throughout this essay, I track a black feminist conversation that uses or gestures to the terms *public, publicity,* and *the public sphere* interchangeably and posits some version of the public as oppositional to silence. Though I am not making the argument that these feminists' uses of the public are comparable, I am suggesting that black feminists have embraced some version of the public and denounced silence. I am not positing an antithetical relation between silence and the public; rather, I am mapping a black feminist discussion that sets up this opposition and reifies the public/silence binary in the process.

4   My use of *fungibility* is indebted to Tiffany King's brilliant theorization of fungibility through the work of Spillers and Hartman. Following Hartman, King draws out the economic notion of fungibility, which speaks to a commodity's elasticity and exchangeability. She joins Hartman in mapping the commodification of the captive body, specifically, the construction of the captive black body as exchangeable within the transatlantic slave economy. Perhaps more aligned with my project here, King also reads exchangeability vis-à-vis Spillers's discussion of the hypervisibility of black women and black female sex and sexuality's polymorphous symbolic and anthropomorphic potential. I join King in extending the metaphor of fungibility beyond the captive body as commodity to articulate black female sexuality as an open sign with "unlimited figurative and metaphorical value" (1025).

5   See Patricia Hill Collins's *Black Feminist Thought* for a discussion of how mainstream discursive representations of black women obscure and justify institutional and interpersonal violence against

black women. See Chimamanda Ngozi Adichie's TED talk "The Danger of a Single Story" for a discussion of how one-sided narratives about people and places inhibit heterogeneous ways of viewing people and moving through the world.

6   See Hemmings; Holland; Nash; and Wiegman for vibrant considerations of the material consequences of particular modes of feminist storytelling.

7   Hammonds cites Higginbotham's notion of the politics of silence to develop her own thinking on silence. Higginbotham discusses silence, along with the politics of respectability, as a practice that antebellum black women developed to thwart violent sexual mythologies of black women and persistent sexual violence against black women. This is in part why silence is sometimes conflated with respectability. Higginbotham's view is related to Darlene Clark Hine's conception of the

culture of dissemblance, a strategy of self-protection and preservation, not sexual conservatism, as it is often taken up.

8   See, for example, L. H. Stallings's *Funk the Erotic* for a brilliant discussion of how feminist and queer critics have historically denounced "the erotic," which Stallings productively reworks and redeploys through the analytic of "funk."

9   Hammonds is notably indebted to Spillers's 1984 essay "Interstices."

10   Lorde's "Uses of the Erotic" and Spillers's "Interstices" are among those essays black feminists cite when they negotiate the move away from silence and toward the public.

11   See black feminist pornography scholars Ariane Cruz, Mireille Miller-Young, Jennifer C. Nash, and L. H. Stallings for critiques of some black feminists' antipornography stance.

Works Cited

Adichie, Chimamanda Ngozi. "The Danger of a Single Story." TED July 2009. https://www.ted.com/talks/chimamanda_adichie_the_danger_of_a_single_story.

Alexander, M. Jacqui. *Pedagogies of Crossing: Meditations on Feminism, Sexual Politics, Memory, and the Sacred.* Durham: Duke UP, 2005.

Badu, Erykah. "Other Side of the Game." *Baduizm.* Kedar Records, 1997.

—————. "Other Side of the Game." *YouTube* 16 Jun. 2009. https://www.youtube.com/watch?v=3qpyDUfMq-8.

—————. "Rimshot." *Baduizm.* Kedar Records, 1997.

Brooks, Daphne A. "It's Not Right, But It's Okay: Black Women's R&B and the House That Terry McMillan Built." *Souls* 5.1 (2003): 32–45.

Browne, Simone. *Dark Matters: On the Surveillance of Blackness.* Durham: Duke UP, 2015.

Carby, Hazel V. "It Jus Be's Dat Way Sometime: The Sexual Politics of Women's Blues." *The Jazz Cadence of American Culture.* Ed. Robert G. O'Meally. New York: Columbia UP, 1998. 471–83.

Cohen, Cathy J. "Punks, Bulldaggers, and Welfare Queens: The Radical Potential of Queer Politics?" *GLQ* 4 (1997): 437–65.

Combahee River Collective. "A Black Feminist Statement." 1977. *Words of Fire: An Anthology of African-American Feminist Thought.* Ed. Beverly Guy-Sheftall. New York: New Press, 1995. 231–40.

Cruz, Ariane. *The Color of Kink: Black Women, BDSM, and Pornography.* New York: New York UP, 2016.

David, Marlo D. "Afrofuturism and Post-Soul Possibility in Black Popular Music." *African American Review* 41.4 (2007): 695–707.

——————————. *Mama's Gun: Black Maternal Figures and the Politics of Transgression.* Columbus: Ohio State UP, 2016.

Davis, Adrienne. "'Don't Let Nobody Bother Yo' Principle: The Sexual Economy of American Slavery." *Sister Circle: Black Women and Work.* Ed. Sharon Harley. New Brunswick: Rutgers UP, 2002. 103–25.

Davis, Angela Y. *Blues Legacies and Black Feminism: Gertrude "Ma" Rainey, Bessie Smith, and Billie Holliday.* New York: Pantheon, 1998.

duCille, Ann. *The Coupling Convention: Sex, Text, and Tradition in Black Women's Fiction.* New York: Oxford UP, 1993.

Edwards, Erica R. "Sex after the Black Normal." *Queer Theory without Antinormativity.* Spec. issue of *differences* 26.1 (2015): 141–67.

"Erykah Badu Has 3 Kids & 3 Baby Daddy's All by Rappers . . . Is It Voodoo? Kendrick Lamar Next???" *ViralCocaine* 20 Jan. 2014. http://viralcocaine.com/erykah-badu-has-4-kids-3-baby -daddys-all-by-rappers-is-it-voodoo-kendrick-lamar-next/.

Fleetwood, Nicole R. *Troubling Vision: Performance, Visuality, and Blackness.* Chicago: U of Chicago P, 2011.

Hammonds, Evelynn M. "Black (W)holes and the Geometry of Black Female Sexuality." *More Gender Trouble: Feminism Meets Queer Theory.* Spec. issue of *differences* 6.2–3 (1994): 126–45.

——————————. "Toward a Genealogy of Black Female Sexuality: The Problematic of Silence." *Feminist Theory and the Body: A Reader.* Ed. Janet Price and Margrit Shildrick. New York: Routledge, 1999. 93–104.

Hartman, Saidiya V. *Scenes of Subjection: Terror, Slavery, and Self-Making in Nineteenth-Century America.* New York: Oxford UP, 1997.

Hemmings, Clare. *Why Stories Matter: The Political Grammar of Feminist Theory.* Durham: Duke UP, 2011.

Higginbotham, Evelyn Brooks. *Righteous Discontent: The Women's Movement in the Black Baptist Church, 1880–1920.* Cambridge, MA: Harvard UP, 1994.

Hill Collins, Patricia. *Black Feminist Thought: Knowledge, Consciousness, and the Politics of Empowerment.* Boston: Unwin Hyman, 1990.

Hine, Darlene Clark. "Rape and the Inner Lives of Black Women in the Middle West: Preliminary Thoughts on the Culture of Dissemblance." *Unequal Sisters: A Multicultural Reader in U.S. Women's History.* Ed. Ellen Carol DuBois and Vicki L. Ruiz. New York: Routledge, 1990. 292–97.

Holland, Sharon Patricia. *The Erotic Life of Racism.* Durham: Duke UP, 2012.

Iton, Richard. *In Search of the Black Fantastic: Politics and Popular Culture in the Post–Civil Rights Era.* New York: Oxford UP, 2010.

Kelley, Robin D. G. *Freedom Dreams: The Black Radical Imagination.* Boston: Beacon, 2002.

King, Jason. "When Autobiography Becomes Soul: Erykah Badu and the Cultural Politics of Black Feminism." *Women & Performance* 10.1–2 (1999): 211–43.

King, Tiffany Lethabo. "The Labor of (Re)reading Plantation Landscapes Fungible(ly)." *Antipode* 48.4 (2016): 1022–39.

Lindsey, Treva B., and Jessica Marie Johnson. "Searching for Climax: Black Erotic Lives in Slavery and Freedom." *Meridians* 12.2 (2014): 169–95.

Lorde, Audre. "The Transformation of Silence into Language and Action." *The Cancer Journals.* 1980. San Francisco: Aunt Lute Books, 2006. 40–44.

Lordi, Emily. "'Window Seat': Erykah Badu, Projective Cultural Politics, and the Obama Era." *Post45* 4 Dec. 2011. http://post45.research.yale.edu/2011/12/window-seat-erykah-badu -projective-cultural-politics-and-the-obama-era/.

McKittrick, Katherine. *Demonic Grounds: Black Women and the Cartographies of Struggle.* Minneapolis: U of Minnesota P, 2006.

Miller-Young, Mireille. *A Taste for Brown Sugar: Black Women in Pornography.* Durham: Duke UP, 2014.

Mitchell, Gail. "Soul Resurrection: What's So New about Neo-Soul?" *Billboard* 1 June 2002: 30, 36.

Morgan, Joan. "Why We Get Off: Moving towards a Black Feminist Politics of Pleasure." *Black Scholar* 45.4 (2015): 36–46.

Muñoz, José Esteban. *Disidentifications: Queers of Color and the Performance of Politics.* Minneapolis: U of Minnesota P, 1999.

Nash, Jennifer C. *The Black Body in Ecstasy: Reading Race, Reading Pornography.* Durham: Duke UP, 2014.

—————. "Strange Bedfellows: Black Feminism and Antipornography Feminism." *Social Text* 97 (2008): 51–76.

Pough, Gwendolyn D. *Check It While I Wreck It: Black Womanhood, Hip-Hop Culture, and the Public Sphere.* Lebanon: Northeastern UP, 2004.

Quashie, Kevin. *Sovereignty of Quiet: Beyond Resistance in Black Culture.* New Brunswick: Rutgers UP, 2012.

Reed, Ryan. "Golden Globes 2018: Watch Oprah Winfrey's Inspirational Call-to-Arms Speech." *Rolling Stone* 8 Jan. 2018. https://www.rollingstone.com/tv/tv-news/golden-globes-2018-watch -oprah-winfreys-inspirational-call-to-arms-speech-202342/.

Rose, Tricia. *Longing to Tell: Black Women Talk about Sexuality and Intimacy.* New York: Picador, 2004.

Samuels, Allison. "Wall of Soul: Jill Scott Is Part of a Generation of 'Neo-Soul' Artists Who Are Reinventing a Classic Tradition While Still 'Keeping It Real' for Black Audiences." *Newsweek* 9 Apr. 2001. https://www.highbeam.com/doc/1G1-72732636.html.

Silvera, Makeda. "Man Royals and Sodomites: Some Thoughts on the Invisibility of Afro-Caribbean Lesbians." *Feminist Studies* 18.3 (1992): 52–532.

Sista. "Erykah Badu Responds to Her Critics." *brown sista* 13 Jul. 2008. http://brownsista.com/erykah-badu-responds-to-her-critics/.

Spillers, Hortense J. *Black, White, and in Color: Essays on American Literature and Culture.* Chicago: U of Chicago P, 2003. 152–75.

——————. "Mama's Baby, Papa's Maybe: An American Grammar Book." *Culture and Countermemory: The "American" Connection.* Spec. issue of *diacritics* 17.2 (1987): 64–81.

Stallings, L. H. *Funk the Erotic: Transaesthetics and Black Sexual Cultures.* Urbana: U of Illinois P, 2015.

——————. *Mutha' Is Half a Word: Intersections of Folklore, Vernacular, Myth, and Queerness in Black Female Culture.* Columbus: Ohio State UP, 2007.

Tambe, Ashwini. "Reckoning with the Silences of #MeToo." *Feminist Studies* 44.1 (2018): 197–203.

Teish, Luisah. "A Quiet Subversion." *Take Back the Night: Women on Pornography.* Ed. Laura Lederer. New York: Harper Perennial, 1980. 115–18.

Tinsley, Omise'eke Natasha. "Black Atlantic, Queer Atlantic: Queer Imaginings of the Middle Passage." *GLQ* 14.2–3: 191–215.

Wekker, Gloria. *The Politics of Passion: Women's Sexual Culture in the Afro-Surinamese Diaspora.* New York: Columbia UP, 2006.

Wiegman, Robyn. *Object Lessons.* Durham: Duke UP, 2012.

Wynter, Sylvia. "Beyond Miranda's Meanings: Un/silencing the 'Demonic Ground' of Caliban's 'Woman.'" *Out of the Kumbla: Caribbean Women and Literature.* Ed. Carole Boyce Davies. Trenton: Africa World, 1990. 355–72.

——————. "On How We Mistook the Map for the Territory, and Reimprisoned Ourselves in Our Unbearable Wrongness of Being, of *Desêtre*: Black Studies toward the Human Project." *A Companion to African-American Studies.* Ed. Lewis R. Gordon and Jane Anna Gordon. Malden: Blackwell, 2007. 107–18.

Consent

*W*hen the *New York Times* published "45 Stories of Sex and Consent on Campus," last year, the student interviewees spoke in one voice: sex on campus is a confused state of affairs. Their stories emphasized an absence of bright lines between violent and nonviolent sex. Instead, the stories suggested a "blurred lines" culture of sex on campus, epitomized by morning-after text message exchanges in which men normalized how "out of it" their prey had been during a sexual encounter through casual jokes. The authors of the piece framed their findings in terms of miseducation and ignorance, concluding that college students are veritable sexual neophytes who remain "confused about what constitutes sexual consent" (Kimmel and Steinem).

This article's conclusion does not stand alone, but joins a chorus of journalistic, activist, and scholarly publications that attempt to unravel and reform the contemporary tenets of American youth sexual culture through the power of a single rubric: consent. Even as feminist activists and scholars disagree about the precise place of consent in an ideal sexual culture, our conversations about sex, pleasure, and safety nonetheless revolve

Volume 30, Number 1   DOI 10.1215/10407391-7481316

© 2019 by Brown University and d i f f e r e n c e s :   A Journal of Feminist Cultural Studies

around the concept.[1] Lost in the consensus is a broader set of questions: Are we not all a little confused about consent? Do we know what we mean (or what we want) when we invoke *consent* as an index of good sex? And who is the "we" that might "know" consent?

This keyword essay locates contemporary feminist consent discourse within the long history of consent in u.s. jurisprudence. This origin story highlights consent's vexatious nature, for the optimism of liberal humanism's freedom of some has historically required the unfreedom of most. The presence of consent has not defied that story of unfreedom, I argue, but has been instead part and parcel of its making. Even putting aside the more sinister applications of consent discourse to serve the needs of u.s. colonial interests,[2] in its imaginary ideal form, consent still betrays the logic of contract, wherein one's freedom is always contingent on exchange. Fundamentally, consent indexes a transaction, such that the scene of consensual exchange can only pretend to ensure the unfettered expression of individual will. In fact, the scene of consent reveals the lie of uninterrupted will and autonomous decision making, for the expression of will always exists in relation to that of another (the other contracting party). This means that an embrace of consent in our sexual politics positions transaction as the fundamental logic of "good" sex.

Centering *transaction* helps us see why consent discourse has produced a literature obsessed with sexual confusion rather than one of sexual safety; in short, replacing *consent* with the vocabulary of *transaction* makes plain why consent isn't working. The history of consent turns on a single question: when one consents to be governed, consents to a labor agreement, or consents to sex, is freedom achieved or abandoned? The transactional obsession of the Consent is Sexy campaign rearticulates this question for the present by asking, on T-shirts, bumper stickers, and posters, *Do you give it? Do you get it?*[3] As a transactional *object* that can be given or taken, consent's power exists particularly, and only, at the site of exchange.

Locating consent as the heart of antiviolence politics in this moment has called feminists toward a few recursive conversations. First, preserving consent as the pinnacle of good/healthy/feminist/sex-positive sexual practice has called us to define what consent is, that is, what we expect from an authentic "yes" claim. Herein lies the evolution of "affirmative," and now, "enthusiastic" consent policies, procedures, and even state laws (California Senate Bill 967). Second, feminist amplification of consent has co-evolved with a project of locating violent sex among young people on campus; this recent conversation insists that violent campus sex is usually the product of ignorance, accident, happenstance, and misunderstanding with respect to what (authentic or real) consent is. Finally, the primacy of consent discourse requires the primacy of the individual. Reducing sexual violence to the absence of consent, and insisting on the rise of consent cultures as the solution to the problem of sexual violence, suggests that violent sex is less the product of structural forces (such as universities and other institutions, including the home, the after-school program, the parish, the nursing home) and more the product of the confused, clumsy, and ultimately unknowable interaction between two individuals, usually performed in private.

At base, insisting on the possibility of a perfected consent culture banks on the promise that the tenets of liberal contract will save us. The turn toward consent as both problem and solution, then, actually reaffirms the logic of he-said, she-said (Honig) by holding up the possibility of a free subject whose expression of will is made possible within the scene of contract, regardless of historical precedent or contemporary institutional forms that curtail the same.

■

The ability to choose one's governing representatives is at the heart of American democratic governance. As such, the origin story of American democracy replays the narrative of Enlightenment liberal philosophy: the self-possessed, autonomous subject departs from tyranny through the assertion of his will and so doing produces a new structure of governance through his own choices. Even among the monied white men who led the American Revolution, this was already a question of social contract, as the acts of departure and choice required an attachment to something new. If democracy held up the possibility of choice over the reality of monarchical force, then the right to choose would also be bound up in a set of responsibilities to the state (Haag). Rights and responsibilities, then, became interlinked. Thus the origin story of political consent in American history begins as much with the expression of liberty as with its curtailment; the question of a freely given will, expressed by a subject who was not entangled in social power (because of his ascendant wealth, masculinity, and whiteness), could not last, as the giving of consent produced a new entanglement with social power.

Yet the history of consent—as a claim on which both political life and sexual culture hinge (Cott, *Public*)—is even more complex with respect to those subjects whom the nation's founders partially or fully excluded from the category of citizen-subject: (at least) women, enslaved people, and children. Through the norm of coverture, white women's consent was valuable only in the private sphere, so that her political consent would not matter, but her consent to marriage would be necessary to solemnify a marriage contract.[4] For early American lawmakers, a lack of capacity to reason was the bedrock justification of enslavement, such that enslaved people's capacity to consent was rendered irrelevant. In the eyes of early American law, enslaved people in general lacked a reasonable will (except in the context of their own criminality) (Hartman) and, as I have argued elsewhere, enslaved women in particular lacked the capacity to consent or withhold consent from sex.[5] The exclusion of white children from the category of consenting subject developed over the early American period to produce and then reify the specific temporality of childhood, in which white people would begin life within a state of innocence[6] that would melt away upon entrance into (white, male) adulthood.[7] Together, this network of exclusions reiterated the developmental logic of reason in Enlightenment philosophy,[8] wherein the ability to express consent was the pinnacle of reasonable citizen-subjecthood, accessible to white boys who would become men; partially accessible to white women whose seductress tendencies[9] made their reasonable capacity suspect but not impossible; and fully inaccessible to enslaved people, whose incapacity to reason justified their continued enslavement.

Sexual consent, as written into early American law, was delimited differently for these different parties, so that exclusion from the ability to give or withhold consent could either protect or produce sexual vulnerability. When lawmakers excluded children from the category of consent through the proliferation of increasingly strict laws about "statutory rape" and "age of consent" in the nineteenth century, they argued that children's lack of reasonable capacity made any assertion of their sexual will irrelevant. These laws argued that children did not (could not) know what they did sexually, which made any sexual contact with a child criminal.[10]

A similar exclusion had the opposite impact on enslaved women. Where the exclusion of unreasonable children from sexual consent spilled much ink in the nineteenth century, the same exclusion of enslaved women was nearly silent in the law; black women, slavery's lawmaker's concluded, would be *un*written from rape law (E. Owens, *Fantasies*). In slavery's jurisprudence, the presumption of black sexual alterity and aggression was backed up by the explicit provision that rape law "shall not apply to any slave."[11] Regardless of legal capacity to consent or refuse to consent to sex, the protective embrace of the law, or its refusal, was intensified by one's access to men of power. As Estelle Freedman writes, "[F]or groups in which men had weak or no claims to citizenship, female [and childhood] vulnerability intensified" (*Redefining* 18).

As the tent of American (formal) citizenship rights incorporated formerly enslaved men, and later women of all races, into the polity over the course of the late nineteenth and early twentieth centuries, previously excluded categories of people gained access to both political and sexual consent. As others have shown, even as black women remained the explicit targets of racialized sexual violence in the immediate aftermath of the Civil War, through the rise of Jim Crow, and into the late twentieth century, their formal inclusion under rape law made it possible for them to "testify" in the face of that violence, that is, to seek redress for that violence.[12] Just as black women mobilized their formal inclusion into the fold of rape law after the end of slavery to put the violence they encountered on the legal record, women of all races fought throughout the twentieth century to increase the visibility of sex crimes in the eyes of the law. The twentieth century saw a flourishing of categories of sexual crime and sexual misdemeanor that specified the meaning of consent, including especially the category of "unwantedness" that grew up within sexual harassment law (MacKinnon and Siegal). Feminist fights to curtail and criminalize some sexual behaviors—such as rape within marriage—worked alongside queer and feminist arguments to decriminalize other sexual behaviors, especially sodomy, through the rubric of consenting adulthood (Halley, "Sexual").

It is in this longer history that we need to consider the politics of consent. Whereas past antisexual violence movements invoked the specter of consent through the expression of negative will—"No means No!"—the new vocabulary of consent ultimately shifts feminist thinking about sex toward the individual, to the sexual pair, and to the contract. To the extent that the concept of consent as an emblem of political and sexual freedom evolved from the logics of liberal humanism, embracing consent in this moment returns us to the primal scene of American democracy, in which the primacy of the autonomous individual is nonetheless bound up in both the responsibilities of contract and in the unfreedom of non-white-male subjects.

■

The contemporary embrace of consent jargon in antiviolence efforts, then, presents as many problems as it presents opportunities. When feminist theoretical interventions center consent in erotic life—and here we might begin to trace the emergence of consent as *the* rubric of good sex to the so-called Sex Wars[13]—we assert the primacy of the individual in sexual and social life. This discursive move has dire consequences, not least of which is that when sexual culture is rendered endlessly individual, sex crimes remain endlessly specific, arguable, and adjudicable. When the presence of consent forms the line between "good sex" and everything else, then feminists must chase the definitional requirements of the consent that makes sex good, which probes even more deeply into the individual, the granular, the affective, and the momentary. How desired was the sex? When was the sex desired? What part of the sex was desired? How enthusiastic was the "yes"?

Hounding the calculus of authentic consent is symptomatic of the greater problem with consent, that is, its dedicated relationship to contract. Consider these scenarios, outlined in the same *New York Times* profile of college students with which I began this essay, but familiar far beyond those pages. Frequently, survivors described participating in sex because they "owed" something–sexual willingness–to a partner. These (mostly) women understood that they had accrued a sort of sexual debt in the scene of consensual–that is, transactional–courtship. That debt could accrue in the face of the partner's kindnesses or purchases, but more often and more classically, her debt had built up because she had previously agreed to some sexual act, or, she imagined, she had "led him on." In other words, these women understood that their sexual partnerships were transactional agreements, in which the expression of sexual, romantic, or social desire was equivalent to inking a contract. Expressing desire, in this context, was not the articulation of a possibility that might change shape over time or across contexts. Instead, expressions of desire were promises, commitments. The expression of desire constituted a contract; breach of contract, these women understood, would have negative consequences.

The voices of these young people demonstrate the perils of consent discourse, wherein the responsibility for sexual safety, sexual pleasure, and sexual egalitarianism lies in the capacities of an individual. It is no wonder that the reality of sexual violence on campus (and elsewhere) remains so susceptible to euphemisms of confusion: when consent–contract–is the baseline of good sex, we must pretend that parties enter a sexual encounter backed by equal structural power. Confusion stems from the extent to which this is simply untrue. Where consent offers both "rights" and "responsibilities," the injured party must consistently cop to her responsibility for violence done to her, hence the repetition of sexual regret underwritten by culpability that composes a veritable leitmotiv in the world of sexual violence prevention.

The clarion call of consent reproduces the fantastical imaginary of American liberalism, in which equality simply exists. Perhaps thinking sex not in terms of imagined, desired, or pretended sex equality, but in terms of a reparative practice of sex equity, making plain the power that exists as a mode of mitigating it, points a different way forward.

EMILY A. OWENS is an assistant professor of history at Brown University and works on the history of sexuality and slavery. Her current book project, *Fantasies of Consent: Sex, Affect, and Commerce in Antebellum Louisiana* is a cultural and legal history of the sex trade in antebellum New Orleans (University of North Carolina Press, 2020). Her work has appeared or is forthcoming in *Louisiana History, Feminist Formations*, and *Signs*. In addition to her appointment in history, Owens also acts as a faculty fellow at the Center for the Study of Slavery and Justice.

Notes

1   If some feminists argue that affirmative consent will revolutionize sexual culture for the better, others register discontent with affirmative-consent-as-panacea. Still others have attempted to name the emergence of a sex panic that reaffirms feminine sexual vulnerability. Finally and most recently, feminist scholars have asked how and why compliance culture has replaced either care or a structural analysis of racialized and gendered oppression in the current flurry of dialogue about violent sex on campus. See, for example, Doyle; Halley; Joint Committees of the American Association of University Professors; Kimmel and Steinem; and Kipnis.

2   See Johnson for more on the dispossession of Choctaw, Creek, and particularly Cherokee Indians through contractual agreements that the U.S. government framed as consensual; in other words, the nineteenth-century U.S. colonial regime achieved near annihilation by legal means. See also Heitala.

3   While the Consent is Sexy campaign no longer seems to maintain an independent website, universities across the country continue to use their materials. See Jennifer C. Nash's contribution to this issue of *differences*.

4   For the history of coverture in the early American republic, see Cott, *Public Vows*. See also Freedman.

5   I have written elsewhere about the particular legal position that enslaved women occupied with respect to sexual consent; see *Fantasies of Consent: Sex, Affect, and Commerce in Antebellum Louisiana*. See also Fuentes.

6   For more on the evolution of ideas about childhood in the nineteenth and twentieth centuries, see Bernstein.

7   For more on the evolution of consent in American law from the eighteenth century onward, see Brewer.

8   For more on the developmental logic of reason, see C. Owens.

9   Freedman writes that in eighteenth-century thought, women were not understood to be credible witnesses to acts of violence done to their own bodies because of their fundamental sexual depravity, represented in the figure of the temptress or seductress. This image shifted over the course of the nineteenth century through the national embrace of the "cult of white womanhood," which distanced white women from women

of color through an emphasis on "passionlessness" (Cott, "Passionlessness").

10   See esp. Sommerville. Sommerville's argument is particularly attentive to class, which intersected with age in important ways to make the category of childhood the exclusive province not only of white children, but primarily *monied* white children. See also Freedman.

11   See E. Owens, *Fantasies*; see also Martin.

12   For more on "testifying," see Rosen.

13   See esp. Gayle Rubin's seminal "Thinking Sex," which argues for an endlessly capacious understanding and embrace of variety within erotic practice in social life, while nonetheless disavowing sexual violence. Even as Rubin critiques the historically exclusive uses of consent in laws about sex, she also relies heavily on the presence of "consenting adults" as a defining factor in acceptable sexual practice (304–6).

Works Cited

Bennet, Jessica, and Daniel Jones. "45 Stories of Sex and Consent on Campus. *New York Times* 10 May 2018. https://www.nytimes.com/interactive/2018/05/10/style/sexual-consent-college-campus.html.

Bernstein, Robin. *Racial Innocence: Performing American Childhood from Slavery to Civil Rights.* New York: New York UP, 2011.

Brewer, Holly. *By Birth or Consent: Children, Law, and the Anglo-American Revolution in Authority.* Chapel Hill: U of North Carolina P, 2005.

California Senate Bill 967. "Student Safety: Sexual Assault." 28 Sept. 2014.

Cott, Nancy F. "Passionlessness: An Interpretation of Victorian Sexual Ideology, 1790–1850." *Signs* 4.2 (1978): 219–36.

————————. *Public Vows: A History of Marriage and the Nation.* Cambridge, MA: Harvard UP, 2002.

Doyle, Jennifer. *Campus Sex, Campus Security.* Cambridge, MA: Massachussetts Institute of Technology UP, 2015.

Freedman, Estelle. *Redefining Rape: Sexual Violence in the Era of Suffrage and Segregation.* Cambridge, MA: Harvard UP, 2002.

Fuentes, Marisa. "Power and Historical Figuring: Rachael Pringle Polgreen's Troubled Archive. *Gender & History* 22.3 (2010). https://onlinelibrary.wiley.com/doi/full/10.1111/j.1468-0424.2010.01616.x.

Haag, Pamela. *Consent: Sexual Rights and the Transformation of American Liberalism.* Ithaca: Cornell UP, 1999.

Halley, Janet. "The Move to Affirmative Consent." *Signs* 42.1 (2016). https://www.journals.uchicago.edu/doi/abs/10.1086/686904.

————————. "Sexuality Harassment." *Left Legalism/Left Critique.* Ed. Wendy Brown and Janet Halley. Durham: Duke UP, 2002. 80–104.

Hartman, Saidiya. *Scenes of Subjection: Terror, Slavery, and Self-Making in Nineteenth-Century America.* New York: Oxford UP, 1997.

Heitala, Thomas. *Manifesto Design: American Exceptionalism and Empire.* Ithaca: Cornell UP, 2002.

Honig, Bonnie. "He Said, He Said: The Feminization of James Comey." *Boston Review* 10 June 2017. http://bostonreview.net/politics-gender-sexuality/bonnie-honig-he-said-he-said -feminization-james-comey.

Johnson, Walter. *River of Dark Dreams: Slavery and Empire in the Cotton Kingdom.* Cambridge, MA: Harvard UP, 2013.

Joint Committees of the American Association of University Professors. "The History, Uses, and Abuses of Title IX." *American Association of University Professors Bulletin*, 2016.

Kimmel, Michael, and Gloria Steinem. "'Yes' Is Better Than 'No.'" *New York Times* 4 Sep. 2014. https://www.nytimes.com/2014/09/05/opinion/michael-kimmel-and-gloria-steinem -on-consensual-sex-on-campus.html.

Kipnis, Laura. *Unwanted Advances: Sexual Paranoia Comes to Campus.* New York: Harper and Row, 2017.

MacKinnon, Catharine, and Reva B. Siegal. *Directions in Sexual Harassment Law.* Cambridge, MA: Harvard UP, 2004.

Martin, François-Xavier. *A General Digest of the Acts the Legislatures of the Late Territory of Orleans and the State of Louisiana and the Ordinances of the Governor under the Territorial Government.* New Orleans: Peter K. Wagner, 1816.

Nash, Jennifer C. "Pedagogies of Desire." *Sexual Politics, Sexual Panics.* Spec. issue of *differences* 30.1 (2019): 198–218.

Owens, Camille. "Blackness and the Human Child." PhD diss. Yale University, forthcoming 2020.

Owens, Emily A. *Fantasies of Consent: Sex, Affect, and Commerce in Antebellum Louisiana.* Chapel Hill: U of North Carolina P, 2020. Forthcoming.

Rosen, Hannah. *Terror in the Heart of Freedom: Citizenship, Sexual Violence, and the Meaning of Race in the Postemancipation South.* Chapel Hill: U of North Carolina P, 2009.

Rubin, Gayle. "Thinking Sex: Notes for a Radical Theory of the Politics of Sexuality." *Pleasure and Danger: Exploring Female Sexuality.* Ed. Carole S. Vance. Boston: Routledge, 1984. 267–319.

Sommerville, Diane Miller. *Rape and Race in the Nineteenth-Century South.* Chapel Hill: U of North Carolina P, 2004.

JENNIFER DOYLE

Harassment and the Privilege of Unknowing: The Case of Larry Nassar

*D*iscourse on sexual harassment is very near where we used to find prohibitions against homosexuality and the discourses of sex panic that enforce those prohibitions. It maps onto the paranoid positions and formations that have interested foundational figures in the field, especially as they have sought to recover terms like *pleasure, knowledge,* and *survival* for queer theory (Sedgwick, "Paranoid"). It shapes our experience of the institutions within which we work. At work, it can feel as if harassment maps onto sexuality itself—the sexualization of work appears as a form of harassment. Within the institution, sexuality itself can feel marked as harassing (Halley, "Sexuality"). But when, exactly, is our work not sexualized? What would it mean to cleanse the workplace of the traces of sex? It is this latter question that makes many of us nervous. We know that this cannot be done; the very idea of such a campaign is harassing. Queer studies begins from a baseline awareness of the violent operations of phobic disavowal, including the disavowal of the fact that we live and work in forms of sexual community, whether or not we have sex with each other. The space supercharged with sexual anxiety is the space coded as "not-sexual"; these are homosocial,

Volume 30, Number 1   DOI 10.1215/10407391-7481330

deeply mystified, and hierarchal structures dedicated to the reproduction of wealth and power.

In the United States, contemporary discourse about campus harassment clusters around Title IX, an amendment to the Higher Education Act that regulates federal funding for schools. Title IX requires that schools address the problem of sex-based forms of discrimination, and it structures the processes used by campus administrators to address discrimination, harassment, and abuse involving students. It promises that "no person in the United States shall, on the basis of sex, be excluded from participation in, be denied the benefits of, or be subjected to discrimination under any education program or activity receiving Federal financial assistance" (Title IX). The questions of what "the basis of sex" means and what about sex is knowable drives the evolution, expansion, and contraction of Title IX's reach. When this regulation passed into law in 1972, people had little sense of where it would lead us. It has been central to the rapid development of women's sports in the United States but also to the normalization of sex segregation in sports. It has facilitated the recognition of sexual assault and sexual harassment as aspects of sex discrimination in education[1] but also made sexual violation a powerful symbolic expression for a school's sense of risk, compliance, and responsibility as well as a container for the conflicts and anxieties that shape how students, staff, and faculty understand their relationships to each other and to the institution.[2]

Somewhat perversely, I think of Title IX as a formal articulation of a wish—a wish for a school in which sex is not a vector for shame, punishment, and social abjection. Title IX regulation describes an evolving sense of *the least* a school can do to make such a world possible. On most of our campuses, an administrative apparatus lifts the responsibility of enforcing that minimum from, especially, a faculty community who would prefer to assign the reproductive labor of working through sex-based forms of harm to a small group of socially abjected service workers. Faculty groan about "sex bureaucrats" (Gerson and Suk) ruining the school while avoiding opportunities to engage their community in the reproductive labor of tending to complaints about their own conduct. Title IX has become a symbolic dumping ground, a figure holding our collective sense of subjectification to the institution. We binge on stories of sexual shame and professional failure, stories of sexual violation, witch hunts, tribunals, and retribution. We flow from rumor-mongering threads on social media and snarky blog posts to polemical op-eds about student paranoia and feminism run amok to news headlines trumpeting the exposure of one predator, then another, then another. Every rumor in this world feels true and every accusation feels false until something breaks. The shape of this discourse is itself harassing.

Many readers will, I think, know the truth of that last sentence. Sexual harassment cases body forth the contradiction of the disavowals that ground our understandings of work and school. The complainant pulls to the surface that which the institution must disavow: the school is a form of sexual community. "Institutions survive the stage of being fragile conventions," Mary Douglas writes, by reproducing the sense that "they are founded in nature and therefore, in reason" (52). These "founding analogies" style our thought about institutions and institutional life—and, Douglas argues, they work only to the extent they are unacknowledged, hidden, even secret. Sex, she writes, appears as one such "natural" ground for institutional stability. This is certainly true for the university. The organization of the relationship between our work and our sexual lives is a key framework through which we understand what a good job supports: the ability to, say, own a home and start a family. It is parental leave, spousal benefits; it is also the explicit prohibition of sex with subordinate coworkers and the implicit sexualization of subordinate bodies. It is the management of that prohibition and the ritualization of violations of those rules. A sense of sex shapes what is recognized as teachable and not teachable; it shapes what is recognized as researchable and unknowable. The gendered foundation of success in the academy bubbles up to the surface of, especially, faculty resistance to antiharassment work precisely because antiharassment activism confronts the forms of sexual entitlement that feel, for some, like earned professional privilege if not sexuality itself. The antiharassment intervention does not expel sex from the workplace: it interrupts the disavowal of the fact that it is always already there. It can become an occasion for staging that disavowal.

The event of sexualized abuse can plug your body into an institution's power grid. Harassment moves through us in waves of dread, anxiety, grief, and alarm. We file complaints when we cannot tolerate this state. Those who can, however, will back away from harassment; harassment is sticky, and speaking out about a harassment case can draw harassment into your life. As Sara Ahmed reminds us, "[W]hen you expose a problem you pose a problem." Bullying and harassment "work" only where a majority of people chooses to minimize and ignore rather than engage and resist these toxic behaviors. Conversations and debates staged around stories of violation, however, can escalate and amplify harassment dynamics, carrying harassment dynamics beyond a case's primary scene to Facebook walls, Twitter threads, and into the basement of unmoderated or barely moderated comments amplifying the "hits" for blog posts and tabloid-style reporting. The energies of violation, dread, anxiety, and anger detach from the people within a case. They become abstractions—accuser and accused become reversible; the truth of an individual case feels unknowable. We sink into this sense of sexual violation and sexual harassment as subjective, as unverifiable. Harassment itself comes to feel both pervasive and somehow unreal. Harassment is exhausting.

In this essay, I think with one badly handled case, a complaint filed against Larry Nassar in 2014 by Amanda Thomashow. Nassar was then on the faculty at Michigan State University's School for Osteopathic Medicine and a clinician at the university's Sports Medicine Clinic. Thomashow had gone to Nassar seeking treatment for hip pain; she accused him of assaulting her. The school's assistant director for institutional equity, Kristine Moore, cleared Nassar of wrongdoing. I am most interested in the July 18, 2014, memo summarizing that investigation and its findings. This is the document that was given to Thomashow to close her case; it is the result of her complaint (Moore).

Less than four years after MSU dismissed Thomashow's complaint, Nassar was sentenced to prison for what is, in essence, the rest of his life. He is responsible for molesting hundreds of girls and women over three decades. I am interested in what made the truth of Thomashow's complaint so difficult to accept. So is Thomashow. She has been asking MSU to reopen that investigation, to look harder at what happened and how it happened. In their negotiations with MSU, Nassar's victims asked for this and for an apology from the university for its failures. The university gave them $500 million dollars but offered no apology admitting to any wrongdoing on the university's part and made no commitment to examining the failure to respond appropriately to Thomashow's complaint.[3] As of this writing, the university's discourse about Nassar has centered on his singular monstrosity—trustees, for example, are sorry that so many were abused by him (Kozlofsky, "Nassar"). They are not sorry, at least not officially, for their own complicity in the institutional culture that enabled him.

Writing about actual cases is hard. Engaging unresolved or poorly resolved cases risks contributing to the harassment dynamics internal to the case's impacted communities. Larry Nassar's abuse of his patients, however, has been addressed in a mind-boggling number of news articles, blog posts, podcasts, and in television coverage. The case grew out of a series of long-form investigative reports on sexual abuse in sports (Evans et al.; Kwiatkoski et al.). Victim testimony is readily available as are court documents, Title IX reports, police reports, and court filings related to the numerous lawsuits against, for example, MSU and USA Gymnastics. We have access to an unusually rich, detailed multimedia archive documenting the experiences of Nassar's victims, police investigation of complaints, and institutional responses to them. Given the scale of material out there, I feel confident that this essay will, at the very least, not make anything worse for Nassar's victims.

Writing about this case requires that I address some of my textual practices and rhetorical decisions. I started writing about particular cases because I have had a case. When I write about other people's cases, I feel keenly aware of the fact that I am working through the trauma of my own. I have not published writing detailing my own experiences as a victim. There are a number of reasons for this. I participated in an awful process that led to the dismissal of a student who had been stalking me. Stalking is inherently sensational. While I have addressed the impact of that experience on me ("Distance"), I do not yet know how to write about being stalked without trafficking in the economies of sensation that undergird harassment dynamics themselves. Harassment has similar effects; writing about a harassment case can feel harassing. Staged without care, that writing can become a form of harassment. It is not all that different, in some ways, from the way one's work as a sexuality studies scholar can be read (as mine was, in our campus's disciplinary proceedings) as sex itself. The fear that our sex-centered work will be experienced by students and by colleagues as harassing haunts many of us who work in sexuality studies. I do not know how to get to the other side of that fear except by writing through it. The scene of violation in Nassar's case (student/patient; faculty/doctor) is quite different from the paradigmatic examples of harassment that rule discourse of the campus sex scandal (professor/student; student/student). Nevertheless, in the story of Thomashow's case we encounter many of the contradictions and forms of resistance that structure sex-based forms of violation and harm, especially as they are baked into hierarchical structures of authority and power. This case also surfaces the reproduction and enforcement of sexual ignorance as a key operation in abusive dynamics.

A few more notes about this essay's vocabulary: I privilege the word *victim* over *survivor* throughout this essay. I draw frequently from statements made by Nassar's victims and their families as recorded by journalists and in police reports and court filings. This is, in essence, a trigger warning. I need to share what Nassar did through the explicit language used by victims because this essay reflects on and pushes back against the representation of the victims in this case as unknowing, sexually innocent and, in Thomashow's case, hysterical. I have tried to avoid trafficking in the sensational economy of harassment narratives, but my aims require being frank. If I prefer the word *victim* in this context, it is because my focus here is not on the recovery and survival experiences of the people he harmed, but on the scene of their disenfranchisement as subjects with the capacity to understand, know, and represent what was happening to their own bodies. This essay focuses on a context in which victims are overwhelmingly cisgendered girls and women and in which the abuser is a cisgendered man. Much of what I say here is likely to resonate, however, with gender nonconforming, genderqueer, nonbinary, and trans readers. I hope my writing, which is oriented by reparative critical models, functions as a hazmat suit that allows the reader to enter these scenes of violation without being dismantled by the subject. Not every reader, however, will want to go there with me.

Victims Proliferate

In 2014, MSU's campus community was deeply engaged in conversation and debate about the problem of sexual violence and sexual harassment. That year, a case of sexual violence and relational abuse at MSU had opened a *Harper's Magazine* article, "Ending College Sexual Assault" (Kang). Local news outlets routinely covered the university's struggles with cases of sexual violence, including high-profile accusations against student athletes. The campus newspaper featured stories about badly handled complaints, op-eds from students describing their experiences with sexual harassment, updates on policy revision and on campus activism. Activists at MSU were part of a national movement that has its roots in Title IX's passage in 1972 but that gained particular momentum in 2013 when students at the University of North Carolina at Chapel Hill founded a knowledge-sharing network that empowers students to engage administrative processes to address the problem of sexual harassment and sexual assault. End Rape on Campus worked with student complainants at MSU (Schuster); they succeeded in pressuring the Department of Education to investigate the university's compliance with Title IX requirements in the adjudication of sex-based complaints. In 2014, when Thomashow filed her complaint, MSU was in the middle of that investigative process (Mencarini, "At MSU"). It was one of dozens of schools across the country then under investigation and in the news. Joan W. Howarth, Dean of MSU Law through the period of the federal investigation of the campus, writes that during this period MSU "faced heavy pressure from the Department of Education, and in some sense that pressure transformed the campus, with new university resources, overhaul of the Title IX regimen, new and visible student activism, and hypersensitivity to Title IX procedural compliance" (718). Sexual violence was addressed at the campus's "Spring Break Safety Fair." That year MSU's administration instituted new mandatory reporting guidelines. In April, the campus launched "No Excuse for Sexual Assault," an awareness program that addressed myths about rape and educated students about the meaning of consent. Volunteers raised awareness about sexual assault in residence halls, the campus hosted "male panels on rape culture," a candlelight vigil, film screenings, and more (Heywood). In the fall, university president Lou Anna Simon announced the campus's participation in "It's On Us," a rape awareness campaign initiated by the White House. A celebrity-packed public service announcement was played at home football games, a fact lauded in an article posted on the White House blog (Lierman).

In 2014, administrators, students, staff, and faculty at MSU were, in other words, fully dialed into the work of addressing sex-based violence and harassment within their community. Given this, many were shocked by the university's decision to invite George Will to give a commencement address at the campus's December ceremony. In June of that year, Will had published an op-ed in the *Washington Post* that denounced antiharassment/ antisexual violence activists and administrators as oversensitive ideologues. He argued that these administrators and activists were "making everyone hypersensitive, even delusional, about victimizations." MSU students and faculty were outraged by his selection as a graduation speaker and as the recipient of an honorary degree. Their anger was concentrated on how Will described sexual assault victims. He argued that the current turn to the problem of sexual harassment and sexual assault on college campuses makes "victimhood a coveted status that confers privileges" and that, as it does so, "victims proliferate" ("Colleges").

Will has been a vocal critic of Title IX for years: before his attention turned to the subject of sexual assault, he often warned that Title IX would be the death of men's sports ("Title IX") and railed against "Title IX imperialists" who want to extend its administrative reach "from locker rooms to classrooms" ("Train"). It seems likely that Will was selected as a commencement speaker precisely because he was (and is) a high-profile figure in conversations about Title IX and campus culture and because the MSU community was engaged in conversation and debate about Title IX compliance. Speakers were announced less than two weeks before the ceremony. Nevertheless, nearly 70,000 people signed a petition protesting Will's selection; students staged a sit-in in the president's office. The Council of Graduate Students passed a resolution condemning the invitation. The General Assembly for the campus undergraduate student government voted by a very strong majority to condemn the choice and asked the university administration to allocate the amount paid him ($47,500) to support victims of sexual assault (C. Mack). Simon responded to this by lecturing student activists on the importance of academic debate. At the graduation ceremony, when Will got up to speak, some students turned their backs to him. Other students staged an alternate ceremony (Ahern; Grasha).

The university invited two other distinguished figures to give commencement addresses that month, Michael Moore and Teresa Sullivan. Sullivan, an MSU alumna, was then president of the University of Virginia. At the time, her campus was roiling in response to the scandal of a sensationalist *Rolling Stone* "exposé" of a gang rape at a fraternity that, it turned out, was spectacularly poor reporting on a false accusation (Coronel et al.). That story was published in November and retracted in early December, not two weeks before her MSU address. By the close of 2014, the subject of false accusations saturated the already intense discourse on campus sexual assault.

Will's take on Title IX and campus harassment is typical of punditry that narrates the issue of sexual harassment as a crisis manufactured by fragile, hysterical students and crusading feminists scrambling for bureaucratic authority. In one think piece after another, Amanda Hess writes, college students have been represented as "whiny, entitled products of helicopter parenting and participation trophies." Greg Lukianodd and Jonathan Heidt, in their 2015 essay "The Coddling of the American Mind," warn that students are increasingly thin skinned, encouraged in their sense of their individual and collective vulnerability by an institutional culture invested in "vindictive protectiveness." Much discourse about Title IX represents this piece of legislation as itself a seducer, luring students into imagining themselves as rape victims and instituting a "neo-Victorian" era (Macdonald). In this narrative, drunken naifs meet the machine of government "overreach" as the administrative apparatus of Title IX bears down on the campus, offering itself to inexperienced youngsters like a morning-after pill.[4] Emily Yoffe, for example, warned that "under the worthy mandate of protecting victims of sexual assault, procedures are being put in place at colleges that presume the guilt of the accused" ("College"). She would, over a period of two years, write a series of op-eds for *Slate* and the *Atlantic* elaborating on this issue, moving smoothly from a critique of alarmist presentations of the campus as a hunting ground ("Problem") to sounding the alarm on behalf of the falsely accused ("Uncomfortable") and advising women to avoid drinking too much ("College"), as a rape-prevention strategy. *New York Times* columnist Ross Douthat joins this chorus of the concerned by observing, "It is very hard for anyone, including the young women and young men involved, to figure out what distinguishes a real assault from a bad or gross or swiftly regretted consensual encounter." In this story, the Title IX administrator arrives on the scene as an ideological predator, exploiting the situation of desire to trick students out of their confusion and into complaint. Under liberalism's pressure, Douthat warns, "the rule of pleasure gives way to the rule of secret tribunals and Title IX administrators." The problem, in these narratives, is that the law can never be adequate to the messiness of sexual desire. Thus Laura Kipnis, in her widely read and discussed *Unwanted Advances*, describes today's students as initiating a "culture of sexual paranoia," "so effectively dumbing down the place that the traditional idea of the university—as a refuge for complexity, a setting for the free exchange of ideas—is getting buried under an avalanche of platitudes and fear" (14).[5]

Discourse on the sexual politics of the campus toggles between warnings that the campus is a hunting ground populated by sexual predators, as depicted in Kirby Dick's *The Hunting Ground*, and laments that the campus is overrun by hysterics who confuse bad sex and rape and are happy to sacrifice academic freedom to the altar of their delicate feelings. We have a national, student-led anti–sexual violence movement responding to the ubiquity of sexual violence, on one hand, and cries of scholars and pundits who fear that the application of Title IX to the administration of sexual life on campus will come at the cost of academic freedom and our collective sexual happiness, on the other. In 2014, the MSU community was very much living in the space between these narratives.

In giving this (very) selective overview of discourse on campus sexual harassment, I have deliberately staged an ugly irony. On March 24, 2014, in a year of change and debate about sexual harassment and Title IX administration, Amanda Thomashow went to see Larry Nassar for treatment for pain related to injuries that she had accrued as an athlete. He had a good reputation and was treating her younger sister. During Thomashow's office visit, Nassar made a strange remark about how "her boyfriend needed to give her better massages" (Moore 3). He sent his assistant out of the room and began to molest her. He "cupped her buttocks, massaged her breasts and vaginal area" (Mencarini, "Woman"). He had reached under her shirt and bra to grope her breast, she explained, like someone would if they were "'making out with you'" (Moore 3). He reached under her clothes and underwear and began to massage her "vaginal area," moving three fingers in a circle. He was not wearing gloves and gave no explanation for what he was doing. "'She was shocked'" (4). She told him to stop. He said he wasn't finished. He was "'extremely close' to inserting a finger into her vagina" (Mencarini, "Attorney"). She stood up and physically pushed him off her body. She observed that he was visibly aroused. He would not let her leave the room until she promised to come back for, as she put it, "a follow-up assault" (Maine). She later cancelled the appointment Nassar had insisted on scheduling and told his assistant that "she was cancelling because she felt violated" (Moore 5). On April 18, she contacted another doctor on staff at MSU and lodged a complaint.[6] The university's office charged with handling Title IX complaints ran an investigation regarding the question of whether or not Nassar had sexually assaulted her. That investigation cleared him.

Nassar did not dispute her account of the session. While he claimed not to remember the details, he told investigators that "Ms. Thomashow's description sounds like standard operating procedure" (Moore 9). The investigator's findings pivoted on the conclusion that Thomashow did not understand the "nuanced difference" between a medical procedure and sexual assault; the report excludes key elements of Thomashow's narrative, including the fact that she had to push Nassar off her and also that she had observed that he had an erection (Graves).

Quite rightly, media coverage of this case makes much of the report's use of the term *nuanced difference*. It has always struck me as odd; it is a strange way of describing the difference between a medical treatment and sexual assault. Moore uses the phrase in a confusing section of the report covering her interviews with four of Nassar's colleagues. These colleagues were consulted as "physicians and treating professionals in this area" who could evaluate the professionalism of his conduct. All of them were women. The three who were practicing osteopaths and therapists said they would not massage a patient underneath her clothing (as was Nassar's practice). Brooke Lemmen, a student of Nassar's and a "good friend," said that "she does not touch under the shirt because she is sensitive to that issue, as a woman" (12). Questioned about Nassar's reaching under Thomashow's underpants, she explained that "she would not use a skin-on-skin method, she would go over clothes [. . .] in part because she is sensitive to what that would mean for the patient" (13). Dr. Lisa Stefano, a classmate and colleague of Nassar's, was described by Moore as making a nearly identical statement regarding her own practice when treating intimate zones of the body. She explained that while there might be benefits to skin-on-skin massage, "as a woman, she is sensitive to the fact that skin-to-skin contact may be uncomfortable to some" (15). Dr. Jennifer Gilmore also testified that, as a matter of "personal preference," she massaged patients over their clothes when using the technique Nassar claimed to be performing. Nassar's practice of reaching under patient's clothing (and without gloves) is shrugged off by all three interviewees and by the investigator. Within the report, these interviewees are presented as having an understanding, as women, of patient vulnerability that Nassar, as a man, does not. This difference is framed as a difference in sex rather one of professionalism.

In this section of the report, Moore goes on to enact a substitution of massage for assault; this displaces the actual nature of Thomashow's complaint. As these women practitioners explain why they do not massage underneath their patients' clothing, they nod to their patients' sense of boundaries. Moore narrates these decisions as made to avoid confusion between therapeutic "manipulation" and "massage," even though it is clear that the potential for confusion addressed by these women is one in which a patient might feel not massaged but violated.

Nassar claimed to be working on Thomashow's sacrotuberous ligament (located in the lower and back part of the pelvis). Gilmore explains that when she performs this kind of release, she tells patients, "I will be right by your butt-bone" (17); DeStefano describes using her fingers on the patient's buttocks (15). In her summary of her interview with Stefano, Moore writes "that this type of manipulation, which is medically appropriate, could be confused with massage" (15). In a note, Moore addresses the fuzzy language used across the report when referring to this area of the body—"the layperson's understanding of the vaginal area could include the 'underwear zone.' When using the term 'vagina area,' [Dr. Lehmen] is talking about palpation outside of the labia" (13). When addressing the body, the language of this report is characterized by the "sketchy" lack of specificity of the "nonfeminist anatomist" (Tuana 212). This confusion is projected onto Thomashow even though her narrative was quite specific. In the report's conclusion, Moore casts ambiguity on the distinction between massage and manipulation and between vagina, labia, and "underwear zone" as the crux of the problem: "The STL (sacrotuberous ligament) is very close to the vaginal area. Manipulation or palpation can be interpreted as massage to someone who is not familiar with osteopathic medicine and would not know the nuanced difference between the two" (19). One might consider the difference between massage and manipulation to be "nuanced"; the difference that Thomashow was drawing, however, was between a therapeutic, medical practice and sexual assault. Nothing in the case literature suggests that Thomashow was confused about the difference between her vagina, labia, and underwear zone. Across this relatively brief document (it is barely twenty-two pages), however, this kind of confusion seems to strike the interviewer and Nassar's witnesses as more plausible than the possibility that Thomashow knew exactly what she was talking about when she reported that Nassar was "extremely close to inserting a finger into her vaginal opening" (4).

The language of the report's conclusion is confusing on another score. Moore legitimizes Thomashow's experience of Nassar's behavior as harassing and yet concludes that she was not harassed. She writes, "[T]he trauma suffered by [Thomashow] is deeply felt and not short term" (22). Moore contextualizes that trauma with Nassar's failure to explain what he was doing: "[W]ithout adequate knowledge about this procedure and without choice related to the procedure, a reasonable person could feel shock, shame, embarrassment and violated." Her trauma, in other words, is reasonable; *reasonableness* is a key term in definitions of sexual harassment. As Moore explains, "[A] person's subjective belief that behavior is offensive does not make that behavior sexual harassment. That behavior must also be objectively unreasonable" (19). That Nassar touched a sexual part of Thomashow's body without her consent is not in dispute; that Moore found that a "reasonable person could feel shock" in response to Nassar's conduct could have supported a harassment complaint. Moore, assuming that Nassar did not, in fact, try to insert a finger into Thomashow's vagina, focuses instead on whether his touching of her "underwear zone" was sexual for Nassar—and on whether Thomashow was capable of understanding the nature of the procedure he told investigators (but not Thomashow) he was performing.

Every signature of a sexual assault is present in Thomashow's account. Nassar groped her; he began trying to penetrate her. She asked him to stop; he refused. She physically pushed him off of her body. She told the receptionist that she felt "violated." She was not confused about what happened. Her narrative as well as those of her friends, family, and colleagues is clear and consistent. Moore might have concluded that she was unable to decide on the validity of Thomashow's charge. Nassar had, after all, sent his assistant out of the room. Instead, she decides that Thomashow was wrong. "The touching," she writes, "was medically appropriate," and "so none of these factors [e.g., the absence of informed consent] create a hostile environment" as defined by school policy. "We cannot find that the conduct was of a sexual nature. Thus, it did not violate the Sexual Harassment Policy. However, we find the claim helpful in that it allows us to examine certain practices at the MSU Sports Medicine Clinic" (22). In essence, Moore found that Thomashow had sexualized the interaction, not Nassar.

Four years after this report was written, following a cascade of criminal complaints and lawsuits filed in courts in Michigan, California, and Texas, Larry Nassar would plead guilty to criminal sexual abuse charges. He was sentenced to prison for the rest of his life. Michigan State University agreed to a 500 million dollar settlement with over three hundred victims of the sexual abuse that he perpetrated while working at MSU and that he presented to his patients, if he bothered to explain it at all, as "intravaginal adjustment" (Howley). There are many more victims, of course: there are all the people he abused while working for USA Gymnastics.

Today, when we look at the 2014 report and its conclusion, we gasp in astonishment: how could the people receiving this complaint not have known what Nassar was doing?[7]

Epistemic Injustice and the Privileges of Unknowing

The 2014 report that cleared Larry Nassar is a stunning example of what philosopher Miranda Fricker theorizes as "epistemic injustice," where a "wrong is done to someone specifically in their capacity as a knower" (1). Fricker's writing on epistemic injustice takes up two vectors of this form of harm. "Testimonial injustice" describes the impact of the bias that renders a person's word meaningless. "Hermeneutical injustice" describes "a gap in collective interpretive resources [that] puts someone at an unfair disadvantage when it comes to making sense of their social experience" (1). In Fricker's work, sexual harassment cases are of paradigmatic importance for understanding the nature of hermeneutical injustice insofar as they often manifest how "extant collective hermeneutical resources can have a lacuna where the name of a distinctive social experience should be" (150). Thus, victims of harassment may struggle to find the language to describe, make sense of, and respond to their experiences. Fricker's examination of the overdetermination of problems of knowing with regard to sexual harassment echoes the work of other feminist theorists of sex, violence, and agency. Sharon Marcus argues, for example, that "a feminist politics which would fight rape" requires more than "developing a language about rape"; it requires "understanding rape to be a language" (387). Sex-based forms of violence are presented as an "inevitable material fact of life" (387). Within this "gendered grammar of violence" (382), the category *woman* is marked as "always already rapeable" (386). "What founds these languages," Marcus explains, "are neither real nor objective criteria, but political decisions to exclude certain interpretations and perspectives and to privilege others" (387). Marcus does not argue that rape is "merely" discursive; she instead situates sexualized forms of violence within a material practice of disenfranchisement. That practice expresses itself in law, in language, and in the body. It shapes our sense of the thinkable and the speakable.

Knowledge problems collect around sexual violence. For example, a cultural reinforcement of the relationship between sexual assault and trauma positions the rape victim as an inherently bad witness. The rape victim is either traumatized and therefore suffers from memory lapses or she is not traumatized and therefore is not really a victim, because rape is, in the discourse of rape, always traumatic. As Bianca Crewe and Jonathan Ichikawa write, "[I]f, according to the available hermeneutics, the trauma of sexual assault damages a potential testifier specifically in terms of their capacities *qua* testifiers, then it will be impossible for their testimony to convey knowledge" (6). Marcus's work suggests, however, that this problem is not localized to the event of a sexual assault; the precondition for this crisis of knowing is the sexual subject's status as always already violated, always already traumatized. She is the embodiment of a truth problem.

The difficulty of Thomashow's position as a witness to her own experience resonates with the contradictions surrounding the discourse of rape. MSU investigators affirmed that Thomashow's feelings (anger, betrayal, shock) were reasonable ("a reasonable person could feel shock"). Although the report affirms that Thomashow suffered trauma, the investigator here decided that she was traumatized not by her doctor's betrayal of her trust, but by what she did not know. The trauma invoked in the language of the report's conclusion unfolds in the domain of the always already described by Marcus—a baseline state of sexualized vulnerability that is coincident with having, in essence, the wrong kind of sexual knowledge. Her shock is framed as a woman's natural reaction to a man approaching this part of her body. Her response is sexual; his action is not.

Within the report, furthermore, the witnesses for accuser and accused are drawn from their personal circles of friends and colleagues. Of Thomashow's four witnesses, at least two are health-care professionals. One of those two worked with Nassar. In the report, she says that Nassar's behavior, as described by Thomashow, "sounds extremely inappropriate." She refers to a woman whose daughter had been treated by Nassar at her workplace; that woman "had been very uncomfortable with what [Nassar] did to her daughter" (8). Another interviewee described Nassar as "creepy and goofy" and said that she would not see him again. All of Thomashow's witnesses are presented in the report as friends and family; the report does not record any sustained questioning of their understanding of the professionalism of the behavior described by Thomashow. All of Nassar's witnesses were friends and/or colleagues. All four are presented in the report as experts.

Thomashow is furthermore structurally positioned as the subject of the investigation and not as, say, a member of the community of readers to whom the investigative report is addressed. msu actually produced two versions of the investigative report, one shared with Thomashow and another written for msu officials. The conclusion for the latter report is longer and explicitly identifies Nassar's behavior as dangerous for the institution: "We find that whether medically sound or not, the failure to adequately explain procedures such as these invasive, sensitive procedures, is opening the practice up to liability and is exposing patients to unnecessary trauma based on the possibility of perceived inappropriate sexual conduct. In addition, we find that the failure to obtain consent from patients prior to the procedure is likewise exposing the practice to liability" (qtd. by Mencarini in "msu"). This in-house report separates the question of the professionalism of Nassar's practice (even regarding something as basic as informing patients regarding the treatment he claimed to be offering) from the question of "inappropriate sexual conduct," reducing the difference between the two to a matter of perception regarding the nature of his touch. It seems to have occurred to no one at msu that professional misconduct might also be sexual misconduct and that this misconduct might include not only touching, but a failure to adhere to the most basic protocols used in addressing especially intimate parts of the body. In keeping with this, Moore's report does not address Thomashow's observations regarding Nassar's joke about her boyfriend needing to give her better massages and the testimony of witnesses who describe Nassar's behavior toward other patients as "creepy." The report reenforces the implicit, common-sense positioning of sexual and professional misconduct as separate issues while reinforcing a contradictory normalization of overt sexism within professional life (and so the boyfriend joke is just talk).

Hermeneutical and testimonial forms of injustice mirror and amplify each other when sexual harassment cases land in the hands of people who are deeply uncomfortable with any direct discussion of sex and sexuality. Nassar assumed the mantle of sexual knowledge for his community; that community deferred to him, to his assertion that what he was doing was not sexual. The 2014 report clearing Nassar is just one manifestation of the negation of the complaints girls and women (nearly all of whom were athletes seeking treatment for injuries)[8] had been staging within their training and coaching relationships, friendships, athletic departments and teams, and complaint systems. Athletes who complained about Nassar, who disclosed but did not file official complaints, describe feeling "crazy," especially as the people around them participated in a group gaslighting, tagging them as "whores" and leaving them feeling that it was they who had sexualized their experience of Nassar's "treatments" (Kozlofsky, "Victim"). In 1997, MSU gymnast Larissa Boyce told her coach Kathy Klages that Nassar was molesting her. Klages convinced her that Boyce was "misunderstanding it" and discouraged Boyce from reporting, even though a second athlete had come forward with an identical complaint. She was asked to apologize to Nassar, and did. To demonstrate to her coaches that she did not have a "dirty mind," she submitted herself to more "treatments" (J. Mack; North; Well). In 2011, after a particularly abusive session, national team gymnast McKayla Maroney told her coach, "Last night it was like Larry was fingering me." That disclosure, witnessed by three other athletes, was met with silence (Fitzpatrick and Conner).

The narratives of Nassar's victims take on the form of crises of knowing—of feeling stupid/not stupid—a feeling that also revolves around the difficulty of squaring their sense of what was happening with the shame of being the subject who names his conduct as sexual. Rachel Denhollander (the first victim to come forward publicly) told investigators that she "felt stupid for not knowing better" (Wang 6). She responded to her sense that something was wrong by educating herself about pelvic floor physiotherapy. Kamerin Moore was so plagued by injury that she became Nassar's "guinea pig." "I don't blame myself," she testified, "for being the innocent child that I was" (MLive, "Kamerin"). In 2004 Brianne Patricia Randall told police she "was 'scared' and 'uncomfortable'" when Nassar, during an appointment to treat back pain, massaged her breasts and "placed his hand on her bare vagina." She "didn't know if it was possible that this type of touching was normal in this type of doctor visit," so she told her mother, who called the police. The police dropped the investigation after talking to Nassar. Nassar had shared a slide presentation on the biomechanics of the sacrotuberous ligament; no element of that presentation explains why he would place a hand directly on a patient's genitals or grope and squeeze her breasts (Rambo). Investigators in that case never discussed his treatment practice with professionals. At Nassar's sentencing, the mother of "victim 105" testified that when she questioned him about the fact that he was not using gloves when he penetrated her daughter, Nassar "made me feel stupid for asking. I told myself, 'He's an Olympic doctor. Be quiet.'" Another victim: "I was unaware not because I was naive but because I was a child" (Rahal and Kozlowski). National team gymnast Jordyn Wieber testified that "the worst part is that I had no idea that he was sexually abusing me [. . .]. I knew it felt strange [. . .] but he was the national team doctor." She talked with her teammates: "[N]one of us really understood it." "I am angry with myself for not recognizing the abuse" (MLive, "Olympian"). A number of his victims describe Nassar bringing them to orgasm; many were so young that they did not understand what was happening to them (Shireen Ahmed).

      Amanda Thomashow, as she explained in a statement delivered at Nassar's sentencing, was not a child "without the words to explain what he did. I was a woman in my mid-twenties studying at a medical school and working at a pediatrician's office. I knew he had abused me" (MLive, "Amanda"). During the investigation of Thomashow's 2014 complaint, when researching his so-called medical practice, MSU officials spoke to only people who had close ties to Nassar. Brooke Lemmen, in fact, would later move patient files at his request when he was under another investigation (Mencarini, "Nassar"). When MSU's police department investigated Thomashow's complaint, Nassar told detectives that he was a "body whisperer." He offered to demonstrate his technique on a volunteer, said he "wasn't a deviant," and, as evidence of this, explained that he didn't even have sex until his honeymoon: "[T]hat's the essence of who I am" (Casarez et al.). His description of his practice is, on its face, creepy: "Most of the time my eyes are closed [. . .]. Use the force, you feel it." "It is a conceptual thing. It is you, the patient, and the spirit" (Levenson). During the MSU investigation, Nassar shared a PowerPoint presentation that he used to explain his practice. One slide featured an image drawn from Star Trek and was titled "Pelvic floor: Where No Man Has Gone Before" (Caserez et al.). Again, these statements are from Nassar himself, submitted as evidence of his professionalism.

      Reading available materials related to investigations of Nassar, it becomes clear that the people running them knew less about the physiology of the pelvic region than his victims. They seem eager to let Nassar do the explaining for them. His defenses of himself are incoherent and contradictory, and this is what people, when listening to sex talk, expect. It is as if, in these investigations, the pelvis itself were cordoned off as beyond investigation, as if this part of the body were beyond knowing ("where no man has gone before"). Those who tried to talk about the abuse had to argue not only for their reasonableness but for something even more basic: for their awareness, their consciousness—for an intentional relationship to their bodies. They needed to map the relationship of one part of the body (genitals, breasts) to another (hips, back, shoulder, neck). They argued against the metonymic substitution of the vagina for their entire being, and lost.

Pelvic Floor Work

It is worth pausing to discuss the treatment that Nassar claimed to be offering. In Thomashow's case, Nassar claimed to be working on the sacrotuberous ligament (the release of which can require working on a patient's backside, near the coccyx); in other instances, in which he was penetrating his patients, he told his patients he described his actions as "pelvic floor therapy." Pelvic floor physiotherapy is not included in standard training and certification for physical therapists (Frawley and Neumann). It is a specialization. Pelvic floor physiotherapy is usually given to people who suffer from incontinence and/or painful intercourse and may be used for hip and low back pain (American; Rabin). It does have benefits for athletes, and for men (Frawley and Neumann). Patients tend to be older than the athletes Nassar treated; American Physical Therapy Association guidelines, in fact, are clear regarding its inappropriateness for young children and for people who have never had a gynecological exam. Some of the symptoms addressed by this treatment (e.g., uterine prolapse, urinary incontinence) are more prevalent in older people and in people who have given birth. These are, furthermore, not uncommon ailments. The treatment, in fact, is not as rare as discourse in coverage of this case would suggest. Patients are referred to specialists, and standard practice is to align the therapist and patient's gender and for the patient to be heavily involved in conversations about the treatment and its protocols. Informed consent is solicited with every treatment and should be reaffirmed (and can be withdrawn) during a session (Frawley and Neumann; Mize). Literature on the subject stresses the importance of this nonsurgical, nonpharmaceutical treatment for common debilitating and humiliating ailments and the necessity for the development of professional guidelines to prevent not only sexual abuse but also the traumatization of patients. The importance of this latter issue is amplified by a number of studies that link pelvic dysfunction to histories of sexual abuse (Postma et al.).

So much shame clings to this part of human anatomy that patients seek this therapy only as a last resort (Rabin). Misogyny and sexism, racism, homo-, and transphobia target this part of the body. Pelvic floor physiotherapy addresses the only load-bearing muscle complex in the standing body, a muscle group that supports a sense of containment, of bodily integrity. How many of us who practice yoga have been undone by the emotion released in poses that address this part of the body? Pelvic floor work is personal and political body work. People investigating complaints against Nassar shrugged off the absence of basic professional protocols in a practice that is, perhaps of all forms of physiotherapy, the one around which there is the most intense awareness of patient vulnerability.

Nassar's packaging of the sexual abuse of his patients as pelvic massage therapy has a recognizable medical history that serves to normalize the vulnerability of the patient. Gynecology's origins are in abuse: grisly experimentation on enslaved women (Owens); forced medical exams on women identified as prostitutes and disease vectors (Walkowitz); the systematic production of women's sexual anatomy as understanding (Tuana); and the more or less genteel practice of "pelvic massage" (as it was called in the nineteenth century), in which doctors massaged women to orgasm as a service for the depressed, anxious, and demoralized (Maines). The examination of women's sex parts is also baked into sports institutions in the form of sex-segregated athletic competition, a structure that can only be produced in and through sexualized forms of abuse and violence (Doyle, "Dirt"). In 1966 the International Olympic Committee required mandatory evaluation of the genitals of women athletes (Pieper). A few years later, this ugly ritual (which could be staged as a parade of athletes before doctors or close individual inspection) was replaced by a chromosome test. That test produced its own problems and has since been replaced by another miserable process centered on hormone levels and racist, sexist, and homophobic standards of gender normativity. Once identified as embodying a gender problem (often by competitors or by athletic officials), these athletes are subjected to hormone tests and a "protocol [that] involves measuring and palpating the clitoris, vagina and labia, as well as evaluating breast size and pubic hair scored on an illustrated five-grade scale" (Padawar). Today, a handful of women from the Global South are hunted by teams of creepy doctors and sports officials intent on running them out of the category "woman." It is not a stretch to say that the whole of women's sports is haunted by sexual violence. Athletes today are fighting policies that require them to subject themselves to unnecessary medical interventions, including surgery, to bring their bodies into compliance with arbitrary standards of gender difference based on junk science (Karkazis and Jordan-Young).

All of the forms of violence I describe in the above paragraph have been framed in terms of care and protection (e.g., the protection of women from disease, the protection of fairness in sports). Sameena Mulla, in her analysis of the entanglement of care and violence in the scene of sexual assault intervention, *The Violence of Care*, offers important insight into the ways that traditions of care can enforce an alienation from one's sexual body, especially when one turns to an institution for help. Mulla's close reading of postassault treatment of victims receiving care in a Baltimore emergency room surfaces a number of practices that might support our understanding of what happened to Nassar's victims. Traditionally, for example, during pelvic exams, an apron is draped over a patient's bent legs, separating person from pelvis as well as patient from doctor. I quote Mulla at some length, because her observations are important for understanding the space of the encounter between Nassar and his victims.

> *The potential intimacy and awkwardness of performing a pelvic examination are mitigated by a process of objectification. That is, a distinction between the patient as person and as a pelvis are rigorously maintained in the way that gazes are mediated. In many traditions of gynecological practice, the ideal patient is one who can shed her personhood while on the exam table and succumb to the transformation of person into a pelvis. Gynecological professionalism demands that during the examination, practitioners orient toward their patient solely as a pelvis. Thus, a gynecologist will encourage the use of a drape or robe that isolates the patient's genitals, and while the patient is in the lithotomy position [in stirrups], she will ignore face-to-face interactions and will rarely maintain eye contact with the patient, even when she is addressing the patient. The patient, in turn, does not subject the practitioner to her gaze. Rather, she directs her eyes to some fixed point on the ceiling and responds to the practitioner's queries as though the pelvis under scrutiny is not her own. (140)*

Nassar was not performing gynecological exams, and these protocols are actually not those of physiotherapy. But he could depend on the fact that even his youngest victims and (especially) their adult chaperones would have had a broad sense of the above described practice of disassociation as, in essence, the requirements of being a good patient, especially when the doctor approaches one's genitals. This compliant patient agrees to interact indirectly with their caregiver through an abstracted, segmented body—an assemblage of parts. Nassar, according to statements made by a number of victims, often hid what he was doing from their sightlines (sometimes by using draping, sometimes by having victims change into baggy shorts, sometimes by positioning and approaching their bodies in a way that obscured their vision); this was also how he hid his behavior from parents chaperoning treatment of their children. When alone with patients, Nassar sometimes engaged in sexual patter, layering chit-chat about massages, blowjobs, and boyfriends over his molestation of their bodies while pretending that he was giving them physical therapy. He did this to Thomashow when, before groping her breast, he joked that her boyfriend needed to give her better massages. In a very real sense, he presented himself as a friend to the girls and women he abused, verbally disavowing the power he exerted over the bodies of those who were required to be treated by Nassar while they competed as members of the U.S.A national gymnastics squad or as members of MSU sports teams.

Mulla's analysis of the forensic encounter sheds additional light on other problems encountered in the history of complaints against Nassar. A standard part of the forensic examination of victims of sexual violence is the photographing of the victim's body. For a wide range of reasons, surprisingly little comes of these photographs. Very few cases make it to a jury trial, and when they do, prosecutors may avoid using the photos because juries, Mulla explains, can be deeply uncomfortable with close-up photographs of a person's genitals. Showing such material can work against the victim's interests. Members of a jury cannot be counted on to understand the content of such images and are unlikely to be familiar enough with such representations to recognize, for example, a wound. They might also experience a visceral repugnance that would make contemplating the images impossible. Such photographs are apt to provoke shame and a desire to look away (Mulla 136–37). Many of the investigators who interviewed Nassar showed this level of discomfort and thus put no pressure on his own explanations for what he was doing. For example, he claimed he was working near genitals but not on or in them, but he also claimed to be an expert in pelvic massage therapy. He presented himself to his victims as an expert in pelvic floor work, but when interviewed by the police and by journalists in a later case, he said he had never received training in it. In an interview with a police detective investigating Thomashow's complaint, he deflected a question about past complaints by claiming that while three patients had complained, they had all been victims of sexual abuse ("Believed"). He denied penetrating his patients and routinely left the fact that he was doing so out of their medical records (Gibbs). MSU's community of faculty and administrators might have responded to the evidence produced around Thomashow's complaint quite differently had they been willing to examine their own impulses to look away from the case and its details.

■

Title IX, as a tool, spotlights the place of sexual violation in the founding mythologies, archaic histories, and traditions that define the space of the school. The fact that there are laws prohibiting sex-based discrimination, however, does not guarantee a good or fair outcome for a complaint. An investigation and disciplinary process has the capacity to ritualize something quite different: it may stage the articulation of an institution's mythology. It will produce the truth that the institution needs. An investigation can force an encounter with forms of unbearable knowledge, requiring a confrontation with not just the singular event of a violation but the ongoingness of the sexualized abuse of power in the everyday. One must work through the latter, unlearn one's unknowing in order to grasp the truth of the former.

The narrative structures offered by a university's administrative culture can reproduce, amplify, nurture, and sustain the forms of incoherence that support the reproduction of sexualized forms of harm. The problem is not that most people are explicitly invested in reproducing sexual violence, but that sexual violence and violation are grounding forces in our lives and institutions present themselves as structures that regulate and manage that problem for us. This may be particularly true for the school, which carries us from early childhood through adolescence and into adulthood (Crewe and Ichikawa). Within the institution, the need to understand and value what a person says about their experience with harassment is all too often deferred to a process, projected onto a structure of institutional authority. This yields a phenomenon that Félix Guattari described as "a fixed transference, a rigid mechanism, like the relationship of nurses and patients with the doctor, an obligatory, predetermined 'territorialised' transference onto a particular role or stereotype." Much of Guattari's clinical practice centered on the relationship between individuals, groups, and institutions (e.g., patient and doctor to clinic and university). For him, the hardening of these relationships "is a way of interiorizing bourgeois repression by the repetitive, archaic, and artificial re-emergence of the phenomena of caste, with all the spell-binding and reactionary group phantasies they bring in their train" (111). Some antiharassment and antidiscrimination complaints cannot be addressed without breaking the cemented social forms that pattern and limit our work with each other and our relationships to each other. As we receive word of new complaints on our campuses, our responses carry our feelings about sex and about work, as well as our feelings about our relationships to the institution. We might understand our relationships to each other through that structure (e.g., as teacher and student, athlete and coach, patient and doctor), but we must not understand our relationships to each other only through that structure. An institution, social structure, group, or organizational culture may be deeply invested in what Eve Sedgwick called "the privilege of unknowing." The mythologies of these structures may, in fact, originate in profound forms of disavowal experienced by members of that institution as fundamentally necessary to the institution's well-being and to the individual's sense of order and survival. When we adopt a paranoid and defensive posture that expresses our most conservative sense of what the institution requires of us, and when we internalize and then manifest that version of the institution in our own behavior, it becomes impossible to listen to and learn from, especially, those whom the institution positions as subordinate.

Speaking with reporters hosting a podcast on the Nassar case, Amanda Thomashow recalls the day she went to campus so that she could learn, in person, of the results of the Title IX investigation (Smith and Wells). When she took her seat at a table across from Kristine Moore, Moore showed her "a simple diagram of a human body." She pointed to it and said, "This is where this manipulation happens." She began to walk out her story of a woman's confusion of manipulation and massage, underwear zone and vaginal opening. Thomashow recalls thinking, "Oh my gosh, you are explaining to me that I wasn't sexually assaulted." As Moore reviewed her conclusions, she told Thomashow, "We talked to a lot of doctors, we talked to four women." Thomashow's voice shifts when she speaks that last word. You can hear her anger. One imagines her looking across the table, refusing Moore's suggestion that a woman is a man's best alibi. "Oh, women, *well . . .*" she says, leaving the rest of the thought unfinished. Incredibly, as their meeting concluded, Moore gave Thomashow a brochure addressed to sexual assault survivors. This, most likely, expressed Moore's willingness to take up Nassar's suggestion that if Thomashow thought she was violated by Nassar, it was not because he assaulted her, but because she had already been violated sometime, somewhere outside the frame of this story.

"Knowledge," Sedgwick writes, "is not itself power; it is a magnetic field of power. Ignorance and opacity collude or compete with it in mobilizing the flows of energy, desire, goods, meanings, persons" ("Privilege" 23). The Nassar case brings to the surface the proximity of knowingness and ignorance, innocence and shame where sex is concerned. It reveals sexual violation not as outside the boundaries of professional conduct, but as, in fact, the very center of patriarchal expressions of capacity and expertise. Nassar's women colleagues, for example, can imagine how their patients feel when their doctor slides an ungloved hand down their pants. Nassar's privilege was that his colleagues were deeply invested in the idea that he could not.

JENNIFER DOYLE is a professor of English at the University of California, Riverside. She is the author of *Campus Sex, Campus Security* (Semiotext[e], 2015), *Hold It against Me: Difficulty and Emotion in Contemporary Art* (Duke University Press, 2013), and *Sex Objects: Art and the Dialectic of Desire* (University of Minnesota Press, 2006). She is compiling two collections of essays, one exploring queer theory at its limits and another on sports, art, and the politics of the body.

Notes

1 Sexual coercion is a central component to quid-pro-quo sexual harassment and has been a major aspect of employment law since the 1970s, when courts first established that employees could sue their employers for sexual harassment. The sexual harassment of students was recognized as a form of sex-based discrimination in 1980 in *Alexander v. Yale*. Ronni Alexander, one of five complainants, claimed that she had been harassed and sexually coerced by one of her teachers. Sexual harassment has fallen under the domain of Title IX governance since that case. The legal precedents for linking sexual violence to sexual harassment and discrimination within Title IX frameworks have been unfolding continuously since then, with a range of decisions expanding and limiting school liability in relation to cases of sexualized forms of harm. For informed feminist scholarship representing different political perspectives on sexual harassment, compliance, and antidiscrimination law, see MacKinnon and Siegel. For more recent scholarship and informed commentary on Title IX, sexual violence, and harassment, see Brodsky and Deutsch; Halley ("Trading"); and Gerson and Suk. Title IX is closely related to Title VII, which amends the 1964 Civil Rights Act and bans discrimination in employment. For recent overviews of the development of antidiscrimination law around Title VII and Title IX, see Grossman; Schultz et al.

2 The bibliography of writing on discrimination, sexual misconduct, sexual violence, and higher education policy is deep and broad. There are very thoughtful critics of the administrative culture that has grown up around Title IX regulation. See, for example, Cantalupo and Kidder; Gerson and Suk; and Howarth. Feminist scholars have long been at the leading edge of the analysis of the sexual politics of civil and

criminal law (see Halley; MacKinnon; Place; and Schultz et al.) as well as of sexuality and pedagogy (see Gallop; Gilbert; hooks; Johnson; and Pellegrini). There is a growing body of work mapping the traumatic impact of the poor administration of sexual assault and harassment cases (e.g., Smith and Freyd) and on efforts to create alternatives to the criminal justice system (see Chen et al.; Deer; Koss, Wilgus, and Williams; and Patterson). There is a world of white papers issued by risk management groups, best practices guidelines written by scholars who study student advising, and law journal articles on the impact of court decisions and shifts in enforcement. My own work on campus harassment focuses on the intersection of discourses of sexual security and campus policing (see *Campus*).

3   This is likely an effect of the university's struggle with its insurers: MSU filed a lawsuit against its insurers in July 2018 (Jesse, "Michigan").

4   In a recent article addressing the distortions of law and policy circulating through public discourse on rape and Title IX, Anne McClintock presents a convincing argument that the widespread characterization of the application of Title IX to sexual assault cases as a form of government overreach "is part of a [right-wing] strategy to infiltrate academia, push back Obama-era policies, undermine collective civil rights and impose large-scale deregulation." She maps a frightening collaboration among Koch-funded groups: the far-right American Legislative Exchange Council, the Foundation for Individual Rights in Education (a right-wing "free speech" organization), and the antifeminist Independent Women's Forum. Their campaign exploits meaningful

debates about the administration of sexual life to launch a broad attack on support for public education as a whole. Misogyny and the discourse of rape are instrumentalized in the service of a decredentialization of the idea of public education itself.

5   Nancy Chi Cantalupo and Bill Kidder describe the rhetorical movement from the subject of sexual assault to academic freedom as a stereotype about harassment that, in discourse about Title IX, "turn[s] attention to physical conduct into discussions about speech" (676). They discuss Kipnis's work in particular because while her polemic centers on academic and sexual freedom, the case that initiated her work (and that she discusses at length in *Unwanted Advances*) involves a faculty member whose defense of his behavior with two students who accused him of sexual misconduct and assault was not a denial of the sexual behavior, but an insistence on it having been consensual.

6   Thomashow is not the first person to file a complaint against Nassar. The earliest complaints at MSU about his behavior were made in 1997 and were expressed in disclosures to coaching staff. In 2004, Brianne Randall-Gay, then fifteen, filed a complaint with Meridian Township Police (Rambo); the police did not forward her complaint to prosecutors.

7   There is more to the story of the Nassar case than I can engage in this context. For example, not long after Nassar was sentenced, William Stremple, the dean under whom Nassar worked, was arrested and accused of "using his position to 'harass, discriminate, demean, sexually proposition, and sexually assault female students'" (Jesse, "MSU"). In three

performance reviews (staged at five-year intervals), employees complained that he sexualized his interactions with them and with students. Each review yielded a caution and a vague commitment to monitor Strample. The question of what monitoring might have looked like went unasked.

8   An ugly and important part of this story: as individual victims have been reconciling themselves with their experiences, they have sought out new doctors to address the injuries that brought them to Nassar's office in the first place. Victim narratives now include revelations that Nassar avoided diagnosing addressable issues, likely in order to keep victims coming back. Alexandra Nelson, for example, reporting on the experiences of gymnast Selena Brennan writes: "After Nassar was arrested, Angie started looking for a new doctor for her daughter—this time, a woman, because Selena didn't want to see male doctors anymore. For at least a year, Nassar had been unable to find the source of the pain. But the next sports physician Selena saw administered a single MRI and immediately offered a new diagnosis: a degenerative disc."

Works Cited

Ahern, Louise Knott. "Hundreds to Protest Michigan State Commencement Speaker." *Lansing State Journal* 10 Dec. 2014. https://eu.usatoday.com/story/news/nation/2014/12/10/michigan-state-university-protest-george-will-commencement/20183947/.

Ahmed, Sara. "The Problem of Perception." *Feminist Killjoys* (blog) 17 Feb. 2014. https://feministkilljoys.com/2014/02/17/the-problem-of-perception/.

Ahmed, Shireen. "The Women Who Brought Down Larry Nasser (Trigger Warning)." *Burn It All Down*, episode 31. 5 Dec. 2017. http://burnitalldownpod.com/episode-31-the-women-who-brought-down-larry-nassar-trigger-warning/.

Alexander v. Yale. 631 F.2d 178. Court of Appeals, 2nd Circuit 1980.

American Physical Therapy Association. "In Wake of Nassar Conviction, PT Points to Need for Education on Legitimate Pelvic Physical Therapy." *PT in Motion* 31 Jan. 2018. http://www.apta.org/PTinMotion/News/2018/01/31/NassarResponseHUFFPOST/.

Barr, John, and Dan Murphy. "Nassar Surrounded by Adults Who Enabled His Predatory Behavior." *ESPN* 16 Jan. 2018. http://www.espn.com/espn/otl/story/_/id/22046031/michigan-state-university-doctor-larry-nassar-surrounded-enablers-abused-athletes-espn.

Brodsky, Alexandra, and Elizabeth Deutsch. "The Promise of Title IX: Sexual Violence and the Law." *Dissent* 62.4 (2015). https://www.dissentmagazine.org/article/title-ix-activism-sexual-violence-law.

Cantalupo, Nancy Chi, and Bill Kidder. "A Systemic Look at a Serial Problem: Sexual Harassment of Students by University Faculty." *Utah Law Review* 2018.3 (2018). https://dc.law.utah.edu/ulr/vol2018/iss3/4.

Casarez, Jean, Emanuella Grinberg, Sonia Moghe, and Linh Tran. "Amanda Thomashow Reported Larry Nassar in 2014. Nothing Happened." *cnn.com* 1 Feb. 2018. https://edition.cnn.com/2018/02/01/us/msu-amanda-thomashow-complaint-larry-nassar/index.html.

Chen, Ching-In, Jai Dulani, and Leah Lakshmi Piepzna-Samarasinha, eds. *The Revolution Starts at Home: Confronting Intimate Violence within Activist Communities.* 2nd ed. Chico: AK Press, 2016.

Coronel, Sheila, Steve Coll, and Derek Kravitz. "Rolling Stone and UVA: The Columbia University Graduate School of Journalism Report." *Rolling Stone* 5 Apr. 2015. https://www.rollingstone.com/culture/culture-news/rolling-stone-and-uva-the-columbia-university-graduate-school-of-journalism-report-44930/.

Crewe, Briana, and Jonathan Jenkins Ichikawa. "Rape Culture and Epistemology." *Applied Epistemology*. Ed. Jennifer Lackey. Oxford: Oxford UP, forthcoming. Preprint, 18 Feb. 2018. https://philarchive.org/archive/CRERCA-2.

Deer, Sarah. *The Beginning and End of Rape: Confronting Sexual Violence in America*. Minneapolis: U of Minnesota P, 2017.

Douglas, Mary. *How Institutions Think*. Syracuse: Syracuse UP, 1986.

Douthat, Ross. "Liberalism and the Campus Rape Tribunals." *New York Times* 13 Sept. 2017. https://www.nytimes.com/2017/09/13/opinion/devos-campus-rape-liberalism.html.

Doyle, Jennifer. *Campus Sex, Campus Security*. Los Angeles: Semiotext(e), 2015.

———. "Dirt off Her Shoulders." *GLQ* 19.4 (2013): 419–33.

———. "Distance Relation: On Being with Adrian Howells." *It's All Allowed: The Performances of Adrian Howells*. Ed. Dominic Johnson and Deirdre Heddon. London: Intellect Books, 2016. 305–19.

Evans, Tim, Mark Alesia, and Marisa Kwiatkowski. "Former USA Gymnastics Doctor Accused of Abuse." *Indy Star* 12 Sep. 2016. https://www.indystar.com/story/news/2016/09/12/former-usa-gymnastics-doctor-accused-abuse/89995734/.

Fitzpatrick, Sarah, and Tracy Conner. "McKayla Maroney Says She Tried to Raise the Sex Abuse Alarm in 2011." *NBC News* 22 Apr. 2018. https://www.nbcnews.com/news/us-news/mckayla-maroney-says-she-tried-raise-sex-abuse-alarm-2011-n867911.

Frawley, Helena C., and Patricia Neumann. "An Argument for Competency-based Training in Pelvic Floor Physiotherapy Practice." *Physiotherapy Theory and Practice*. Published online ahead of print, 10 May 2018. https://www.tandfonline.com/doi/full/10.1080/09593985.2018.1470706.

Fricker, Miranda. *Epistemic Injustice: Power and the Ethics of Knowing*. Oxford: Oxford UP, 2007.

Gallop, Jane. *Feminist Accused of Sexual Harassment*. Durham: Duke UP, 1997.

Gerson, Jacob, and Jeannie Suk. "The Sex Bureaucracy." *California Law Review* 104 (2016): 881–948.

Gilbert, Jennifer. *Sexuality in School: The Limits of Education*. Minneapolis: U of Minnesota P, 2014.

Grasha, Kevin. "MSU Students Turn Backs on George Will at Commencement." *Lansing State Journal* 13 Dec. 2014. https://www.lansingstatejournal.com/story/news/local/2014/12/13/protesters-turn-msu-commencement/20352147/.

Graves, James F. Letter to Candice Jackson, U.S. Department of Education, Office for Civil Rights. 9 Mar. 2018. https://media.woodtv.com/nxs-woodtv-media-us-east-1/document_dev/2018/03/09/Candice%20Jackson%20letter%203-9-18_1520631236409_36509831_ver1.0.PDF.

Grossman, Joanna L. "Moving Forward Looking Back: A Retrospective on Sexual Harassment Law." *Boston Law Review* 95.3 (2015): 1029–49.

Guattari, Félix. *Psychoanalysis and Transversality: Texts and Interviews 1955–1971.* Trans. Ames Hodges. Los Angeles: Semiotext(e), 2015.

Halley, Janet. "Paranoia, Feminism, Law: Reflections on the Possibilities for Queer Legal Studies." *New Directions in Law and Literature.* Ed. Elizabeth S. Anker and Bernadette Meyler. Oxford: Oxford UP, 2017. 123–43.

——————. "Sexuality Harassment." *Left Legalism, Left Critique.* Ed. Janet Halley and Wendy Brown. Durham: Duke UP, 2002. 80–104.

——————. "Trading the Megaphone for the Gavel in Title IX Enforcement." *Harvard Law Review* 128.103 (2015): 103–17.

Halley, Janet, Prabha Kotiswaran, Rachel Rechoubé, and Hila Shamir. *Governance Feminism: An Introduction.* Minneapolis: U of Minnesota P, 2018.

Hess, Amanda. "How 'Snowflake' Became America's Inescapable Tough-guy Taunt." *New York Times* 13 June 2017. https://www.nytimes.com/2017/06/13/magazine/how-snowflake-became-americas-inescapable-tough-guy-taunt.html.

Heywood, Todd. "Battling Sexual Assault at MSU." *Lansing State Journal* 2 Apr. 2014. http://lansingcitypulse.com/article-10046-Battling-sexual-assault-at-MSU.html.

hooks, bell. *Teaching to Transgress: Education and the Practice of Freedom.* New York: Routledge, 1994.

Howarth, Joan W. "Shame Agent." *Journal of Legal Education* 66 (2017): 717–18.

Howley, Kerry. "How Did Larry Nassar Deceive So Many for So Long?" *The Cut* 12 Nov. 2018. https://www.thecut.com/2018/11/how-did-larry-nassar-deceive-so-many-for-so-long.html.

The Hunting Ground. Dir. Kirby Dick. Chain Camera Pictures. 2015.

Jenks, Emily. "Student Section Booing 'It's On Us' Campaign Ad Is Disrespectful." *State News* 7 Oct. 2014. https://statenews.com/article/2014/10/student-section-booing-its-on-us.

Jesse, David. "Michigan State Sues Insurers Seeking Payment for Nassar Settlement." *Detroit Free Press* 27 July 2018. https://www.freep.com/story/news/local/michigan/2018/07/26/michigan-state-lawsuit-insurers-larry-nassar/845859002/.

——————. "MSU Knew about Ex-dean's Sex Comments in '05. It Didn't End There." *Detroit Free Press* 10 May 2018. https://www.freep.com/story/news/local/michigan/2018/05/10/michigan-state-university-william-strampel/590146002/.

Johnson, Barbara. "Teaching Ignorance: *L'école des femmes.*" *Yale French Studies* 63 (1982): 166–82.

Kang, Jay Caspian. "Ending College Sexual Assault." *Harper's* 9 Sept. 2014. https://harpers.org/blog/2014/09/ending-college-sexual-assault/.

Karkazis, Katrina, and Rebecca M. Jordan-Young. "The Powers of Testosterone: Obscuring Race and Regional Bias in the Regulation of Women Athletes." *Feminist Formations* 30.2 (2018): 1–39.

Kipnis, Laura. *Unwanted Advances: Sexual Paranoia Comes to Campus.* New York: Harper & Row, 2017.

Koss, Mary P., Jay Wilgus, and Kaaren M. Williams. "Campus Sexual Misconduct: Restorative Justice Approaches to Enhance Compliance with Title IX Guidance." *Trauma, Violence, and Abuse* 15.3 (2014): 242–57.

Kozlofsky, Kim. "Nassar Accusers Wish MSU Deal Included Apology." *Detroit News* 4 June 2018. https://eu.detroitnews.com/story/news/local/michigan/2018/06/04/nassar-accusers-say-msu -settlement-lacks-accountability/656840002/.

————————. "What MSU Knew: 14 Were Warned of Nassar Abuse." *Detroit News* 18 Jan. 2018. https://www.detroitnews.com/story/tech/2018/01/18/msu-president-told-nassar-complaint -2014/1042071001/.

Kozlofsky, Kim, and Sarah Rahal. "Victim Confronts Nassar: 'Why Should We Forgive You?'" *Detroit News* 19 Jan. 2018. https://www.detroitnews.com/story/news/local/michigan/2018/01 /18/nassar-sentencing-testimony-third-day/109571420/.

Kwiatkosky, Marisa, Mark Alesia, and Tim Evans. "A Blind Eye to Sex Abuse: How USA Gymnastics Failed to Report Cases." *Indy Star* 4 Aug. 2016. https://www.indystar.com/story/news /investigations/2016/08/04/usa-gymnastics-sex-abuse-protected-coaches/85829732/.

Lay, Sierra. "University Dedicates Thursday to Sexual Assault Education." *State News* 17 Apr. 2014. https://statenews.com/article/2014/04/university-dedicates-thursday-to-sexual-assault -education.

LeBlanc, Beth. "2004 Police Report: Teen Felt 'Uncomfortable,' 'Scared,' after Nassar Appointment." *Lansing State Journal* 1 Feb. 2018. https://www.lansingstatejournal.com/story/news /local/2018/01/30/meridian-twp-apologize-woman-whose-nassar-complaint-never-sent -prosecutors/1078230001/.

Levenson, Eric. "Larry Nassar Claimed He Was 'the Body Whisperer' in Police Interview." CNN 2 Feb. 2018. https://www.cnn.com/2018/02/01/us/larry-nassar-police-interview/.

Lierman, Kyle. "It's On Us, a Growing Movement to End Campus Sexual Assault." *The White House: President Barak Obama* (blog) 24 Sep. 2014. https://obamawhitehouse.archives.gov /blog/2014/09/24/its-us-growing-movement-end-campus-sexual-assault.

Lukianodd, Greg, and Jonathan Heidt. "The Coddling of the American Mind." *Atlantic* Sept. 2015. https://www.theatlantic.com/magazine/archive/2015/09/the-coddling-of-the-american -mind/399356/.

Luther, Jessica. *Unsportsmanlike Conduct: College Football and the Politics of Rape.* Brooklyn: Edge of Sports / Akashic, 2016.

MacDonald, Heather. "Neo-Victorianism on Campus." *Weekly Standard* 20 Oct. 2014. https:// www.weeklystandard.com/heather-mac-donald/neo-victorianism-on-campus.

Mack, Cameron. "ASMSU Becomes Latest Group to Condemn George Will's Appearance." *State News* 9 Dec. 2014. https://statenews.com/article/2014/12/asmsu-condemns-george-will.

Mack, Julie. "Nassar Victim Describes Telling MSU Coach in 1997 about Abuse." *MLive* 20 Jan. 2018. https://www.mlive.com/news/index.ssf/2018/01/nassar_victim_describes_tellin.html.

MacKinnon, Catherine A. *Sexual Harassment of Working Women: A Case of Sex Discrimination.* New Haven: Yale UP, 1979.

MacKinnon, Catherine A., and Reva B. Siegel, eds. *Directions in Sexual Harassment Law*. New Haven: Yale UP, 2014.

Maine, D'Arcy. "Hear Larry Nassar's Victims in Their Own (Brave and Powerful) Words." *espnW.com* 24 Jan. 2018. http://www.espn.com/espnw/voices/article/22145563/hear-larry -nassar-victims-their-own-powerful-brave-words.

Maines, Rachel. *The Technology of Orgasm: Hysteria, the Vibrator, and Women's Sexual Satisfaction*. Baltimore: Johns Hopkins UP, 1999.

Marcus, Sharon. "Fighting Bodies, Fighting Words: A Theory and Politics of Rape Prevention." *Feminist Theorize the Political*. Ed. Judith Butler and Joan Wallach Scott. New York: Routledge, 2002. 385–403.

McClintock, Anne. "Who's Afraid of Title IX?" *Jacobin* 24 Oct. 2017. https://www.jacobinmag .com/2017/10/title-ix-betsy-devos-doe-colleges-assault-dear-colleague.

Mencarini, Matt. "At MSU: Assault, Harassment, and Secrecy." *Lansing State Journal* 15 Dec. 2016. https://www.lansingstatejournal.com/story/news/local/2016/12/15/michigan-state -sexual-assault-harassment-larry-nassar/94993582/.

—————. "Attorney: MSU Failed to 'Adequately Investigate' Nassar Complaint." *Lansing State Journal* 20 Mar. 2017. https://www.lansingstatejournal.com/story/news/local/2017/03 /20/attorney-msu-failed-adequately-investigate-2014-nassar-complaint/99413154/.

—————. "MSU Hid Full Conclusions of 2014 Nassar Report from Victim." *Lansing State Journal* 26 Jan. 2018. https://lansingstatejournal.com/story/news/local/2018/01/26/michigan -state-larry-nassar-title-ix/1069493001/.

—————. "Nassar Recommended Expert Who Helped Clear Him in 2014." *Lansing State Journal* 10 Apr. 2017. https://lansingstatejournal.com/story/news/local/2017/04/10/nassar -recommended-expert-who-helped-clear-him-2014/100065222/.

—————. "Woman Who Reported Nassar in 2014: 'It destroyed me but I lived.'" *Lansing State Journal* 16 Jan. 2018. https://www.lansingstatejournal.com/story/news/local/2018/01 /16/larry-nassar-michigan-state-amanda-thomashow/1034302001/.

Mize, Lori. "Nassar's Atrocities Stigmatize a Legitimate Medical Treatment." *Huffington Post* 24 Jan. 2018. https://www.huffingtonpost.com/entry/opinion-mize-pelvic-therapy_us _5a67f62ae4b0e5630074aa9b.

MLive. "Amanda Thomashow Speaks about Filing a MSU Title IX Report against Larry Nassar in 2014." *YouTube* 17 Jan. 2018. https://youtu.be/teR7QaOrUQ8.

—————. "Kamerin Moore Talks about Being Larry Nassar's 'Guinea Pig' during Sentencing." *YouTube* 22 Jan. 2018. https://youtu.be/FjB0u27J4xU.

—————. "Olympian Jordyn Wieber Breaks Silence as She Confronts Larry Nassar." *YouTube* 19 Jan. 2018. https://youtu.be/Tsdz_-m9uLE.

Mocumel, Linsey. "Secret Report: Nassar's Actions Caused 'Trauma.'" *WoodTV.com* 9 Mar. 2018. https://www.woodtv.com/news/michigan/secret-report-nassars-actions-caused-trauma /1026866960.

Moore, Kristine. "Report on Investigation into Allegations of Sexual Harassment: Claimant Final Report." Office for Inclusion and Intercultural Initiatives, Michigan State University. 18 July 2014.

Mulla, Sameena. *The Violence of Care: Rape Victims, Forensic Nurses, and Sexual Assault Intervention*. New York: New York UP, 2014.

Nelson, Alexandria. "The Woman Coming for Nassar's Job." *Bleacher Report* 19 July 2018. https://bleacherreport.com/articles/2786857-the-woman-coming-for-larry-nassars-job.

North, Amanda. "Young Women Reported Larry Nassar for Years. No One Took Them Seriously until Now." *Vox* 25 Jan. 2018. https://www.vox.com/identities/2018/1/25/16928994/larry-nassar-mckayla-maroney-gymnastics-me-too.

Owens, Deirdre Cooper. *Medical Bondage: Race, Gender, and the Origins of American Gynecology*. Athens: U of Georgia P, 2017.

Padawar, Ruth. "The Humiliating Practice of Sex-Testing Female Athletes." *New York Times* 28 June 2016. https://www.nytimes.com/2016/07/03/magazine/the-humiliating-practice-of-sex-testing-female-athletes.html.

Patterson, Jennifer, ed. *Queer Sexual Violence: Radical Voices from within the Antiviolence Movement*. Riverdale: Riverdale Avenue, 2016.

Pellegrini, Ann. "Pedagogy's Turn: Observations on Students, Teachers, and Transference-Love." *Critical Inquiry* 25.3 (1999): 617–25.

Pieper, Lindsay Parks. *Sex Testing: Gender Policing in Women's Sports*. Urbana: U of Illinois P, 2016.

Place, Vanessa. *The Guilt Project: Rape, Morality, and the Law*. New York: Other Press, 2010.

Postma, Rienke, Iva Bicanic, Huub van der Vaart, and Ellen Laan. "Pelvic Floor Muscle Problems Mediate Sexual Problems in Young Adult Rape Victims." *Journal of Sexual Medicine* 10.8 (2013): 1978–87.

Rabin, Roni Caryn. "Pelvic Massage Can Be Legitimate but Not in Larry Nassar's Hands." *New York Times* 31 Jan. 2018. https://www.nytimes.com/2018/01/31/well/live/pelvic-massage-can-be-legitimate-but-not-in-larry-nassars-hands.html.

Rahal, Sarah, and Kim Kozlowski. "204 Impact Statements, 9 Days, 2 Counties, a Life Sentence for Larry Nassar." *Detroit News* 16 Jan. 2018. https://www.detroitnews.com/story/news/local/michigan/2018/02/08/204-impact-statements-9-days-2-counties-life-sentence-larry-nassar/1066335001/.

Rambo, Paul. Meridian Township Police Department Narrative Report: Incident 04-18086. 17 Sept. 2004.

Randolph, Mary, and Diane M Reddy. "Sexual Abuse and Sexual Functioning in a Chronic Pelvic Pain Sample." *Journal of Child Sexual Abuse* 15.3 (2006): 61–78.

Schultz, Vicki, et al. "Open Statement on Sexual Harassment from Employment Discrimination Law Scholars." *Stanford Law Review* (June 2018). https://www.stanfordlawreview.org/online/open-statement-on-sexual-harassment-from-employment-discrimination-law-scholars/.

Schuster, Simon. "MSU's Loudest Survivor Refuses to Be Silenced." *State News* 4 Feb. 2015. https://statenews.com/article/2015/02/emily-kollaritsch.

Sedgwick, Eve Kosofsky. "Paranoid Reading and Reparative Reading, or You're So Paranoid You Probably Think This Essay Is about You." *Touching Feeling: Affect, Pedagogy, Performativity*. Durham: Duke UP, 2003. 123–52.

————————. "The Privilege of Unknowing: Diderot's *The Nun.*" *Tendencies.* Durham: Duke UP, 1993. 23–51.

Smith, Carly Parnitzke, and Jennifer J. Freyd. "Institutional Betrayal." *American Psychologist* 69.6 (2014): 575–87.

Smith, Lindsay, and Kate Wells, hosts. "Gaslighting." *Believed.* Michigan Radio, 12 Nov. 2018. https://believed.michiganradio.org/gaslighting-larry-nassar-msu/.

Title IX of the Education Amendments of 1972, 20 U.S.C. §§1681–Ed Seq.

Tuana, Nancy. "Coming to Understand: Orgasm and the Epistemology of Ignorance." *Hypatia* 19.1 (2012): 194–232.

Walkowitz, Judith. *Prostitution and Victorian Society: Women, Class, and the State.* Cambridge: Cambridge UP, 1980.

Wang, Lin-Chi. "Final Investigative Report re Rachael Denhollander and Larry Nassar." Michigan State University, Office of Institutional Equity. 17 Mar. 2017.

Well, Kate. "The Day a Young Gymnast Tried to Tell MSU about Sexual Abuse." *Michigan Radio* 27 Apr. 2017. http://michiganradio.org/post/day-young-gymnast-tried-tell-msu-about -sexual-abuse.

Will, George. "Colleges Become the Victims of Progressivism." *Washington Post* 6 June 2014. https://www.washingtonpost.com/opinions/george-will-college-become-the-victims-of -progressivism/2014/06/06/e90e73b4-eb50-11e3-9f5c-9075d5508f0a_story.html.

————————. "Title IX." *ABC News* 5 Jan. 2013. https://abcnews.go.com/ThisWeek/story?id= 132569.

————————. "A Train Wreck Called Title IX." *Newsweek* 25 May 2002. https://www.newsweek .com/train-wreck-called-title-ix-145717.

Yoffe, Emily. "The College Rape Overcorrection." *Slate* 7 Dec. 2014. http://www.slate.com /articles/double_x/doublex/2014/12/college_rape_campus_sexual_assault_is_a_serious _problem_but_the_efforts.html.

————————. "College Women: Stop Getting Drunk." *Slate* 15 Oct. 2013. http://www.slate .com/articles/double_x/doublex/2013/10/sexual_assault_and_drinking_teach_women_the _connection.html.

————————. "The Problem with Campus Sexual Assault Surveys." *Slate* 24 Sep. 2015. http:// www.slate.com/articles/double_x/doublex/2015/09/aau_campus_sexual_assault_survey_why _such_surveys_don_t_paint_an_accurate.html.

————————. "The Uncomfortable Truth about Campus Sexual Assault." *Atlantic* 6 Sep. 2017. https://www.theatlantic.com/education/archive/2017/09/the-uncomfortable-truth-about -campus-rape-policy/538974/.

KEYWORD 8

Trigger Warnings

*T*here has been a great deal of commentary over the past few years on the rise of "trigger warnings" in the college classroom: debates have raged in universities over the sexual, cultural, and democratic (or antidemocratic) politics of employing such content warnings.[1] Do they allow students valuably to prepare themselves to deal with disturbing material that could otherwise inflict misogynist, transphobic, racist, classist, and colonialist violent fantasies upon them? Or do they coddle students, preventing them from learning how to confront those histories, fantasies, and violences? Those who challenge gender and sexual norms have been at the forefront of these debates, even if often in opposition to one another: feminist and queer scholars and educators are both those most likely to want to discuss the intersections of sex, race, class, imperialism, power, and violence (thus making them most likely to include readings or films with disturbing content in their classes) and those most likely to want to empower their students, whether they see that as best achieved by giving students advance warnings of things they might choose to avoid or by challenging them directly and immediately to face such content.

Volume 30, Number 1   DOI 10.1215/10407391-7481344

Of course, there are no "immediate" confrontations, since even (or especially) if not recognized, our encounters are always mediated by dis-cursive, ideological, economic, political, and indeed literal media frames—and particularly so for our encounters with trigger warnings and "trigger warnable" content. For at the same time that these debates have arisen in the context of today's neoliberal university, they have also arisen within less academic, more popular media forums: the rise of trigger warnings has been noted in articles published in standard-bearers like the *New York Times* and the *Guardian*, featured at online news sites like the *Huffington Post* and *BuzzFeed*, discussed on National Public Radio and in the *Chronicle of Higher Education*, and quipped about on the *Rush Limbaugh Show*, on Fox News opinion programs, on late-night network comedy shows, and in HBO's *Girls*. Yet for all this media attention, there has been very little awareness or acknowledgment of warning labels' own origins in media practices. Though rarely mentioned or even known in popular and scholarly discourses, trig-ger and content warnings first emerged in fan cultures surrounding media properties—more specifically, in primarily women's and queer fan cultures surrounding television programs, in which writers of fan fiction expanding upon television shows alert readers in their peer fan community by marking their creations with information about, for example, referenced characters, romantic pairings, categories of sexual practices, possible violence, and affective tone.[2]

Given the emergence of this trend within televisual cultural formations, one might be tempted to make a broad argument about the televisualization and "fan-atization" of education (related to what might be said about the televisualization and, indeed, fanaticism of politics today, as is so evident in the U.S. presidency of Donald J. Trump [Joyrich]). Still, these deployments of content information and trigger warnings in academic and fan communities occur in quite different contexts with quite different implications. In TV fandom, trigger warnings have been used to mark fan productions since at least the early 2000s, deployed (again, especially by women and LGBTQ+) as a way of managing both the terms of address and the inherently transgressive and transformative status of fan works, as these are texts that are based not on claims of sole originality, authorship, and ownership, but on reworking known—and typically commodified, corpora-tized, and copyrighted—material.[3] These warnings for content thus appear alongside disclaimers of ownership and profit-generating capacity, together signaling a participation in fandom's "gift economy" (the "free labor" and "free exchange" that define fan communities and counterpublics) even as they may also serve, in a sense, as a kind of marketing device—indeed, as perhaps the best kind of marketing device in an antimarket field.

In this way, as much as such warnings for fan works might function to turn away potential readers or viewers, they function equally, if not more so, to lure readers and viewers, "selling" the fan productions via claims of pleasure and danger, expectation and surprise, knowledge and its discomforts in an arena that is otherwise not for sale, at least not in traditional market terms. A transgression of the terms of the capitalist media marketplace is thus supported by these statements of other kinds of transgressions—of charged (as in emotionally volatile) content that might yield knowledges, affects, and economies that are troubling for some and tempting for others, different from the usual charged (as in requiring payment) knowledges, affects, and economies of commercialized media productions, texts, and receptions.

Trigger warnings exist in quite a different relationship, though, to the economies and epistemologies of academia. Here, rather than operating as part of a set of strategies that allows for challenges to dominant financial, epistemological, and affective economies, I would suggest that the discourse of content and trigger warnings has often had the effect of stifling such challenges, particularly as the subtleties and complexities that have characterized fandoms' discussions of the use of warning labels have largely been flattened and simplified as these discussions migrated from companionate fan communities to increasingly corporatized academic ones. Indeed, the particular way in which this discourse has generally been deployed in academia supports and is in turn supported by the rise of the neoliberal model of the university. In this model, students are increasingly seen, and see themselves, as consumers, with rights not only to self-select among offerings—here, modes of knowledge production likened to produced commodities—but also to be satisfied with the results. The language of "choice" among "goods" yields the demand that the "big bads" (itself a TV trope that fans use to caricature the evil adversaries in a text) be clearly labeled as such so that students might avoid these dangers. Correspondingly, faculty members must now assume the responsibility for not only students' learning but their comfort—despite the fact that often, if not necessarily, one comes at the expense of the other. That is, there is something inherently discomforting in knowledge production, in the emergence of new thoughts that unsettle taken-for-granted assumptions—in, precisely, "critical thinking."

In fact (and ironically, given the ties between academic and televisual discourses I have been tracing), this may be particularly true when it comes to the production of knowledge about things like television, one of our most taken-for-granted cultural institutions and one that is typically dismissed in both popular and academic discourses alike as "mere entertainment" rather than anything having to do with education (beyond the exception of some children's programming teaching the building blocks of the ABCs—along with, of course, teaching kids the building blocks of segmented and ongoing TV form itself). The way, then, in which television teaches neoliberal thinking—training us, as if in a reality program, to manage risks and resources, to calculate personal yet not social responsibility, to optimize self-care and reward, and to demonstrate entrepreneurial acumen so as to feature more favorably in the story or to move on in the competition—may be neglected as a topic for serious scholarly inquiry even as this thinking has come more and more to define the very parameters of scholastic life (McCarthy; Ouellette; Ouellette and Hay). This includes feminist campus life, much of which, too, has "leaned in" toward modes of self-optimization and self-promotion that can rigidify identities, categories, and meanings more than (as in the best tradition of feminist fan production) transform, transgress, and recreate them.[4]

Televisual discourse—or perhaps more accurately, the discourse of convergent media, with its emphasis on multiple means of content delivery, packaging, promotion, and customizability—has also helped to produce a particular way of thinking about "content" that is operative in the discourse of trigger warnings. For now that television texts can easily be accessed and travel across media technologies (with, for example, a gag or dramatic moment from a television program becoming a GIF, a viral video, or an Internet meme, not to mention perhaps the inspiration for "extras" or "bonus" features ranging from DVD commentary to online tie-in games to alternative cuts), cultural material is increasingly thought of in cut-and-paste terms. In other words, content is assumed to be a transportable, divisible entity, somehow floating beyond the operations of textuality. Not only does this reiterate old binaries between form and content; more significantly, it suggests that meanings, and the knowledges and affects thereby generated, are themselves isolatable, definable, fungible. According to this logic, then, it should not be a problem to label content, whether in a DVR menu or a university course, and, depending on demand, replace it with something that, instead of triggering trauma and pain, enhances for optimal pleasure and value.

Yet for all the concern with trauma in the discourse on trigger warnings, there is often a surprising lack of engagement on the part of those calling for such warnings with the voluminous scholarly work on the subject of trauma, ranging from early psychoanalytic accounts of hysteria, "shellshock," and melancholia to more recent trauma theory developed in the humanities and social sciences.[5] This is a large and complex field, full of its own debates; but across the work, there is a fairly consistent understanding of trauma as something that, precisely, is not simply translatable into content: it is very often described as unrepresentable, unsignifiable, and irrational, knowable more by the gaps, absences, and displacements it yields than by any identifiable presence. Someone who has been traumatized is thus as, if not more, likely to be "triggered" by something that has an oblique, not referential, relation to the past trauma—for instance, a smell, a rhythm or pitch of sound, a color or effect of light—than by what is misrecognized as simply representational content.

Further, while questions of textuality, with its slippages, differences, and deferrals, are typically omitted from demands for trigger warnings (as if, say, representations of rape are all the same, with the same likelihood of producing a traumatic effect, regardless of the mode of portrayal, aesthetic treatment, narrative and genre conventions, and so on), these clearly play a role in such demands. Not surprisingly, the more unfamiliar texts (whether from another era, culture, or aesthetic tradition that thus make use of conventions that aren't as naturalized for students or that attempt to undermine conventionality entirely) tend to be the most likely targets of trigger warning demands: I have heard of cases of students in media studies courses complaining about preclassical, non-Western, or avant-garde films, but not about popular u.s. television programs even if these too are, say, full of violence. In this way too, then, demands for trigger warnings can play into, rather than combat, troubling developments in the university: the move away from unconventional material and uncomfortable knowledge toward educational offerings designed to satisfy students-as-consumers (material that will keep them "content," in the sense of comfortable, via a program of easily digestible content).

This trajectory, then, almost reverses the goals of the fan productions from which trigger warnings developed. Media fandom offers transformative works that are not content with dominant consumer discourses, works that play with pleasure and danger so as to devise new modes of address, new significations, and new economies. Rather than supporting neoliberal logics of authorized "choice" and personal responsibility, commodity constructions of knowledge and meaning production, and mainstream media models of individually customizable content, fan communities appropriate media texts in ways that can unsettle, rather than stabilize, these logics and definitions—for instance, challenging and resignifying the very definitions of ownership and consumption, authorization and meaning production, public and private, personal and social, form and content, identity and difference, benefit and loss. They thus open up these terms for debate rather than closing debate down, as demands for trigger warnings in education are often wont to do.

What fandom can therefore best warn us about is not crisis-ridden or troubling material per se but the material troubles—as well as the pedagogical, epistemological, and political troubles—that emerge from the crises of neoliberal, mediatized, commodity culture. Likewise, what feminist academic communities can most usefully learn from feminist fan communities and media counterpublics are the dangers of reifying and rigidifying meanings—of, say, categories of identity, desire, harm, and victimization as much as of the supposed content of the things that we encounter in the classroom, in the media, and in everyday life. That is, rather than avoiding triggers, we might, like the most adventurous fans, seek out the open exchanges, transformations, and recreations that encounters with charged material, whether in media or academic forums, can yield.

LYNNE JOYRICH is a professor of modern culture and media at Brown University and a member of the editorial collective of the journal *Camera Obscura: Feminism, Culture, and Media Studies*. She is the author of *Re-viewing Reception: Television, Gender, and Postmodern Culture* (Indiana University Press, 1996) and articles on film, television, and gender and sexuality studies.

Notes

1   There are so many discussions of trigger warnings that it is impossible to cite them all. For some histories and summaries of these debates, see Brown; Flaherty; Halberstam; Knox; Lukianoff and Haidt; Smith; and Vingiano. See also "Digital Archive: Trigger Warnings" (which includes a useful bibliography).

2   One of the few texts to link the discussions about trigger warnings in the classroom to the originating discussions about such warnings in fandom is by Alexis Lothian, whose very thoughtful analysis emphasizes, in turn, how thoughtful discussions about this issue in fan cultures have been.

3   For some interesting discussions of women's, feminist, and queer fandom, see Coppa; Hellekson and Busse, "Introduction"; Lothian, Busse, and Reid; and Russo. An excellent source of fan productions is *Archive of Our Own*, described as "a fan-created, fan-run, non-profit, non-commercial archive for transformative fanworks, like fanfiction, fanart, fan videos, and podfic." See also the fan studies journal *Transformative Works and Cultures*, which, in its very title, emphasizes the transformative nature of fan production.

4   The kind of feminist activism found on many college campuses today may seem deeply opposed to the entrepreneurial "lean in" movement for women's leadership (based on the 2013 book by Sheryl Sandberg), and, of course, in many ways, they are quite distinct (in terms of a radical or accommodationist approach, an interest in gender-inclusive communities or in female individuals, a breadth of concern with intersectionality or a more singular concern with women's career advancement and leadership). Yet I am suggesting that, in certain presumptions about and emphases on selfhood and self-definition—presumptions tied to those about the knowable content both of texts and of categories of identity that I see as undergirding calls for trigger warnings—there are troubling similarities and overlaps between these feminisms that need to be interrogated.

5   Trauma studies is a rich field, to which I cannot do justice with just a few references, but for some key texts, see Caruth; Freud; Kaplan; LaCapra; and Leys. For useful bibliographies of the field, see Flores; and Radstone, Walker, and Shenker.

Works Cited

Archive of Our Own. https://archiveofourown.org (accessed 6 Oct. 2018).

Brown, Sarah. "A Brief Guide to the Battle over Trigger Warnings." *Chronicle of Higher Education* 26 Aug. 2016. https://www.chronicle.com/article/A-Brief-Guide-to-the-Battle/237600.

Caruth, Cathy. *Unclaimed Experience: Trauma, Narrative, and History*. Baltimore: Johns Hopkins UP, 1996.

Coppa, Francesca. "A Brief History of Media Fandom." Hellekson and Busse, *Fan Fiction* 41–59.

"Digital Archive: Trigger Warnings." Currents: Feminist Key Concepts and Controversies. *Signs*. http://signsjournal.org/currents-trigger-warnings/ (accessed 6 Oct. 2018).

Flaherty, Colleen. "Trigger Unhappy." *Inside Higher Ed* 14 Apr. 2014. https://www.inside highered.com/news/2014/04/14/oberlin-backs-down-triggerwarnings-professors-who-teach -sensitive-material.

Flores, Stephan. "Trauma Theory Bibliography." http://www.webpages.uidaho.edu/~sflores /TraumaTheoryBib.html (accessed 6 Oct. 2018).

Freud, Sigmund. "Beyond the Pleasure Principle." 1920. *The Standard Edition of the Complete Psychological Works of Sigmund Freud*. Trans. and ed. James Strachey. Vol. 18. London: Hogarth, 1955. 3–64. 24 vols. 1953–74.

Halberstam, Jack. "Trigger Happy: From Content Warning to Censorship." *Signs* 42.2 (2017): 535–42.

Hellekson, Karen, and Kristina Busse, eds. *Fan Fiction and Fan Communities in the Age of the Internet*. Jefferson: McFarland, 2006.

——————. "Introduction: Work in Progress." Hellekson and Busse, *Fan Fiction* 5–32.

Joyrich, Lynne. "TV Trumps." *Unwatchable*. Ed. Nicholas Baer, Maggie Hennefeld, Laura Horak, Gunnar Iversen. New Brunswick: Rutgers UP, 2019. 293–98.

Kaplan, E. Ann, ed. *Trauma Culture: The Politics of Terror and Loss in Media and Literature*. New Brunswick: Rutgers UP, 2005.

Knox, Emily J. M., ed. *Trigger Warnings: History, Theory, Context.* Lanham: Rowman and Littlefield, 2017.

LaCapra, Dominick. *Writing History, Writing Trauma.* 2nd ed. Baltimore: Johns Hopkins UP, 2014.

Leys, Ruth. *Trauma: A Genealogy.* Chicago: U of Chicago P, 2000.

Lothian, Alexis. "Choose Not to Warn: Trigger Warnings and Content Notes from Fan Culture to Feminist Pedagogy." *Feminist Studies* 42.3 (2016): 743–56.

Lothian, Alexis, Kristina Busse, and Robin Anne Reid. "'Yearning Void and Infinite Potential': Online Slash Fandom as Queer Female Space." *English Language Notes* 45.2 (2007): 103–11.

Lukianoff, Greg, and Jonathan Haidt. "The Coddling of the American Mind." *Atlantic* Sept. 2015. https://www.theatlantic.com/magazine/archive/2015/09/the-coddling-of-the-american-mind/399356/.

McCarthy, Anna. "Reality Television: A Neoliberal Theater of Suffering." *Social Text* 93 (2007): 17–41.

Ouellette, Laurie. "'Take Responsibility For Yourself': *Judge Judy* and the Neoliberal Citizen." *Reality TV: Remaking Television Culture.* Ed. Susan Murray and Laurie Ouellette. New York: New York UP, 2004, 231–50.

Ouellette, Laurie, and James Hay. *Better Living through Reality TV: Television and Post-Welfare Citizenship.* Malden: Blackwell, 2008.

Radstone, Susannah, Janet Walker, and Noah Shenker. "Trauma Theory." *Oxford Bibliographies.* http://www.oxfordbibliographies.com/view/document/obo-9780199791286/obo-9780199791286-0147.xml (accessed 6 Oct. 2018).

Russo, Julie Levin. "The Queer Politics of Femslash." *The Routledge Companion to Media Fandom.* Ed. Suzanne Scott and Melissa Click. New York: Routledge, 2017. 155–64.

Sandberg, Sheryl. *Lean In: Women, Work, and the Will to Lead.* New York: Knopf, 2013.

Smith, Erika. "Inside the Trigger Warning Debate." *Bust* 18 Jan. 2017. https://bust.com/feminism/18911-trigger-warnings.html.

Transformative Works and Cultures. http://journal.transformativeworks.org/index.php/twc (accessed 6 Oct. 2018).

Vingiano, Ali. "How the 'Trigger Warning' Took Over the Internet." *BuzzFeed News* 5 May 2014. https://www.buzzfeednews.com/article/alisonvingiano/how-the-trigger-warning-took-over-the-internet.

Pedagogies of Desire

*I*n 1993, *Saturday Night Live* aired a gameshow skit: "Is it Date Rape?" The skit was a parody of contemporary feminism's imagined puritanical ethics, with seemingly benign sexual practices classified as abusive; it was also, more specifically, a parody of Antioch College's affirmative consent policy. Passed in 1991, thanks to efforts by the Womyn of Antioch and other campus activists, and in a moment marked by campus speak-outs about sexual violence across the U.S., Antioch's policy mandated affirmative verbal consent to ensure legal sexual conduct. For *Saturday Night Live*, though, Antioch's mandate that students secure verbal consent "at each new level of physical and/or sexual behavior in any given interaction, regardless of who initiates it" was imagined to require students to pose robotic questions like "May I compliment you on your halter top?" and "May I elevate the level of sexual intimacy by feeling your buttocks?" (qtd. in Humphreys and Herold 36). *Saturday Night Live*'s representation of Antioch was echoed in myriad popular venues. The *New York Times* noted, "Adolescents will always make mistakes—sometimes serious ones. Telling them what's unacceptable, in no uncertain terms, is fine. But legislating kisses won't save them from

Volume 30, Number 1   DOI 10.1215/10407391-7481358

themselves" ("'Ask'"), and Sarah Crichton described Antioch's policy as "criminaliz[ing] the delicious unexpectedness of sex" (52). Antioch, then, was imagined as the end of sex, and feminism as the social movement that had finally destroyed eroticism.

While the notion of Antioch as invested in disciplining sex circulated widely in the 1990s, in our contemporary #MeToo moment, Antioch has been celebrated for its vision of creating a campus culture of "positive, consensual sexuality" (Bussel 43). In the last decade, campus sexual assault has become highly publicized. The Obama administration's "It's on Us" and "1 is 2 Many" campaigns highlighted an epidemic of campus sexual assault, and its 2011 "Dear Colleague" letter urging colleges and universities to use a "preponderance of evidence" standard to adjudicate campus sexual assault cases made swift institutional response and accountability a mandate (a policy initiative that was rolled back by Secretary of Education Betsy DeVos, who alerted universities that they could use a much higher "clear and convincing evidence" standard to determine if a student committed sexual assault) (Ali 10). Activist labor like Emma Sulkowicz's "Carry the Weight" project at Columbia University (2014–15), and documentaries like *The Hunting Ground* (2015) have further revealed both the ubiquity of sexual violence on college campuses and a widespread institutional unwillingness to protect survivors and punish perpetrators. In the wake of the new attention to campus sexual assault, affirmative consent has become a prevailing campus policy, and in some states—New York and California—it has become law.[1] In other words, Antioch's "yes means yes" mantra—a reversal of an older feminist mantra, "no means no"—has become the new mandate of campus sexual life, and Antioch is often hailed as an institution that had the requisite commitment to eradicating sexual violence long before Title IX transformed campus life (Rosman).[2]

This article thinks through these competing historical and cultural narratives of Antioch's articulations of the value of affirmative consent in order to ask how women's studies—a field that has long engaged sex as a space steeped in power, hierarchy, and inequality—has come to invest in affirmative consent as the sexual ethic that can produce sex as a territory free of violence. This article explores that question, raising it neither as a diagnosis of the failure of one of feminism's institutional projects nor as part of a genre of texts that expose feminism's ugly underpinnings (biopower, carcerality, governance, neoliberalism, to name a few),[3] but as an exploration of the challenges facing one iteration of institutional feminism. In thinking through this question, I bridge two scholarly conversations: a set of persistent conversations in women's studies about the politics and ethics of feminism's institutional projects and a set of conversations emerging from an array of fields including critical legal studies and black feminist historiography thinking critically about the idiom of consent in precisely the moment that consent—particularly "enthusiastic" affirmative consent—has been hailed as how we are to secure sexual freedom. My exploration of institutional feminism's imbrications with affirmative consent focuses on the space of the university precisely because it is the location of an emphatic amplification of affirmative consent as the paradigmatic form of ethical, legal, and Left political sex and because this amplification has been made possible by the labor of student activists, often under the mantle of feminism.

Antioch's legacy—once bemoaned and now celebrated—is that affirmative consent is the primary idiom structuring sexual and legal life on college campuses, an idiom designed to ensure ethical and legal sexual relations. The magnitude of this shift cannot be understated. While affirmative consent policies aspire to shift campus sexual cultures, they also fundamentally rewrite the landscape of law's relationship to sex. Describing affirmative consent laws in the context of criminal rape prosecutions, Katharine K. Baker and Michelle Oberman note, "In essence, the affirmative consent requirement resets the baseline in rape prosecutions. The baseline becomes no. [. . .] In the absence of a credible yes, the jury must assume no" (72). If, as the state senators who introduced California's affirmative consent bill to the legislature argue, affirmative consent mandates "affirmative, conscious and voluntary agreement to engage in sexual activity—throughout the encounter, removing ambiguity for both parties," it also suggests that a failure to receive consent constitutes a per se violation of the law (de León and Jackson).

This same idiom is often promoted—by both campus activists and universities—as an erotic project where affirmative consent offers not merely a way to engage in legally compliant sex but an opportunity to enhance sexual pleasure. Rachel Bussel, for example, imagines affirmative consent as a strategy of sexual communication that yields increased pleasure. She writes, "The kind of consent I'm talking about isn't concerned just with whether your partner wants to have sex, but what kind of sex, and why. Do you want to be on top, do it against the wall, doggy-style, missionary? These are questions good lovers ask of one another. [. . .] I don't mean that you need to probe your lover's every thought; I mean that getting some insight into what turns them on will fuel the sexual chemistry for both of you" (44). For students, the representation of affirmative consent as erotic often happens under the mantle of "consent is sexy," a mantra designed to highlight the pleasurable benefits of affirmative consent. The now ubiquitous slogan, though, obscures that it circulates on college campuses not as a student-generated plea for ethical sex, but as a university-purchased campaign. Indeed, Consent is Sexy/The Consent Campaign designs and distributes campus-specific posters, buttons, and shirts, along with educational training materials advertising consent's sexual benefits that they promise "make messages impactful and memorable, and [. . .] engage and stimulate exploration and discussion" (Consent is Sexy Community Facebook Page). Put differently, colleges and universities explicitly marshal the language of eroticism to "sell" affirmative consent, to make affirmative consent seem not simply ethical but also pleasurable. One university notes, "It means that you know your partner wants you and likes the sexual activity between you. Now that's hot" ("Consent is Sexy!" California State University San Marcos). Another suggests telling a sexual partner, "I really want this to be good for you [. . .]. What do you like?" ("Consent," University of North Carolina at Chapel Hill), and another describes consent as "really about communication" ("Consent is Sexy." Governors State University). Students are advised on the Governors State University site that "[t]alking about questions like these can be fun and interesting. And can tell you a lot about whether you are both sexually compatible. Much better to know this before you begin a sexual relationship!" Some of the language emphasizing the "fun and interesting" aspects of frank sexual conversations is cited across multiple college websites and is directly attributed to Consent is Sexy, making visible both that corporation's national reach and the uniformity of the branding of affirmative consent. Here, affirmative consent is rebranded from a regulatory regime that distinguishes legal and illegal sex to a pleasure-maximization strategy.

The embrace of affirmative consent as the idiom that can transform sex from a space of violence to a site of ethical pleasure has unfolded despite various critiques of consent. For legal scholar Janet Halley, affirmative consent is troubling not as an ethic (she contends, "I myself would never want to have sex with an unconsenting person, and I don't want you to either"), but as a legal norm (258). Put differently, she raises critical questions about "the desirability of putting the weight of the state and of punishment behind that norm" (258). The potential damage of affirmative consent is that it uses law to empower "people who enthusiastically participated in sex to deny it later and punish their partners" (Halley 259). Jacob Gersen and Jeannie Suk also amplify a concern about placing the regulatory and punitive force of law behind consent. They trace the expansion of the "sex bureaucracy," where "nonviolent, non-harassing, voluntary sexual conduct— whether considered normal, idiosyncratic, or perverse—is totally regulated by the bureaucracy" (885). This bureaucracy is not simply regulatory; it is also pedagogical, preoccupied with "teaching people how to have good sex in healthy relationships" (948). For Joseph Fischel, consent's violence hinges on its incessant production of the (white) child as the (asexual) subject in need of protection and the sex offender as the (queer) subject who needs to be regulated and surveilled. Fischel suggests that we "deprioritize [consent's] juridical claim as a metric for permissible sex and [. . .] demagnetize its cultural appeal as a slogan for good sex" (11), instead centering other analytics like autonomy, peremption, and vulnerability.

For black feminist historians, consent is problematic because it masks its roots in ideas of white liberal personhood, ignoring the ways in which black women have, historically, been unable to offer or withhold consent. In her analysis of "fantasies of consent" in antebellum New Orleans, Emily Alyssa Owens writes, "The focus on willingness in the debate about sexual labor indexes the larger framework for understanding sex in slavery as either rape or consent. Although this framework has created a useable heuristic for understanding black women's experiences of sexuality within the totalizing violence of slavery, the lexicon of rape and consent ultimately limits our capacity to make intelligible the deep and complex vulnerabilities that these women faced" (17). What this body of work shares is a commitment to interrogating the celebration of consent as a framework for antiviolence and for freedom in the midst of a moment that hails consent generally, and affirmative consent particularly, as the site of women's freedom.

This paper unfolds this shifting paradigm of sex in the university in a few moves: first, I trace the conditions of the present by examining the university's production of the student as a sexual citizen. I argue that the university incessantly produces student sexual citizens whose sexual practices are organized around a singular ethic: affirmative consent. I treat this contemporary iteration of the sexual student as a key production of the neoliberal university, exploring how the university's production of an ethic of affirmative consent neatly aligns with neoliberal ideas of risk mitigation and self-management, even as it seems to do that work in the guise of making sex both nonviolent and pleasurable. In the second portion of the essay, I turn attention to Sex Signals, one of the myriad performances staged on college and university campuses during the "red zone"—a term developed to describe a "time at the beginning of the school year when a disproportionate number of campus sexual assaults take place"—designed to introduce students to the key idiom of affirmative consent, to provide students a common vocabulary (Redden). In the final section, I conclude by considering the particular challenges this moment poses for the institutional project of feminism. In so doing, I center discourses of management and self-regulation as key sites for continued feminist inquiry.

The Contemporary Sexual Student-Citizen

The question "What is a student?" is one that feminism has been at the heart of both posing and transforming. From canonical pieces like Adrienne Rich's "Claiming an Education" that have urged women students that "claiming" an education "for women [. . .] can literally mean the difference between life and death" (231) to work on the "imperial university" (Chatterjee and Maira) that has revealed the construction of students as consumers, donors, and future-returns for universities, feminist scholars have been at the forefront of treating "student" as a political category rather than simply a descriptive one, and imagining the transformation of this category as itself a site of struggle. As Robyn Wiegman, Wahneema Lubiano, and Michael Hardt reveal, feminism was at the heart of 1960s student movements to reconceptualize the student from a child into "citizens with rights and responsibilities" (8). They write, "[I]n the course of these multiple and sweeping demands, students dismantled much of the prior edifice of the *in loco parentis* logic. Simple things such as parents receiving grades were replaced with the authority of students to represent themselves as legitimately adult subjects of the institution" (8). Feminism, then, constituted a critical framework that enabled students to make the demand to be seen not as children, but as adults, or at least as adult-like.

The shift from child to adult, from student as belonging to the biological family to student belonging to the institutional family, has been replaced by another transformation: the student has been reimagined as a consumer. Indeed, scholarly work on the rapid corporatization of the university has highlighted the institutional production of a different kind of student, one who imagines education as a commodity, a change that corrodes relationships between faculty and students, transforming professors into "customer service representatives," education into commodity, and students into purchasers (Lugo-Lugo). For some scholars, this shift is best understood as emblematic of the birth and rise of a different kind of university—administrative, corporate, neoliberal. As Benjamin Ginsberg observes, the administrative view of the university has imagined it as "the equivalent of a firm manufacturing goods and services whose main products happen to be various forms of knowledge rather than automobiles, computers, or widgets. [. . .] From an administrative perspective, generally speaking, forms of knowledge that cannot profitably be sold to customers—be they students, corporations, the government, or private donors—should be scrapped in favor of investments in more financially promising areas of inquiry" (168). Scholars have persuasively demonstrated that this transformation puts its most profound affective, corporeal, and psychic pressure on scholars of color who are often called upon to be "brown-faced entertainer[s]," or to perform affective labor (including diversity labor) for students, colleagues, and the institution (Lugo-Lugo 48).

The contemporary neoliberal university produces the student as both a consumer and a particular kind of sexual subject. Of course, colleges and universities have long had interests in regulating the sexual lives of their students, yet in the contemporary moment, students are transformed into sexual citizens through learning to align their sexual practices with the prevailing politic and ethic of the day: affirmative consent. Affirmative consent's rise to the university's prevailing norm has emerged out of legal rather than ethical mandates, most particularly Title IX, a civil rights law enacted in 1972, that has been most culturally associated with athletics and campus sexual assault.[4] The act mandates that "[n]o person in the United States shall, on the basis of sex, be excluded from participation in, be denied the benefits of, or be subjected to discrimination under any education program or activity receiving Federal financial assistance" (Title IX). (Both sexual harassment and rape constitute forms of sex discrimination for purposes of Title IX.) The Department of Education's Office of Civil Rights (ocr)—which enforces Title IX—requires schools to "take prompt and effective action to end harassment, prevent it from recurring, and remedy the effects of the harassment on the victim" ("Sexual"). Thus, colleges have prevention (often interpreted as education) responsibilities and investigatory and adjudicatory responsibilities when they receive reports of sexual violence. Colleges that fail to comply with Title IX are, theoretically, at risk of losing federal funding, though this punishment has never been meted out, and can be subjected to a lengthy ocr investigation. Moreover, colleges that are under ocr investigation are often also the subjects of intense media and activist scrutiny, which can tarnish the public images of universities, even if only temporarily. At the close of the Obama administration, 223 colleges and universities were under ocr investigation, and ocr made public the list of universities that were subjected to review. As Nick Anderson notes, "The schools were not at all pleased to be spotlighted on the issue. They were even less pleased when many investigations continued for years without resolution." At times, it seems the public scrutiny—rather than the threat of losing funding—drives colleges' risk-management efforts toward sexual violence. Thus, we inhabit a moment where, as Jennifer Doyle notes, the "management of sexuality has been sewn into the campus. Sex has its own administrative unit" (46). And this "administrative unit" has one end: "reduc[ing] the risk of sexual violence" (50), an imperative that is all the more urgent because failures produce an institutional feeling of intense "vulnerability" and "exposure" (24). That risk management is multifaceted and increasingly involves the enlisting of various bodies—from faculty as mandatory reporters to the "student affairs complex," from first-year orientation leaders to student activists offering peer education—speaks to the breadth of this mandate (Tompkins).

It is in this context that the university has continued the labor of transforming students into sexual citizens, now tasking students with organizing their desires around affirmative consent precisely because this collective effort mitigates risk, particularly the risk of university exposure to Title IX investigations and to highly visible antisexual assault activist efforts. Put differently, universities transform students into sexual citizens who perform precisely what universities need them to perform: risk management. Through university-sponsored preventative education, students become responsible self-managing subjects, often in the name of feminism but ultimately supporting the corporate university model. Michael A. Peters treats the "responsibilizing of the self" as a hallmark of neoliberalism and notes, "The duty to the self—simultaneously, its responsibilization as moral agent and its construction as a calculative rational choice actor—becomes the basis for a series of investment decisions concerning one's health, education, security, employment, and retirement" (92). Neoliberalism, then, produces a different form of self, one marked by "the encouragement of a political regime of ethical self-constitution as consumer-citizens. 'Responsiblization' refers to modern forms of governments of the self where individuals are called upon to make choices about lifestyles, their bodies, their education, and health at critical points in the life cycle—birth, 'starting school,' 'going to university,' 'first job,' marriage, retirement" (Besley and Peters 160). This process, Besley and Peters note, is "at once economic and moral" and ultimately is undergirded by a citizen who "applies certain managerial, economic and actuarial techniques to themselves" (172). Thus, the idiom of affirmative consent is a key way that universities produce students as "entrepreneurial," as vigilant and risk averse, and cloak those ideologies in the language of desire and pleasure, thus accessing the long history of feminism's intervention into how "the student" is constructed as a citizen and subject.

As a *New York Times* article about campus sexual assault indicates, "There is a whole new vocabulary to memorize, with terms like 'enthusiastic consent,' 'implied consent,' 'spectrum of consent,' 'reluctant permission,' 'coercion' and 'unintentional rape.' Even 'yes means yes,' the slogan of the anti-rape movement, is sort of confusing" (Bennett, "Campus"). This new sexual taxonomy is, for Doyle, part of the "sexual security" movement, one that produces a prevailing ethic of risk management in the guise of prevention. Here, the idea is that the university is in the midst of producing new social norms that distinguish legal and illegal sex but that more importantly introduce students to ethical sexual behavior. But in constructing and instructing students in affirmative consent, universities produce student sexual citizens whose ethics align with those of the institution: risk prevention. It is not simply that universities mitigate risk through their education and prevention programs but that students are enlisted in the service of becoming self-managing risk-preventing subjects who both treat their own sexual practices as in need of risk mitigation and vigilantly monitor the sexual practices of their colleagues for potential violations. Students are encouraged to treat sexual interactions as risk-reduction exercises, using affirmative consent as a tool for ensuring that the self is not exposed to potential risk. Here, encouraging "active," "enthusiastic," "verbal" consent is not merely a strategy of engaging in ethical sex; it is also a tactic of avoiding exposure to liability, to investigation, to tarnished reputation, to expulsion.

Some colleges explicitly detail "risk reduction strategies" that students should deploy when managing their sexual lives. They emphasize that these "strategies" are not meant to engage in "victim-blaming," but instead to act as guidelines for organizing sexual conduct—and desire—in compliant ways that decrease exposure to risk. Colleges encourage students to ensure that one "clearly receive[s] consent for every aspect of sexual activity" ("Risk Reduction Strategies," Bowdoin), to "understand that mixing alcohol or drugs with sexual activity is always risky. Do not engage in sexual activity if either or both parties are intoxicated," ("Reducing Risk," Carnegie Mellon University), and to remember that "mixed messages from a partner are a clear indicator that you should stop, listen to his or her wishes, and communicate better. You must respect the timeline with which they are comfortable" ("Title IX and Risk Reduction," Wayne State College). Other universities explicitly offer strategies for "reducing the risk of being accused of sexual misconduct," including "avoid ambiguity," "respect the timeline for sexual behaviors with which others are comfortable, and understand that they are entitled to change their minds," and "understanding that exerting power and control over another through sex is unacceptable conduct" ("Risk Reduction for Intimate Partner Violence," Napa Valley College). Colleges also circulate information on "reducing the risk of being sexually assaulted," including encouraging students to "know your sexual intentions and limits," "communicate your limits firmly and directly," "listen to your gut feelings," and "attend large parties with friends you trust. [. . .] Leave with the group, not alone. Avoid leaving with people that you don't know very well" ("Risk Reduction Strategies: A Guide," Lee College). Here, sexual assault prevention training—undergirded by an idiom of affirmative consent—takes on the form of a pedagogy of risk management, urging students to limit their exposure to the threat of accusation and to the threat of violation.

Similarly, the language of "bystander intervention" training—increasingly the lingua franca of prevention training—also shores up the notion of consistent self-management as the hallmark of the student sexual citizen. "Bystander intervention" programs "train students to recognize warning signs, and then intervene to stop sexual assaults from occurring. BIPS [Bystander Intervention Programs] also teach students to feel empowered to act when others are in danger" (Murphy 801–2). In short, bystander programs emphasize that "preventing harassment [is] everybody's responsibility" (Miller). The notion of the collective responsibility to prevent sexual violence is often analogized to "successful" programs for designated drivers. Michael Winerip notes, "The hope is that bystander programs will have the same impact on campus culture that the designated driver campaign has had in reducing drunken driving deaths (to 9,878 in 2011 from 15,827 in 1991). And that it can be inculcated in a relatively short time; Mothers Against Drunk Driving was founded in 1980 and within a decade was making a difference. Both take the same tack: Drinking to excess can't be stopped but the collateral damage can." The logic of the bystander program is that everyone is a witness to potential violence, and thus everyone should be enlisted in laboring to "prevent" or eliminate violence. On the one hand, the call for collective investment in violence eradication resonates with a feminist conception of the ubiquity of (male) violence and the necessity of exposing and disrupting it. On the other hand, the centrality of bystander intervention to campus sex training suggests that the task of the student sexual citizen is to be in "harassment prevention" mode constantly. The student sexual citizen should not only manage his or her own sexual conduct to ensure it is compliant but also should act as a constantly vigilant citizen monitoring and surveilling others' conduct. We can then think about how the notion of student as part of the institutional family who is effectively given responsibility for ending campus sexual violence is part of the larger erosion of university responsibility for campus sexual assault. In her analysis of the security state, Inderpal Grewal argues that neoliberalism is marked by a sense that "the state is unable to provide security and thus it disavows its ability to protect all citizens" (28). Grewal's analysis of so-called security moms reveals that citizens—here, maternal citizens—are enlisted to perform the labor of security in intimate spaces and "privatization turns the personal into the political and defines the work of security as everyone's job" (29). We see the same idea at work in the logics of the production of the contemporary student sexual citizen who is enlisted to be educated in the work of campus security, not simply regulating her own sexual behavior but also engaged in "bystander" work that insists that "if you see something, say something." The student sexual citizen, the student consumer citizen, the student corporate citizen, labors with feminism—and corporate institutionality—in a neoliberal education of desire, one that requires surveillance and vigilant brand management.

Ultimately, my goal is not to critique the critical and political desire for nonviolent sex, but to think deeply about an institutional orientation toward risk management that produces student sexual citizens who are also appropriately oriented toward harm mitigation and prevention, who are self-managing subjects (and relentlessly oriented toward self-management). Moreover, I want to place critical pressure on the mobilization of pleasure to mask the incessant production of students as self-managing, risk-mitigating, entrepreneurial subjects who treat sexual encounters not as practices of vulnerability, but as moments of avoiding injury through adherence to "risk reduction" strategies. That all of this work happens under the auspices of affirmative consent and its promise of ethical and pleasurable sex reveals the complexities of institutional feminism and its relationship to the corporate university's security model of political subjectivity.

Training the Sexual Student

At the heart of the practice of "prevention," one of the pillars of many universities' sexual assault efforts, are interactive programs and trainings designed to introduce students to concepts like affirmative consent and to help students consider the "social and cultural dynamics involved in sexual assault and identify ways to effectively prevent and respond to interpersonal violence" ("Prevention and Training," George Washington University). Indeed, the Center for Disease Control (CDC) has advocated campus-based prevention strategies that aim their pedagogical work along multiple dimensions: *individual* (here, there is often an emphasis on "bystander education") and sessions that teach students about gendered and sexual norms, *relationship* (dorms, coaches), *community* (engaging "campus leadership"), and *social* (largely focused on alcohol). As the CDC indicates, it is crucial to "make prevention a part of everyone's job on campus. From students to staff and administrators, there should be a common language around prevention. Are leadership, staff, and students talking about primary prevention? Are leadership and staff knowledgeable about primary prevention concepts and principles? Are prevention messages and policies a part of the fabric of the organization and communication?" Training programs have largely been hailed as successful interventions. A *New York Times* article found that one program significantly lowered female college students' risk of being assaulted. They report:

> *In a randomized trial, published in* The New England Journal of Medicine, *first-year students at three Canadian campuses attended sessions on assessing risk, learning self-defense and defining personal sexual boundaries. The students were surveyed a year after they completed the intervention. The risk of rape for 451 women randomly assigned to the program was about 5 percent, compared with nearly 10 percent among 442 women in a control group who were given brochures and a brief information session. (Hoffman)*

If the first-year orientation is the space where students are often first introduced to affirmative consent as a virtuous practice, the training skit is often the vehicle for imparting this crucial knowledge. (Importantly, these same training skits are now used in the military and in workplaces and might be in even more demand in the wake of #MeToo highlighting the ubiquity of sexual harassment; in other words, these theatrical productions have become institutional genres.)

It is crucial to note that women's studies, in particular, is deeply implicated in the kinds of pedagogies of desire that are staged in campus sex training theater. As women's studies has often been at the vanguard of "service learning" programs and "practical learning" initiatives that allow students to put feminist theory into practice (often through domestic violence and sexual assault prevention work), the field has also historically been invested in laboring in and against the university, with its faculty working alongside student activists to demand institutional transparency, fairness, and student safety. In other words, women's studies is often the academic space that offers students political and theoretical tools for performing and staging anti–sexual violence activist work on campus. It is women's studies programs and departments that regularly sponsor campus events like Take Back the Night, that invite activist speakers laboring to eradicate sexual violence, and that partner with student-led campus feminist organizations to support efforts to ensure gender equity. While the women's studies classroom is often a space where students read theoretical texts focused on sexual violence and injury, it is also a space that performs advocacy work on college campuses, galvanizing students to imagine different sexual futures, sexual futures that are marked by justice, bodily autonomy, and integrity.

Sex Signals, a popular sexual assault prevention program that has been performed more than 3,500 times on u.s. campuses, bills itself as "one of the most popular sexual assault prevention programs on college campuses through its unorthodox, humor-facilitated, and inclusive approach to examining our culture, sex, and prevention strategies like bystander intervention" ("Sex"). Sex Signals started in 1999 and has been hired by an array of colleges and universities to conduct sexual assault prevention education. Across campuses, varied groups hire Sex Signals, including Women's Resource Centers, Offices of Student Life, Counseling Centers, Freshmen Dean's Offices, One Book One College Initiatives, First-Year Experience Coordinators (where it is often a required component of first-year orientation), Student Activities Councils, and feminist activist groups. It is, then, crucial to note that Sex Signals is part of the outsourcing of the sexual citizenship education. In the same moment that sexual education is considered a significant part of university risk mitigation, universities increasingly outsource this seemingly crucial portion of risk-mitigation work. Sexual citizenship education, then, is subcontracted to a seemingly feminist company that makes the bulk of its money from universities that hire it to train sexual citizens who are oriented toward prevention.

Sex Signals begins its interactive skits with an intensive focus on gender roles. It treats everyday campus interactions as mediated by gendered expectations and logics and reveals that notions like "act like a lady" conscript students into confining socially constructed roles. For Sex Signals, what is most important—and most problematic—about these roles is that they shape campus sexual mores and, when mixed with alcohol (and the toxic conditions of Greek life), generate the dangerous conditions that produce campus sexual assault. Indeed, as the skits unfold, performers remind the audience that perpetrators frequently assert "I *really* didn't rape that girl" even when "no" was clearly uttered or when "yes" was never unambiguously spoken. The inability to see a violent assault as rape is made possible by the gendered roles that Sex Signals carefully charts. The performers then encourage audience members to pose questions of performers who remain in character for the duration of the performance ("did she say no?," "How much did you drink?"), allowing performers the chance to dispel pervasive "rape myths" and to show how the "not my fault" logic "gives people the chance to prove they are not responsible for hurting someone." Ultimately, the show concludes by emphasizing that an emphasis on "no" can be confusing. In other words, the question of "did she say no?" obfuscates conversations about sexual violence, allowing "victim blaming" and obscuring perpetrator responsibility. What the show reveals is that sexual encounters—the very encounters that are steeped in patriarchal gender logics, alcohol consumption, and unequal bargaining power—can be made simpler and more equitable by the "one word we want to hear": "Yes." It is affirmative consent, Sex Signals concludes, that can make sexual interactions both equitable and legal, both transparent and just, both sexy and safe. It is affirmative consent that can produce new kinds of campus climates that reject the toxicity of gender roles and that foreground open and pleasurable sexual communication.

Part of what is fascinating about Sex Signals is its paradoxical insistence that campus sexual climates and interactions are marked by the complexity of gender roles *and* that these complex interactions can be made simple through an investment in affirmative consent. In other words, while the old "no means no" is imagined to produce certain kinds of murkiness, the requirement of "yes"—particularly an enthusiastic and pleasurable "yes"—is a guarantee of mutuality and shared desire, as well as a guarantee of legally compliant sex. Even as Sex Signals insists on naming the tenacity of gender roles in shaping sexual encounters, it presumes that gender roles can be diffused simply through a mandate of receiving a "yes"—and that students can effectively be taught this in a thirty-minute skit.

While Sex Signals is most intimately associated with its centrality to first-year orientation programming in u.s. colleges and universities, it has increasingly turned its attention to corporate landscapes, bringing its same emphasis on consent, honesty, and humor to u.s. workplaces. In its corporate iterations, Sex Signals focuses on both racial bias and sexual harassment, working to underscore the legal and ethical importance of "civil" work environments. In its "The Canary in the Coal Mine" and "Not Suitable for Work" programs, for example, Sex Signals emphasizes the urgency of creating workplace cultures rooted in respect. As the organizers note, their programming is "a perfect part of your tool box to dismantle bias culture, help employees learn to recognize bias and create a more equitable and healthier working environment for everyone." In their framing of it, a "productive working environment" aligns with an "aware" one, a space where employees have grappled with bias and collectively labored to create a "welcoming" environment for everyone through the pedagogical value of the feminist, antiracist skit. While Sex Signals' campus programming focuses more specifically on alcohol consumption and consent, and its corporate programming focuses more on bias, the programming shares a fundamental sense of the production of a singular sexual (and racial) ethic. Here, we can see how part of the task of sexual citizenship education is aligning university ethics with workplace ethics, ensuring that students are well prepared for the ethics and legal mandates of a corporate workplace. Sex training, then, is a form of work training, and both are imagined as feminist endeavors.

Women's Studies in Present Tense

The conditions of the present are, then, marked by the installation of affirmative consent as the university's key idiom, one that seems to do its work around the promotion of a sexual ethic and an ethically trained student sexual citizen but that actually produces the student as embodying and performing the risk-management ethic of the university. What, then, is the place of institutional feminism in all of this? How do we understand a moment where institutional feminism has trained the student activists who champion affirmative consent, a moment in which the women's studies classroom is a laboratory both for activism and for neoliberalism? How do we square our field's sense of sex as a terrain of inequality, violence, and hierarchy—and, indeed, eroticism's imbrication with inequality, violence, and hierarchy—with the notion that affirmative consent can produce a kind, *the* kind, of sex that can liberate us? Indeed, why have some scholars and activists laboring under the mantle of feminism imagined sex as a place that can liberate us, if freedom is imagined to be a removal from structural inequality, intimate violence, and structures of domination that seem to define sex?

The contention that sex is a terrain of violence is often imagined—and caricatured—as an "anti-sex" position, as a key contribution of feminist scholars like Catharine MacKinnon and Andrea Dworkin who underscored the violence of heterosexual sex and the ways that patriarchal control eviscerates women's sexual bargaining power. The sex positivity that marked feminist theory and popular culture in a pre-#MeToo moment was often imagined to eschew that position, to champion sexual agency as the hallmark of feminist praxis, to center sex work as a radical practice, and to embrace pleasure as the route to freedom. Yet even in the midst of this theoretical and political turn, feminist and queer scholars—particularly those working on black erotics and racialized longings—have taken up the mantle of describing sexual pleasure as a technology of racial domination. Scholars including Darieck Scott, Tan Hoang Nguyen, Ariane Cruz, and Mireille Miller-Young trace how abjection is mobilized by racially marked subjects as a technology of pleasure and ecstasy. Here, sex does its work not because it is excised from violence, but because hierarchy is put to work for fleshy electricity, for sensual pleasures. We are not, this body of work suggests, ever free, and sex isn't the terrain that can get us there. Instead, this work suggests, we can sit in unfreedom, and thus the unfreedom-ness of sex, by mobilizing the structures that wound and putting them to erotic work, even if that erotic work is built on an edifice of oppression that solidifies and cements the conditions of our oppression. Ultimately, this body of scholarship has advanced the notion that we can make use of sex's multiple and conflicting meanings for pleasurable ends, even if those "funky" pleasures also make us feel politically uncomfortable (Stallings). This scholarly intervention—largely rooted in black feminist theory, women of color feminist theory, and queer of color studies—emphasizes a vision of feminist theory (and queer theory) that is not so far removed from the often-disavowed (at least pre-#MeToo) "antisex" politic that foregrounds violence and sex as always mutually constitutive. This vision of sex as violence (and, perhaps, violence as sex) is a conception of sex fundamentally at odds with the affirmative consent idiom that presumes that violence can be excised from sex through securing "enthusiastic," verbal, affirmative consent.

Ultimately, what I have endeavored to show is that feminism's engagement with neoliberalism's stronghold on the university must extend far beyond simply naming the neoliberal or corporate university, and instead contend with how neoliberalism does its work through the rhetoric of risk *and* in the name of feminism (and pleasure). Those of us invested in feminism's institutional iterations need to grapple with how neoliberalism has produced an entrepreneurial student engaged in the seemingly necessary work of risk mitigation and consider how this preparation of student as good worker and as good sexual citizen does its work through the language and promise of pleasure. Women's studies, as an institutional project, must struggle to think through its role in educating feminism as an ethic of self-regulation and management. We must contend with how our conception of sex as steeped in violence, as shaped by hierarchy, as a site of unfreedom gets transformed in the neoliberal university into a conception of sex as a space that can be made safe. It is, then, crucial that we begin to ask if there are other ways to teach sex, other kinds of pedagogies of desire, that refuse ideas of risk mitigation and instead center other idioms, including vulnerability.

Here, my analysis is informed by Fischel's critical work on vulnerability, which can serve as an invitation to the field to consider what it might mean for women's studies to sit with—rather than eschew—vulnerability. This includes embracing the sense that sex is inevitably and constitutively a site of vulnerability and that this is precisely what has made it a rich site for staging feminist and queer analysis. Ultimately, feminist theory has again reminded us that we can be undone in and through sex, that erotics can make and rupture worlds. Of course, the contention that sex can not be made free of violence—and that it might be its capacity to undo and unmake us that has made it a rich site for decades of feminist and queer inquiry—puts the field at odds with the university's mantra of risk management and perhaps even at odds with the students we have trained and productively empowered with a feminist theory of affirmative consent as the solution to pervasive sexual violence. It places the field in a vulnerable position in a place—the university—where feminist inquiry has long been vulnerable. Can women's studies risk a feminism that does not assume an answer or a solution to sex, and can it imagine "teaching" an ethics of vulnerability within a university that disavows harm through a pedagogy of risk management as self-management? What would that vulnerable feminist pedagogy look like, within and against the university culture that defines our current political moment? This article has attempted to trace the evolving role of feminism in the construction of the student and of sexual ethics in the late twentieth and twenty-first centuries so that we might, without abandoning the terrifying reality of sexual violence, imagine ourselves vulnerable to our own complicity with the institutions that disavow eroticism's, and feminism's, potentially destabilizing force.

JENNIFER C. NASH is an associate professor of African American studies and gender and sexuality studies at Northwestern University. She is the author of *The Black Body in Ecstasy: Reading Race, Reading Pornography* (Duke University Press, 2014) and *Black Feminism Reimagined: After Intersectionality* (Duke University Press, 2019), as well as articles published in journals including *Signs, GLQ, Social Text, Feminist Theory*, and *Feminist Review*. She is currently working on a manuscript titled "Black Maternal Politics."

Notes

1   See Cal. Educ. Code §67386 (2015); and N.Y. Educ. Law §6441 (2015). Janet Halley notes, "I am unaware of a reliable count of all campuses that have adopted affirmative consent requirements. But the trend is clear, and appears in universities as well as colleges, in private as well as public institutions, and in Eastern, Western, Southern and Midwestern institutions" (257).

2   See also Stark.

3   For biopower, see, for example, Schuller; on carcerality, see Bernstein; on governance, see Halley, Kotiswaran, Rebouché, and Shamir; on neoliberalism, see, for example, Bumiller.

4   Title IX's mandates, along with the Clery Act and the Campus Sexual Violence Elimination Act (Campus SAVE ACT) requirement that universities maintain and publish information about crime on and near campus, including sexual assault, intimate partner violence, and stalking, have made risk management the hallmark of the administrative response to sexual violence as universities seek to avoid the publicity.

Works Cited

Ali, Russlynn. Dear Colleague Letter. United States Department of Education 4 April 2011. https://www2.ed.gov/about/offices/list/ocr/letters/colleague-201104.pdf.

Anderson, Nick. "At First, 55 Schools Faced Sexual Violence Investigations." *Washington Post* 18 Jan. 2017. https://www.washingtonpost.com/news/grade-point/wp/2017/01/18/at-first-55-schools-faced-sexual-violence-investigations-now-the-list-has-quadrupled/.

"'Ask First' at Antioch." Op-ed. *New York Times* 11 Oct. 1993. https://www.nytimes.com/1993/10/11/opinion/ask-first-at-antioch.html.

Baker, Katherine K., and Michelle Oberman. "Women's Sexual Agency and the Law of Rape in the 21st Century." *Studies in Law, Politics, and Society* 69 (2016): 63–111.

Bennett, Jessica. "Campus Sex . . . With a Syllabus." *New York Times* 9 Jan. 2016. https://www.nytimes.com/2016/01/10/fashion/sexual-consent-assault-college-campuses.html.

————. "The #MeToo Moment: When the Blinders Come Off." *New York Times* 30 Nov. 2017. https://www.nytimes.com/2017/11/30/us/the-metoo-moment.html.

Bernstein, Elizabeth. "Militarized Humanitarianism Meets Carceral Feminism: The Politics of Sex, Rights, and Freedom in Contemporary Antitrafficking Campaigns." *Signs* 36.1 (2010): 45–72.

Besley, Tina, and Michael A. Peters. "Enterprise Culture and the Rise of the Entrepreneurial Self." *Counterpoints* 303 (2007): 155–74.

Bumiller, Kristin. *In an Abusive State: How Neoliberalism Appropriated the Feminist Movement against Sexual Violence*. Durham: Duke UP, 2008.

Bussel, Rachel Kramer. "Beyond Yes or No: Consent as Sexual Process." *Yes Means Yes! Visions of Female Sexual Power and a World without Rape.* Ed. Jaclyn Friedman and Jessica Valenti. Berkeley: Seal Press, 2008. 43–52.

Cal. Educ. Code §67386 (2015).

Center for Disease Control. "Sexual Violence on Campus: Strategies for Prevention." 2016. https://www.cdc.gov/violenceprevention/pdf/campussvprevention.pdf.

Chatterjee, Piya, and Sunaina Maira, eds. *The Imperial University: Academic Repression and Scholarly Dissent.* Minneapolis: U of Minnesota P, 2014.

"Consent." University of North Carolina at Chapel Hill. https://safe.unc.edu/learn-more /consent/ (accessed 2 Nov. 2018).

"Consent is Sexy!" California State University San Marcos. https://www.csusm.edu/stars /issues/consent.html (accessed 24 Oct. 2018).

"Consent is Sexy." Governors State University. http://www.govst.edu/consent/ (accessed 24 Oct. 2018).

Consent is Sexy Community. *Facebook.* https://www.facebook.com/uiconsent/ (accessed 10 Nov. 2018).

Cossman, Brenda. "Sexing Citizenship, Privatizing Sex." *Citizenship Studies* 4 (2002): 483–506.

Crichton, Sarah. "Sexual Correctness: Has It Gone Too Far?" *Newsweek* 25 Oct. 1993: 52–56.

de León, Kevin, and Hannah-Beth Jackson. "Why We Made 'Yes Means Yes' California Law." *Washington Post* 13 Oct. 2015. https://www.washingtonpost.com/news/in-theory/wp/2015/10 /13/why-we-made-yes-means-yes-california-law/.

Doyle, Jennifer. *Campus Sex, Campus Security.* Cambridge, MA: MIT P, 2015.

Fischel, Joseph. *Sex and Harm in the Age of Consent.* Minneapolis: U of Minnesota P, 2016.

Gersen, Jacob, and Jeannie Suk. "The Sex Bureaucracy." *California Law Review* 104 (2016): 881–948.

Ginsberg, Benjamin. *The Fall of the Faculty.* New York: Oxford UP, 2011.

Grewal, Inderpal. "'Security Moms' in the Early 20th Century United States: The Gender of Security in Neoliberalism." *Women's Studies Quarterly* 34.1–2 (2006) 25–39.

Halley, Janet. "The Move to Affirmative Consent." *Signs* 42.1 (2016): 257–79.

Halley, Janet, Prabha Kotiswaran, Rachel Rebouché, and Hila Shamir. *Governance Feminism: An Introduction.* Minneapolis: U of Minnesota P, 2018.

Hoffman, Jan. "College Rape Prevention Program Proves a Rare Success." *New York Times* 10 June 2015. https://www.nytimes.com/2015/06/12/health/college-rape-prevention-program -proves-a-rare-success.html.

Humphreys, Terry, and Ed Herold. "Should Universities and Colleges Mandate Sexual Behavior?" *Journal of Psychology and Human Sexuality* 1 (2003): 35–51.

Khazan, Olga. "A Viral Short Story for the #MeToo Moment." *Atlantic* 11 Dec. 2017. https://www.theatlantic.com/technology/archive/2017/12/a-viral-short-story-for-the-metoo-moment/548009/.

Lugo-Lugo, Carmen R. "A Prostitute, A Servant, and a Customer-Service Representative: A Latina in Academia." *Presumed Incompetent: The Intersections of Race and Class for Women in Academia.* Ed. Gabrielle Gutiérrez y Muhs, Yolanda Flores Niemann, Carmen G. González, and Angela P. Harris. Boulder: U of Colorado P, 2012. 40–49.

MacKinnon, Catharine. *Women's Lives, Men's Laws.* Cambridge, MA: Harvard UP, 2007.

Miller, Claire Cain. "The #MeToo Moment: How to Be a (Good) Bystander." *New York Times* 12 Dec. 2017. https://www.nytimes.com/2017/12/12/us/the-metoo-moment-how-to-be-a-good-bystander.html.

Murphy, Wendy. "Bystander Intervention Policies for Campus Sexual Assault Should Be Framed as Civil Rights Programs, and Made Broadly Applicable to All Protected Class Offenses." *Utah Law Review* 4 (2017): 801–14.

New York Educ. Law §6441 (2015).

Owens, Emily Alyssa. "Fantasies of Consent: Black Women's Sexual Labor in 19th-Century New Orleans." PhD diss. Harvard University, 2015.

Peters, Michael A. "Neoliberalism, Education, and the Crisis of Western Capitalism." *Policy Futures in Education* 48.2 (2007): 85–102.

"Prevention and Training." George Washington University. https://haven.gwu.edu/prevention-training (accessed 2 Nov. 2018).

Redden, Molly. "Welcome to the Red Zone: What's Wrong with Sexual Assault Training on Campus." *Guardian* 26 Aug. 2016. https://www.theguardian.com/society/2016/aug/26/campus-sexual-assault-training-red-zone.

"Reducing Risk." Carnegie Mellon University. https://www.cmu.edu/title-ix/prevention/risk-reduction.html (accessed 2 Nov. 2018)

Rich, Adrienne. *On Lies, Secrets, and Silence: Selected Prose.* New York: Norton, 1995.

"Risk Reduction for Intimate Partner Violence, Sexual Harassment, and Sexual Violence." Napa Valley College. http://www.napavalley.edu/HR/Documents/Risk%20Reduction%20for%20Intimate%20Partner%20Violence.pdf (accessed 2 Nov. 2018).

"Risk Reduction Strategies." Bowdoin College. https://www.bowdoin.edu/title-ix/prevention-and-education/risk-reduction-strategies.shtml (accessed 2 Nov. 2018).

"Risk Reduction Strategies: A Guide." Lee College. http://www.lee.edu/know-more/risk-reduction-strategies-a-guide/ (accessed 2 Nov. 2018).

Rosenbury, Laura. "Work Wives." *Harvard Journal of Law and Gender* 36 (2013): 345–404.

Rosman, Katherine. "At the College That Pioneered the Rules on Consent, Some Students Want More." *New York Times* 24 Feb. 2018. https://www.nytimes.com/2018/02/24/style/antioch-college-sexual-offense-prevention-policy.html.

Schuller, Kyla. *The Biopolitics of Feeling: Race, Sex, and Science in the Nineteenth Century.* Durham: Duke UP, 2017.

Schultz, Vicki. "The Sanitized Workplace." *Yale Law Review* 112.8 (2002): 2061–193.

"Sex Signals—College." *Catharsis Productions.* http://www.catharsisproductions.com/programs/sex-signals (accessed 24 Oct. 2018).

"Sexual Harassment: It's Not Academic." u.s. Department of Education. Office for Civil Rights. https://www2.ed.gov/about/offices/list/ocr/docs/ocrshpam.html (accessed 24 Oct. 2018).

Stallings, L. H. *Funk the Erotic: Transaesthetics and Black Sexual Cultures.* Urbana: u of Illinois p, 2015.

Stark, Samantha. "'I Kept Thinking of Antioch': Long before #MeToo, a Times Video Journalist Remembered a Form She Signed in 2004." *New York Times* 8 Apr. 2018. https://www.nytimes.com/2018/04/08/insider/antioch-sexual-consent-form-metoo-video.html.

Title IX. The Education Amendments of 1972, 20 u.s.c. A§ 1681.

"Title IX and Risk Reduction." Wayne State College. https://www.wsc.edu/info/20160/title_ix/531/title_ix_and_risk_reduction (accessed 2 Nov. 2018).

Tompkins, Kyla Wazana. "We Aren't Here to Learn What We Already Know." *Los Angeles Review of Books* 13 Sep. 2016. http://avidly.lareviewofbooks.org/2016/09/13/we-arent-here-to-learn-what-we-know-we-already-know/.

Weeks, Jeffrey. "The Sexual Citizen." *Theory, Culture, and Society* 15.3–4 (1998): 35–52.

Wiegman, Robyn, Wahneema Lubiano, and Michael Hardt. "In the Afterlife of the Duke Case." *Social Text* 93 (2007): 1–16.

Winerip, Michael. "Stepping Up to Stop Sexual Assault." *New York Times* 9 Feb. 2014. https://www.nytimes.com/2014/02/09/education/edlife/stepping-up-to-stop-sexual-assault.html.

Help Students Cite Any Source Easily

MLA HANDBOOK, 8TH EDITION

"This is the most succinct and sensible revision to MLA documentation style in my long career."

—Andrea A. Lunsford, Stanford University

Lower-priced, shorter, and redesigned for writers at all levels, this groundbreaking edition of the *MLA Handbook* recommends one universal set of guidelines, which writers can apply to any type of source.

Paperback edition
146 pp. • 6 × 9
List price: $15.00

Large-print edition
146 pp. • 8 × 12
List price: $20.00

Also available in e-book formats.

Modern Language Association **MLA**

style.mla.org • www.mla.org

DISCOVER MORE RESOURCES ONLINE

style.mla.org

Keep up to date on new scholarship

Issue alerts are a great way to stay current on all the cutting-edge scholarship from your favorite Duke University Press journals. This free service delivers tables of contents directly to your inbox, informing you of the latest groundbreaking work as soon as it is published.

To sign up for issue alerts:

1. Visit **dukeu.press/register** and register for an account. You do not need to provide a customer number.

2. After registering, visit **dukeu.press/alerts**.

3. Go to "Latest Issue Alerts" and click on "Add Alerts."

4. Select as many publications as you would like from the pop-up window and click "Add Alerts."

read.dukeupress.edu/journals   **DUKE** UNIVERSITY PRESS

Printed and bound by CPI Group (UK) Ltd, Croydon, CR0 4YY

13/04/2025

14656485-0002